Summary o

HOST YOUR WEB SITE IN THE CLOUD

AMAZON WEB SERVICES MADE EASY

BY **JEFF BARR**

Host Your Web Site in the Cloud: Amazon Web Services Made Easy

by Jeff Barr

Copyright © 2010 Amazon Web Services, LLC, a Delaware limited liability company, 1200 12th Ave S., Suite 1200, Seattle, WA 98144, USA

Program Director: Lisa Lang   **Chief Technical Officer**: Kevin Yank

Technical Editor: Andrew Tetlaw   **Indexer**: Fred Brown

Technical Editor: Louis Simoneau   **Cover Design**: Alex Walker

Editor: Kelly Steele

Expert Reviewer: Keith Hudgins

Printing History:

First Edition: September 2010

Notice of Rights

Notice of Liability

Trademark Notice

Helmet image on the cover is a Davida Jet and was kindly provided by http://motociclo.com.au.

Published by SitePoint Pty Ltd

Web: www.sitepoint.com

Email: business@sitepoint.com

ISBN 978-0-9805768-3-2

Printed and bound in the United States of America

About the Author

Jeff Barr is currently the Senior Evangelist at Amazon Web Services. In this role, Jeff speaks to developers at conferences and user groups all over the world. Jeff joined Amazon.com in 2002 when he realized it was destined to become the next great developer platform, and that he could help make it so. Before coming to Amazon, Jeff ran his own consulting practice, and has also held management and development positions at Microsoft, eByz, KnowNow, and Visix Software.

Jeff earned a Bachelor's degree in Computer Science from the American University in Washington DC and also took some graduate classes at George Washington University in the same city. Jeff resides in Sammamish, Washington with his wife and their five children. In his spare time he enjoys the great outdoors, electronics, and welding.

About the Technical Editors

Andrew Tetlaw has been tinkering with web sites as a web developer since 1997. He's dedicated to making the world a better place through the technical editing of SitePoint books, kits, articles, and newsletters. Andrew's also a busy father of five, enjoys receiving beer showbags, and often neglects his blog at http://tetlaw.id.au/.

Louis Simoneau joined SitePoint in 2009, after traveling from his native Montréal to Calgary and finally Melbourne. He now gets to spend his days learning about cool web technologies, an activity that had previously been relegated to nights and weekends. He enjoys hip-hop, spicy food, and all things geeky. His personal web site is http://louissimoneau.com/ and his latest blog project is http://growbuycookeat.com/.

About the Chief Technical Officer

As Chief Technical Officer for SitePoint, Kevin Yank keeps abreast of all that is new and exciting in web technology. Best known for his book, *Build Your Own Database Driven Web Site Using PHP & MySQL*, he also co-authored *Simply JavaScript* with Cameron Adams and *Everything You Know About CSS Is Wrong!* with Rachel Andrew. In addition, Kevin hosts the *SitePoint Podcast* and co-writes the *SitePoint Tech Times*, a free email newsletter that goes out to over 240,000 subscribers worldwide.

Kevin lives in Melbourne, Australia and enjoys speaking at conferences, as well as visiting friends and family in Canada. He's also passionate about performing improvised comedy theater with Impro Melbourne (http://www.impromelbourne.com.au/) and flying light aircraft. Kevin's personal blog is *Yes, I'm Canadian* (http://yesimcanadian.com/).

About SitePoint

SitePoint specializes in publishing fun, practical, and easy-to-understand content for web professionals. Visit http://www.sitepoint.com/ to access our blogs, books, newsletters, articles, podcasts, and community forums.

To Carmen,

*Thanks for all of your love,
support, and encouragement. I
couldn't have done it without you!*

Table of Contents

Chapter 4   Storing Data with Amazon S3 59

Chapter 5   Web Hosting with Amazon EC2 99

Chapter 6   Building a Scalable Architecture with Amazon SQS

Chapter 8   Amazon SimpleDB: A Cloud Database

Chapter 11 Putting It All Together:
CloudList

Index

Preface

In the spring of 2002, I logged in to my Amazon Associates account one day and saw a little box on the landing page with the magic words: "Amazon Now Has XML!" Amazon had exposed many aspects of its product catalog in XML form. Coupled with the Amazon Associates program, enterprising developers could download the data, use it to create a marketing site, and then earn commissions by sending traffic to the main Amazon.com site.

I thought this was fairly interesting and dived right in. I downloaded the documentation, wrote some code, and was impressed. I saw plenty of promise, but also plenty of room for improvement, so I wrote it all up and sent it to a feedback email address that they'd provided for this purpose.

One situation led to another and by early summer I was Amazon's guest at a very exclusive conference held at their headquarters. They had invited five or six outside developers to Seattle in order to gain some direct customer feedback on their service and talk about their plans for the future. As I sat there and listened, I was definitely impressed. It was clear they were thinking big. They hinted at their plans to open up the Amazon technology platform and invite developers to participate.

Having worked at Microsoft for three years, I had a real appreciation for a platform's power and my mind raced forward. They were going to need a developer program, sample code, more documentation, and all sorts of material in order to make this happen. I thought I could make a contribution, and stepped out to chat with the person who'd extended the invitation to me; I told her I wanted to interview for a role at Amazon to work on this new web services effort!

In order to demonstrate my interest in Amazon, I wrote a set of PHP wrappers for that very first version of AWS and called it PIA, the PHP Interface to Amazon. Amusingly enough, my now quaint announcement can still be found on the AWS Discussion Forums.[1]

I went through the interview process, and before the end of the summer I was hired as a senior member of the Amazon Associates team. My official duty was to write business analytical tools using Perl; however, my manager also indicated that I

---

[1] http://solutions.amazonwebservices.com/connect/thread.jspa?threadID=183

should devote 10-20% of my time to helping out on the web services effort in whatever way seemed appropriate.

Just a few weeks after I started, the manager of the Amazon Associates team asked me if I would mind speaking at a conference. She explained that they had intended to hire a "real" speaker when she accepted the invitation, but it was taking longer than expected to find the right person. I did a lot of public speaking earlier in my career and was happy to take care of this for them. That first event went really well, and before too long they tossed another one my way, and then another. The 10-20% of time allocated to the web services effort quickly grew to 40-50%; I kept busy writing sample code, answering questions on the AWS forums, and doing whatever I could to help the first members of our developer community succeed.

A few months passed and management approached me. "We've been planning to hire an evangelist to take on these speaking gigs, but it appears that you're already doing most of the job. Do you want it?" After some consultation with my family, I decided that I did, and in April of 2003 it was made official. I was the world's first (as far as I know) Web Services Evangelist!

In this role I travel the world and speak at a range of forums: conferences, user groups, college classes, and corporate technology teams. I arrange one-on-one meetings with developers in each city, and use these meetings to learn about what the developers are doing and how we can better serve them.

Over the last couple of years we've released a number of infrastructure services, including the Elastic Compute Cloud (EC2), the Simple Storage Service (S3), the Simple Queue Service (SQS), and the Simple Database (SimpleDB). It has been a real privilege to watch firsthand as the AWS team has designed, implemented, delivered, and operated service after service and to see our developer community grow to include hundreds of thousands of developers.

When I was asked to consider writing a book about AWS earlier this year, I thought it would be the perfect opportunity to share some of what I've learned in the last seven years.

Thanks for Reading

I hope that you enjoy reading this book as much as I've enjoyed writing it. Please feel free to look me up and let me know what you think.

Who Should Read This Book?

This book is aimed at web developers who have built a web application or two, and are ready to leap into the world of cloud computing using Amazon Web Services. This book makes use of the PHP language, but if you have experience in any server-side scripting language, you'll find the examples clear and easy to understand. It's also assumed that you know the fundamentals of HTML and CSS, and that you're comfortable with the Linux command line. Knowledge of basic system administration tasks, such as creating and mounting file systems, will also be helpful.

By the end of this book, you can expect to have a firm grasp of the concept of cloud computing and its role in enabling a whole new class of scalable and reliable web applications. You'll also have gained a clear understanding of the range of Amazon Web Services, such as the Simple Storage Service, the Elastic Compute Cloud, the Simple Queue Service, and SimpleDB. You'll be able to make use of all these services in your web applications as you write commands, tools, and processes in PHP.

What's Covered in This Book?

The book comprises 11 chapters. Chapters 3 through to 10 detail specific Amazon Web Services, and the final chapter explores building a sample application. I would recommend that you read the book from start to finish on your first go, but keep it by your side to dip in and out of the chapters if you need a refresher on a particular web service.

Chapter 1: *Welcome to Cloud Computing*
In this chapter, you'll learn the basics of cloud computing, and how it both builds on but differs from earlier hosting technologies. You will also see how organizations and individuals are putting it to use.

Chapter 2: *Amazon Web Services Overview*
This chapter moves from concept to reality, where you'll learn more about the fundamentals of each of the Amazon Web Services. Each web service is explained in detail and key terminology is introduced.

Chapter 3: *Tooling Up*
By now you're probably anxious to start. But before you jump in and start programming, you'll need to make sure your tools are in order. In Chapter 3, you'll

install and configure visual and command line tools, and the CloudFusion PHP library.

Chapter 4: *Storing Data with Amazon S3*

In Chapter 4, you will write your first PHP scripts. You will dive head-first into Amazon S3 and Amazon CloudFront, and learn how to store, retrieve, and distribute data on a world scale.

Chapter 5: *Web Hosting with Amazon EC2*

Chapter 5 is all about the Elastic Compute Cloud infrastructure and web service. You'll see how to use the AWS Management Console to launch an EC2 instance, create and attach disk storage space, and allocate IP addresses. For the climax, you'll develop a PHP script to do it all in code. To finish off, you'll create your very own Amazon Machine Image.

Chapter 6: *Building a Scalable Architecture with Amazon SQS*

In this chapter, you will learn how to build applications that scale to handle high or variable workloads, using message-passing architecture constructed using the Amazon Simple Queue Service. As an example of how powerful this approach is, you'll build an image downloading and processing pipeline with four queues that can be independently assigned greater or lesser resources.

Chapter 7: *EC2 Monitoring, Auto Scaling, and Elastic Load Balancing*

Chapter 7 will teach you how to use three powerful EC2 features—monitoring, auto scaling, and load balancing. These hardy features will aid you in keeping a watchful eye on system performance, scaling up and down in response to load, and distributing load across any number of EC2 instances.

Chapter 8: *Amazon SimpleDB: A Cloud Database*

In Chapter 8, you'll learn how to store and retrieve any amount of structured or semi-structured data using Amazon SimpleDB. You will also construct an application for parsing and storing RSS feeds, and also make use of Amazon SQS to increase performance.

Chapter 9: *Amazon Relational Database Service*

In Chapter 9, we'll look at Amazon Relational Database Service, which allows you to use relational databases in your applications, and query them using SQL. Amazon RDS is a powerful alternative to SimpleDB for cases in which the full query power of a relational database is required. You'll learn how to create database instances, back them up, scale them up or down, and delete them when they're no longer necessary.

Chapter 10: *Advanced AWS*

In this introspective chapter, you'll learn how to track your AWS usage in SimpleDB. You'll also explore Amazon EC2's Elastic Block Storage feature, see how to do backups, learn about public data sets, and discover how to increase performance or capacity by creating a RAID device on top of multiple EBS volumes. Finally, you will learn how to retrieve EC2 instance metadata, and construct system diagrams.

Chapter 11: *Putting It All Together: CloudList*

Combining all the knowledge gained from the previous chapters, you'll create a classified advertising application using EC2 services, S3, and SimpleDB.

The Book's Web Site

Located at http://www.sitepoint.com/books/cloud1/, the web site that supports this book will give you access to the following facilities.

The Code Archive

As you progress through this book, you'll note file names above many of the code listings. These refer to files in the code archive, a downloadable ZIP file that contains all of the finished examples presented in this book. Simply click the **Code Archive** link on the book's web site to download it.

Updates and Errata

No book is error-free, and attentive readers will no doubt spot at least one or two mistakes in this one. The Corrections and Typos page on the book's web site will provide the latest information about known typographical and code errors, and will offer necessary updates for new releases of browsers and related standards.[2]

---

[2] http://www.sitepoint.com/books/cloud1/errata.php

The SitePoint Forums

If you'd like to communicate with other developers about this book, you should join SitePoint's online community.[3] The forums offer an abundance of information above and beyond the solutions in this book, and a lot of interesting and experienced web developers hang out there. It's a good way to learn new tricks, have questions answered in a hurry, and just have a good time.

The SitePoint Newsletters

In addition to books like this one, SitePoint publishes free email newsletters, such as *The SitePoint Tribune*, *The SitePoint Tech Times*, and *The SitePoint Design View*. Reading them will keep you up to date on the latest news, product releases, trends, tips, and techniques for all aspects of web development. Sign up to one or more SitePoint newsletters at http://www.sitepoint.com/newsletter/.

The SitePoint Podcast

Join the SitePoint Podcast team for news, interviews, opinions, and fresh thinking for web developers and designers. They discuss the latest web industry topics, present guest speakers, and interview some of the best minds in the industry. You can catch up on all the podcasts at http://www.sitepoint.com/podcast/, or subscribe via iTunes.

Your Feedback

If you're unable to find an answer through the forums, or if you wish to contact us for any other reason, the best place to write is books@sitepoint.com. We have an email support system set up to track your inquiries, and friendly support staff members who can answer your questions. Suggestions for improvements, as well as notices of any mistakes you may find, are especially welcome.

---

[3] http://www.sitepoint.com/forums/

Acknowledgments

First and foremost, I need to thank my loving wife, Carmen. When I told her that I was considering an offer to write a book, she offered her enthusiastic support, and wondered why I hadn't taken her advice to do this a decade or more earlier.

Next, my amazing children, Stephen, Andy, Tina, Bianca, and Grace. Your support in the form of patience, peace and quiet, constant encouragement, and healthy snacks and meals has been without par. Now I can take care of all of those things that I promised to do "after the book is done!"

My colleagues at Amazon Web Services deserve more than a passing mention. My then-manager, Steve Rabuchin, championed this project internally and asked for nothing in return—save a mention in the acknowledgements. Jeff Bezos created an amazing company, one that allows innovation and good ideas like AWS to flourish. For my peers in AWS Developer Relations, here's what I've been working on; I hope that it lives up to your expectations! To all of the internal reviewers, your careful and detailed feedback was incredibly helpful.

And finally, thanks to Keith Hudgins (expert reviewer) and Andrew Tetlaw (technical editor) for all your assistance and feedback.

Conventions Used in This Book

You'll notice that we've used certain typographic and layout styles throughout this book to signify different types of information. Look out for the following items.

Markup Samples

Any markup—be that HTML or CSS—will be displayed using a fixed-width font, like so:

```
<h1>A perfect summer's day</h1>
<p>It was a lovely day for a walk in the park. The birds
were singing and the kids were all back at school.</p>
```

If the markup forms part of the book's code archive, the name of the file will appear at the top of the program listing, like this:

```
                                                              example.css
.footer {
  background-color: #CCC;
  border-top: 1px solid #333;
}
```

If only part of the file is displayed, this is indicated by the word *excerpt*:

```
                                                     example.css (excerpt)
  border-top: 1px solid #333;
```

If additional code is to be inserted into an existing example, the new code will be displayed in bold:

```
function animate() {
  new_variable = "Hello";
}
```

Where existing code is required for context, a vertical ellipsis will be displayed (rather than repeat all the code):

```
function animate() {
    ⋮
  return new_variable;
}
```

Some lines of code are intended to be entered on one line, but we've had to wrap them because of page constraints. A ➥ indicates a line break that exists for formatting purposes only, and should be ignored.

```
URL.open("http://www.sitepoint.com/blogs/2007/05/28/user-style-she
➥ets-come-of-age/");
```

Tips, Notes, and Warnings

Hey, You!

Tips will give you helpful little pointers.

Ahem, Excuse Me ...

Notes are useful asides that are related—but not critical—to the topic at hand. Think of them as extra tidbits of information.

 ## Make Sure You Always ...

... pay attention to these important points.

 ## Watch Out!

Warnings will highlight any gotchas that are likely to trip you up along the way.

Chapter  1

Welcome to Cloud Computing

One or two office moves ago, I was able to see Seattle's football and baseball stadiums from the window of my seventh-floor office. Built side-by-side during an economic boom, these expensive and high-capacity facilities sit empty for the most part. By my calculations, these buildings see peak usage one percent of the time at most. On average, they're empty. Hundreds of millions of dollars of capital sit idle. I use this stadium analogy—and have done so many times over the last few years—to help my audiences understand the business value of cloud computing.

Now, instead of a stadium, think of a large-scale corporate data center. It's packed with expensive, rapidly depreciating servers that wait, unutilized, for batch processing jobs, large amounts of data, and a flood of visitors to the company web site. That's because matching predictions and resources for web traffic has historically been problematic. Conservative forecasts lead to under-provisioning and create the risk of a "**success disaster**," where a surge of new users receive substandard service as a result. Overly optimistic forecasts lead to over-provisioning, increased costs, and wasted precious company resources.

As you'll see in this book, cloud computing provides a cost-effective and technically sophisticated solution to this problem. Returning to my opening analogy for a minute, it's as if a stadium of precisely the right size was built, used, and then destroyed each week. The stadium would have just enough seats, parking spaces, restrooms, and additional facilities needed to accommodate the actual number of attendees. With this scenario, a stadium fit for 50 people would be just as cost-effective as one built for 50,000.

Of course, such a situation is impractical with stadiums; custom, just-in-time resource instantiation is, on the other hand, perfectly reasonable and practical with cloud computing. Data processing infrastructure—servers, storage, and bandwidth—can be procured from the cloud, consumed as needed, and then relinquished back to the cloud, all in a matter of minutes. This is a welcome and much-needed change from yesterday's static, non-scalable infrastructure model. Paying for what you actually need instead of what you *think* you might need can change your application's cost profile for the better, enabling you to do more with less.

Avoiding a Success Disaster

Imagine you're a budding entrepreneur with limited resources. You have an idea for a new web site, one you're sure will be more popular than Facebook[1] or Twitter[2] before too long. You start to put together your business plan and draw a chart to predict your anticipated growth for the first six months. Having already run prototypes of your application and benchmarked its performance, you realize that you'll have to purchase and install one new server every month if all goes according to plan. You never want to run out of capacity, so you allow for plenty of time to order, receive, install, and configure each new server. Sufficient capacity in reserve is vital to handle the users that just might show up before your next server arrives; hence, you find you're always spending money you lack in order to support users who may or may not actually decide to visit your site.

You build your site and put it online, and patiently await your users. What happens next? There are three possible outcomes: your traffic estimates turn out to be way too low, just right, or way too high.

Perhaps you were thinking smallish, and your estimate was way too low. Instead of the trickle of users that you anticipated, your growth rate is far higher. Your initial

---

[1] http://facebook.com/
[2] http://twitter.com/

users quickly consume available resources. The site becomes overloaded and too slow, and potential users go away unsatisfied.

Then again, maybe you were thinking big and you procured more resources than you actually needed. You geared up for a big party, and it failed to materialize. Your cost structure is out of control, because there are only enough users to keep your servers partially occupied. Your business may fail because your fixed costs are too high.

Of course, you might have guessed correctly and your user base is growing at the rate you expected. Even then you're still in a vulnerable position. Early one morning you wake up to find that a link to your web site is now on the front page of Digg,[3] Reddit,[4] or Slashdot.[5] Or, a CNN commentator has mentioned your site in an offhand way and your URL is scrolling across the headline crawl at the bottom of the screen. This was the moment you've been waiting for, your chance at fame and fortune! Unfortunately, your fixed-scale infrastructure fails to be up to the task, so all those potential new users go away unhappy. The day, once so promising, ends up as yet another success disaster.

As you can see, making predictions about web traffic is a very difficult endeavor. The odds of guessing wrong are very high, as are the costs.

Cloud computing gives you the tools needed to prepare and cope with a traffic on-slaught, such as the ones I have just described. Providing you've put the time in up-front to architect your system properly and test it for scalability, a solution based on cloud computing will give you the confidence to withstand a traffic surge without melting your servers or sending you into bankruptcy.

Tell Me about Cloud Computing!

Let's dig a bit deeper into the concept of cloud computing now. I should warn you up-front that we'll be talking about *business* in this ostensibly technical book. There's simply no way to avoid the fact that cloud computing is more than just a new technology; it's a new business model as well. The technology is certainly interesting and I'll have plenty to say about it, but a complete discussion of cloud computing

---

[3] http://digg.com/

[4] http://reddit.com/

[5] http://slashdot.org/

will include business models, amortization, and even (gasp) dollars and cents. When I was young I was a hard-core geek and found these kinds of discussions irrelevant, perhaps even insulting. I was there for the technology, not to talk about money! With the benefit of 30 years of hindsight, I can now see that a real entrepreneur is able to use a mix of business and technical skills to create a successful business.

What's a Cloud?

Most of us have seen architecture diagrams like the one in Figure 1.1.

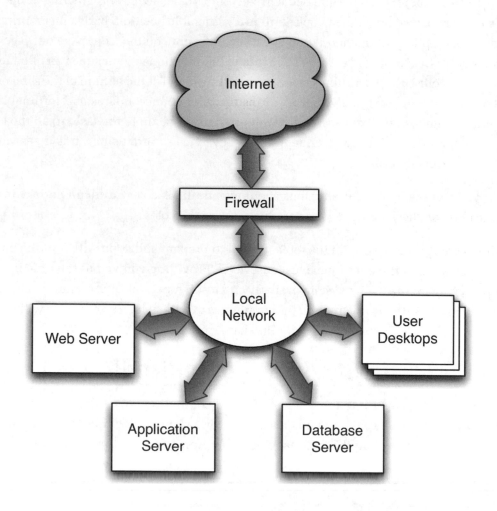

Figure 1.1. The Internet was once represented by a cloud

The cloud was used to indicate the Internet. Over time the meaning of "the Internet" has shifted, where it now includes the resources usually perceived as being *on* the Internet as well as the means to access them.

The term **cloud computing** came into popular use just a few years before this book was written. Some were quick to claim that, rather than a new concept, the term was simply another name for an existing practice. On the other hand, the term has become sufficiently powerful for some existing web applications have to magically turned into examples of cloud computing in action! Such is the power of marketing.

While the specifics may vary from vendor to vendor, you can think of **the cloud** as a coherent, large-scale, publicly accessible collection of compute, storage, and networking resources. These are allocated via web service calls (a programmable interface accessed via HTTP requests), and are available for short- or long-term use in exchange for payment based on actual resources consumed.

The cloud is intrinsically a multi-user environment, operating on behalf of a large number of users simultaneously. As such, it's responsible for managing and verifying user identity, tracking allocation of resources to users, providing exclusive access to the resources owned by each user, and preventing one user from interfering with other users. The software that runs each vendor's cloud is akin to an operating system in this regard.

Cloud computing builds on a number of important foundation-level technologies, including TCP-IP networking, robust internet connectivity, SOAP- and REST-style web services, commodity hardware, virtualization, and online payment systems. The details of many of these technologies are hidden from view; the cloud provides developers with an idealized, abstracted view of the available resources.

The Programmable Data Center

Let's think about the traditional model for allocation of IT resources. In the paragraphs that follow, the resources could be servers, storage, IP addresses, bandwidth, or even firewall entries.

If you're part of a big company and need additional IT resources, you probably find you're required to navigate through a process that includes a substantial amount of person-to-person communication and negotiation. Perhaps you send emails, create an online order or ticket, or simply pick up the phone and discuss your resource requirements. At the other end of the system there's some manual work involved to approve the request; locate, allocate, and configure the hardware; deal with cables, routers, and firewalls; and so forth. It is not unheard of for this process to take 12–18 months in some organizations!

If you are an entrepreneur, you call your ISP (Internet Service Provider), have a discussion, negotiate and then commit to an increased monthly fee, and gain access to your hardware in a time frame measured in hours or sometimes days.

Once you've gone through this process, you've probably made a long-term commitment to operate and pay for the resources. Big companies will charge your internal cost center each month, and will want to keep the hardware around until the end of its useful life. ISPs will be more flexible, but it is the rare ISP that is prepared to make large-scale changes on your behalf every hour or two.

The cloud takes the human response out of the loop. You (or more likely a management application running on your behalf) make web service requests ("calls") to the cloud. The cloud then goes through the following steps to service your request:

1. accepts the request
2. confirms that you have permission to make the request
3. validates the request against account limits
4. locates suitable free resources
5. attaches the resources to your account
6. initializes the resources
7. returns identifiers for the resources to satisfy the request

Your application then has exclusive access to the resources for as much time as needed. When the application no longer needs the resources, the application is responsible for returning them to the cloud. Here they are prepared for reuse (reformatted, erased, or rebooted, as appropriate) and then marked as free.

Since developers are accustomed to thinking in object oriented terms, we could even think of a particular vendor's cloud as an object. Indeed, an idealized definition for a cloud might look like this in PHP:[6]

---

[6] This doesn't map to any actual cloud; the method and parameter names are there only to illustrate my point.

```
class Cloud
{

  public function getDataCenters()
  {
    ⋮
  }

  public function allocateServer($dataCenter, $count)
  {
    ⋮
  }

  public function releaseServer($server)
  {
    ⋮
  }

  public function allocateDiskStorage($dataCenter, $gb)
  {
    ⋮
  }

  public function releaseDiskStorage($storage)
  {
    ⋮
  }

  ⋮
}
```

Here's how this idealized cloud would be used. First, we retrieve a list of available data centers ($d), and store a reference to the first one in the list ($d1):

```
$c = new Cloud();
$d = $c->getDataCenters();
$d1 = $d[0];
```

We can then allocate a server ($server) to the data center and create some storage space ($storage):

```
$server = $c->allocateServer($d1, 1);
$storage = $c->allocateDiskStorage($d1, 100);
```

The important point is that you can now write a program to initiate, control, monitor, and choreograph large-scale resource usage in the cloud. Scaling and partitioning decisions (such as how to add more server capacity or allocate existing capacity) that were once made manually and infrequently by system administrators with great deliberation can now be automated and done with regularity.

Characterizing the Cloud

Now that you have a basic understanding of what a cloud is and how it works, let's enumerate and dive in to some of its most useful attributes and characteristics. After spending years talking about Amazon Web Services in public forums, I've found that characterization is often more effective than definition when it comes to conveying the essence of the Amazon Web Services, and what it can do.

General Characteristics

Here are some general characteristics of the Amazon Web Services.

Elastic

The cloud allows scaling up and scaling down of resource usage on an as-needed basis. Elapsed time to increase or decrease usage is measured in seconds or minutes, rather than weeks or months.

Economies of scale

The cloud provider is able to exploit economies of scale and can procure real estate, power, cooling, bandwidth, and hardware at the best possible prices. Because the provider is supplying infrastructure as a commodity, it's in its best interest to drive costs down over time. The provider is also able to employ dedicated staffers with the sometimes elusive skills needed to operate at world-scale.

Pay-as-you-go

This is a general characteristic rather than a business characteristic for one very good reason: with cloud-based services, technical people will now be making resource allocation decisions that have an immediate effect on resource consumption and the level of overall costs. Running the business efficiently becomes *everyone's* job.

Business Characteristics

Here are some of the defining characteristics of the Amazon Web Services from a business-oriented point of view:

No up-front investment

Because cloud computing is built to satisfy usage on-demand for resources, there's no need to make a large one-time investment before actual demand occurs.

Fixed costs become variable

Instead of making a commitment to use a particular number of resources for the length of a contract (often one or three years), cloud computing allows for resource consumption to change in real time.

CAPEX becomes OPEX

Capital expenditures are made on a long-term basis and reflect a multi-year commitment to using a particular amount of resources. Operation expenditures are made based on actual use of the cloud-powered system and will change in real time.

Allocation is fine-grained

Cloud computing enables minimal usage amounts for both time and resources (for example: hours of server usage, bytes of storage).

The business gains flexibility

Because there's no long-term commitment to resources, the business is able to respond rapidly to changes in volume or the type of business.

Business focus of provider

The cloud provider is in the business of providing the cloud for public use. As such, it has a strong incentive to supply services that are reliable, applicable, and cost-effective. The cloud reflects a provider's core competencies.

Costs are associative

Due to the flexible resource allocation model of the cloud, it's just as easy to acquire and operate 100 servers for one hour as it is to acquire and operate one server for 100 hours. This opens the door to innovative thinking with respect to ways of partitioning large-scale problems.

Technical Characteristics

Here are some of the defining characteristics of the Amazon Web Services from the technical standpoint:

Scaling is quick

New hardware can be brought online in minutes to deal with unanticipated changes in demand, either internally (large compute jobs) or externally (traffic to a web site). Alternatively, resources can be returned to the cloud when no longer needed.

Infinite scalability is an illusion

While not literally true, each consumer can treat the cloud as if it offers near-infinite scalability. There's no need to provision ahead of time; dealing with surges and growth in demand is a problem for the cloud provider, instead of the consumer.

Resources are abstract and undifferentiated

Cloud computing encourages a focus on the relevant details—results and the observable performance—as opposed to the technical specifications of the hardware used. Underlying hardware will change and improve over time, but it's the job of the provider to stay on top of these issues. There's no longer a need to become personally acquainted with the intimate details of a particular dynamic resource.

Clouds are building blocks

The cloud provides IT resources as individual, separately priced, atomic-level building blocks. The consumer can choose to use none, all, or some of the services offered by the cloud.

Experimentation is cheap

The cloud removes the economic barrier to experimentation. You can access temporary resources to try out a new idea without making long-term commitments to hardware.

Some Common Misconceptions

After talking to thousands of people over the last few years, I've learned that there are a lot of misconceptions floating around the cloud. Some of this is due to the inherent unease that many feel with anything new. Other misconceptions reflect the fact that all the technologies are evolving rapidly, with new services and features appearing all the time. What's true one month is overtaken the next by a new and improved offering. With that said, here are some of the most common misconceptions. Parts of this list were adapted from work done at the University of California, Berkeley.[7]

"The cloud is a fad"

Given the number of once-promising technologies that have ended up on history's scrap heap, there's reason to be skeptical. It's important to be able to respond quickly and cost-effectively to changes in one's operating environment; this is a trend that's unlikely to reverse itself anytime soon, and the cloud is a perfect fit for this new world.

"Applications must be re-architected for the cloud"

I hear this one a lot. While it's true that some legacy applications will need to be re-architected to take advantage of the benefits of the cloud, there are also many existing applications using commercial or open source stacks that can be moved to the cloud more or less unchanged. They won't automatically take advantage of all the characteristics enumerated above, but the benefits can still be substantial.

"The cloud is inherently insecure"

Putting valuable corporate data "somewhere else" can be a scary proposition for an IT manager accustomed to full control. Cloud providers are aware of this potential stickling point, taking this aspect of the cloud very seriously. They're generally more than happy to share details of their security practices and policies with you. Advanced security systems, full control of network addressing and support for encryption, coupled with certifications such as SAS 70,[8] can all instill additional confidence in skeptical managers. I'll address the ways that AWS has helped developers, CIOs, and CTOs to get comfortable with the cloud in the next chapter.

---

[7] Michael Armbrust, Armando Fox, Rean Griffith, Anthony D. Joseph, Randy H. Katz, Andrew Konwinski, Gunho Lee, David A. Patterson, Ariel Rabkin, Ion Stoica, and Matei Zaharia, *Above the Clouds: A Berkeley View of Cloud Computing* (Berkeley: University of California, 2009), at http://d1smfj0g31qzek.cloudfront.net/abovetheclouds.pdf.

[8] http://www.sas70.com/

"The cloud is a single point of failure"

Some developers wonder what happens if the cloud goes down? Unlike traditional data centers, the AWS cloud offers a wide variety of options for functional and geographic redundancy to ensure high availability.

"The cloud promotes lock-in"

Because you can run existing applications on the cloud, they can be moved off as easily as they can be moved on. Operating systems, middleware, and applications can often be run in a cloud environment with little or no change. Of course, applications can be updated to take advantage of services offered by the cloud and that's what we'll be exploring in this book.

"The cloud is only good for running open source code"

This argument no longer holds water. Commercial operating system and application software vendors now recognize the cloud as a legitimate software environment and have worked to ensure that their applications have the proper cloud-friendly licenses. Forward-thinking vendors are now making their licensed software available on an hourly, pay-as-you-go basis. Instead of buying, for example, a database license for tens or even hundreds of thousands of dollars, you can gain access to the same database for a few dollars per hour.

"Cloud resources are too expensive"

Making a genuine comparison between internal IT resources and equivalent cloud computing resources has proven to be a difficult task.[9] Establishing the complete, all-inclusive cost of internal resources requires a level of tracking and accounting that's absent in most large- or mid-sized organizations. It's far too easy to neglect obvious costs, or to compare internal resources at a permanent hourly cost to scalable cloud resources that cost nothing when idle.

You'll find more detailed explanations in the remaining chapters of this book as to why these are indeed misconceptions.

---

[9] See, for example, James Hamilton's blog post: *McKinsey Speculates that Cloud Computing May Be More Expensive than Internal IT* at http://perspectives.mvdirona.com/2009/04/21/McKinseySpeculatesThatCloudComputingMayBeMoreExpensiveThanInternalIT.aspx .

Cloud Usage Patterns

Let's now examine some common cloud usage patterns. Armed with this information, you should be in a good position to decide whether your application or workload is a good fit for AWS. Although all these patterns essentially represent usage over time, there are a number of important nuances. In the cases below, "usage" generally represents a combination of common cloud resources—servers, storage, and bandwidth.

Constant usage over time

common for internal applications where there's little variation in usage or load from day to day or hour to hour

Cyclic internal load

characteristic for batch or data processing applications run on a predictable cycle, such as close of business for the day or month; the load, both in time and expected resource consumption, is highly predictable.

Cyclic external load

often applies to web sites that serve a particular market demand; sites related to entertainment and sporting events often fit this pattern.

Spiked internal load

typical in environments where researchers or analysts can submit large-scale, one-time jobs for processing; the demand is usually unpredictable.

Spiked external load

seen on the Web when an unknown site suddenly becomes popular, often for a very short time

Steady growth over time

usually for a mature application or web site; as additional users are added, growth and resources track accordingly.

Cloud Use Cases

Given that you've read this far, you might be wondering how other people are putting clouds to use. In this section I've collected some (but definitely not all) of the most common use cases, starting simple and building to the more complex.

Hosting Static Web Sites and Complex Web Applications

The cloud can easily host a static web site built from static HTML pages, CSS style sheets, and images. In fact, the simplest of such sites can be hosted using only cloud storage, perhaps aided by a content distribution system.

More complex web sites, often with substantial server-side processing and access to a relational database, can also be hosted in the cloud. These sites make use of cloud storage and processing, and often require substantial processing and storage resources to attain the required scale.

Software Development Life Cycle Support

The cloud is a good match for the resource requirements of each phase of the software development life cycle.

During development, using the cloud can ensure that developers have adequate resources for their work. Suppose that a team of developers are building a classic three-tier web application with web, application, and database tiers, each destined to reside on a separate physical server at deployment time. Without AWS, each developer would be supplied with three complete servers, each of which would sit idle for much of the day. Costs grow quickly when new developers are added to the project. Moving to the cloud means that each developer can spin up servers in the morning, develop and test all day, and then return the servers to the cloud at the end of the working day.

The cloud is also valuable during software testing. Developers can spin up testing servers and run unit tests on them without burdening their development servers. If there are numerous unit tests, multiple parallel servers can be used to spread the load around.

The cloud can be used to support a continuous integration environment. In such an environment, each source code commit operation initiates a multistep process of rebuilding, unit testing, and functional testing. If the code is being written for multiple target environments (several different versions or variants of Linux) or platforms (Windows and Linux), the cloud can be a very cost-effective alternative to owning your own infrastructure.

Load and performance testing can be done throughout each development cycle using cloud computing resources. If the application itself will run on the cloud, the testing will ensure that it performs well under a heavy load, adding additional resources as the load grows and removing them as it dissipates.

Testing the performance of a web application intended for public or enterprise deployment becomes easier when the cloud can supply the resources needed to conduct a test at a scale representative of the expected load. Several companies use cloud resources to generate loads that are the equivalent to hundreds of thousands of simultaneous users.

Once the application has been deployed (perhaps also to the cloud), the cloud can supply the resources needed to perform compatibility tests when application middleware layers or common components are updated. Thorough testing can help establish the confidence needed to make substantial upgrades to a production system without the risk of downtime.

Training

The cloud can supply the short-term resources needed to support various types of training programs.

If students are learning how to install, run, and monitor the three-tier application described in the previous section, they can use their own laptops to access cloud resources allocated for the duration of the class. When the class is over for the day the resources are returned to the cloud. The students can start from a single "master" machine image and avoid wasting time (theirs or the instructor's) installing and configuring required packages and applications.

Traditional training classes must impose limits on class size corresponding to the restricted amount of physical hardware that they have available. Leading companies are now conducting online training seminars, backed by per-student cloud-based resources where an additional server is launched as each new student joins the class. This technique has been used by application and database software vendors with impressive results.

Demos

Resources drawn from the cloud can be used to host and deliver demos and trial versions of packaged software applications. Vendors can place demos into the hands of potential customers while the lead is "hot," rather than after the usual protracted delay while a suitable test environment is prepared. Application vendors can create and provide access to a server hosted in the cloud at low cost and on short notice. The sales cycle is shortened and customers have a good experience with the use of cloud-based resources. In some cases, cloud-based demos actually lead to cloud-based deployment.

Data Storage

The cloud is a good place to store private or public data. Scalability, long-term durability, and economy of scale are of paramount importance for this use case. The stored data could be as simple and compact as a few personal files for backup, or it could be as large and complex as a backup of a company's entire digital assets, or anything in between.

Often, use of storage in the cloud turns out to be an excellent first step, a step that inspires confidence and soon leads to considering the cloud for other, more complex, use cases.

Disaster Recovery and Business Continuity

Enterprises with a mission-critical dependence on IT resources must have a plan in place to deal with any setback, be it a temporary or permanent loss of the resources or access to them. The plan must take into account the potential for fires, floods, earthquakes, and terrorist acts to disrupt a company's operations. Many businesses maintain an entire data center in reserve; data is replicated to the backup center on occasion and the entire complex stands ready to be activated at a moment's notice. Needless to say, the cost of building and running a duplicate facility is considerable.

Cloud computing, once again, offers a different way to ensure business continuity. Instead of wasting capital on hardware that will never be put to use under normal circumstances, the entire corporate network can be modeled as a set of cloud resources, captured in template form, and then instantiated when trouble strikes. In this particular use case, you'll need to work with your cloud provider to ensure that the necessary resources will be available when you need them.

Once the corporate network has been modeled for business continuity purposes, other interesting uses come to mind. Traditionally, widespread deployment of up-dated versions of middleware and shared applications components require substantial compatibility and performance testing. This task is fraught with peril! Many companies find themselves slowly slipping behind: they're unable to deploy the newest code due to limitations in their ability to fully test before deployment, and unwilling to risk facing the consequences of a failed deployment.

Imagine spinning up a full copy (or a representative, scaled-down subset) of the corporate network, along with specified versions of the application components to be tested, and then running compatibility and load tests on it, all in the cloud, and at a very reasonable cost.

Media Processing and Rendering

A number of popular web sites support uploading of media files: music, still images, or videos. Once uploaded the files undergo a number of processing steps, which can be compute-intensive, I/O intensive, or both. Files of all types are scanned for viruses and other forms of malware. Music is fingerprinted (to check for copyright violations) and then transcoded to allow for playback at different bit rates. Images are scaled, watermarked, checked for duplication, and rendered in different formats. Videos are also transcoded and scaled, and sometimes broken into shorter chunks. Finally, the finished objects are stored and made available for online viewing or downloading.

Rendoring uses a scene description to generate frames for an animated movie. Each frame can be rendered independently of the others. There's comparatively little input data, but plenty of output data. The process is compute-intensive, since each pixel of each frame must be computed, taking into account light, shadow, color, and motion.

Cloud computing is ideal for processing and rendering use cases due to the amount of storage, processing, and internet bandwidth they can consume.

Business and Scientific Data Processing

Scientific and business data processing often involves extremely large-scale data sets and can consume vast amounts of CPU power. Analysis is often done on an on-demand basis, leading to over-commitments of limited internal resources. In fact,

I'm told that many internal scientific compute grids routinely flip between 0% usage (absolutely no work to be done) and 100% usage (every possible processor is in use). This is a particularly acute problem on university campuses, where usage heats up before the end of the semester and before major conferences.

Business data processing can be ad hoc (unscheduled) or more routine; monthly payroll processing and daily web log processing come to mind as very obvious use cases for cloud computing. A large, busy web site is capable of generating tens of gigabytes of log file data in each 24-hour period. Due to the amount of business intelligence that can be mined from the log files, analysis is a mission-critical function. Gaining access to the usage data on a more timely basis enables better site optimization and a quicker response to changes and trends. The daily analysis process starts to take long and longer, and at some point begins to take almost 24 hours. Once this happens, heavily parallel solutions are brought to bear on the problem, consuming more resources for a shorter amount of time—a perfect case for cloud computing.

Overflow Processing

As companies begin to understand the benefits that cloud computing brings, they look for solutions that allow them to use their existing IT resources for routine work, while pushing the extra work to the cloud. It's like bringing in temporary workers to handle a holiday rush.

Overflow processing allows companies to become comfortable with the cloud. They find more and more ways to use the cloud as their confidence level increases, and as the amount of vital corporate data already present in the cloud grows.

Just Recapping

As you can see, there are a number of different ways to use the cloud to host existing applications, build creative new ones, and improve the cost-effectiveness and efficiency of organizations large and small.

In this chapter we've learned the fundamentals of cloud computing. Using a sporting-venue analogy, we've seen how cloud computing allows individuals and organizations to do a better job of matching available resources to actual demand. We've learned about the notion of a "success disaster" and aim to avoid having one of our own—with the assistance of AWS, of course. From there we covered the characteristics of a cloud, and proposed that the cloud could be thought of as a programmable data center. We examined the cloud from three sides: general, technical, and business, and enumerated some common misconceptions. Finally, we took a quick look at usage patterns and an extended look at actual use cases.

In the next chapter we'll learn more about the Amazon Web Services, and we'll get ready to start writing some code of our own.

Chapter **2**

Amazon Web Services Overview

In the previous chapter we discussed the concept of cloud computing in general terms. We listed and discussed the most interesting and relevant characteristics of the cloud. With that information as background, it's now time to move from concept to reality.

In this chapter I'll introduce Amazon Web Services, or AWS for short. After a review of some key concepts I'll talk about each AWS service.

Amazon and AWS Overview

You've probably made a purchase at the Amazon.com[1] site. Perhaps you even bought this book from Amazon.com. One of my first purchases, way back in November 1996, was a book on Perl programming.

Amazon.com Inc. was founded in 1994 and launched in 1995. In order to attain the scale needed to create a profitable online business, the company made strategic investments in world-scale internet infrastructure, including data centers in multiple locations around the world, high-speed connectivity, a plethora of servers, and the

---

[1] http://www.amazon.com/

creation of a world-class system architecture. With an active customer base in the tens of millions, each and every system component must be reliable, efficient, cost-effective, and highly scalable.

Realizing that developers everywhere could benefit from access to the services that support Amazon's web site, Amazon decided to create a new line of business. In early 2006, the company launched the Amazon Simple Storage Service (S3). Since then Amazon has brought a broad line of infrastructure, payment, workforce, merchant, and web analytic services to market under Amazon Web Services (AWS). In this book I'll focus on the infrastructure services. If you'd like to learn about the other services, please visit the AWS home page.[2]

Building Blocks

AWS consists of a set of building-block services. The services are designed to work independently, so that you can use one without having to sign up for or know anything at all about the others. They are, however, also designed to work well together. For example, they share a common naming convention and authentication system. So, much of what you learn as you use one service is applicable to some or all the other services! This building-block approach also minimizes internal connections and dependencies between the services, which gives Amazon the ability to improve each service independently so that each works as efficiently as possible.

Every function in AWS can be accessed by making a web service call. Starting a server, creating a load balancer, allocating an IP address, or attaching a persistent storage volume (to name just a few actions) are all accomplished by making web service calls to AWS. These calls are the down-to-the-metal, low-level interface to AWS. While it's possible (and simple enough) to make the calls yourself, it's far easier to use a client library written specifically for the programming language of your choice.

Protocols

The web service calls use one of two popular protocols **SOAP** (once short for Simple Object Access Protocol, but now just a pseudo-acronym) and **REST** (an assimilation of Representational State Transfer). Because this book will focus on building useful applications and utilities, I will access AWS using a client library rather than

---

[2] http://aws.amazon.com/

spending much time at the web service protocol layer. Suffice it to say that SOAP and REST are two different ways to initiate a call (or request) to a web service. Libraries and tools are layered on top of the AWS **APIs** (Application Programming Interfaces) to simplify the process of accessing the services.

I guess I have to mention XML here too! XML is a fundamental part of the SOAP protocol. If you access AWS using a SOAP-based library you'll have no dealings with XML tags or elements. However, if you use a REST-based library, you'll have to do some parsing to access the data returned by each call. The examples in this book will use PHP's SimpleXML parser.[3]

Figure 2.1 shows how all the parts that I've outlined in this section fit together. We'll be focusing on building AWS-powered Applications (top-left corner):

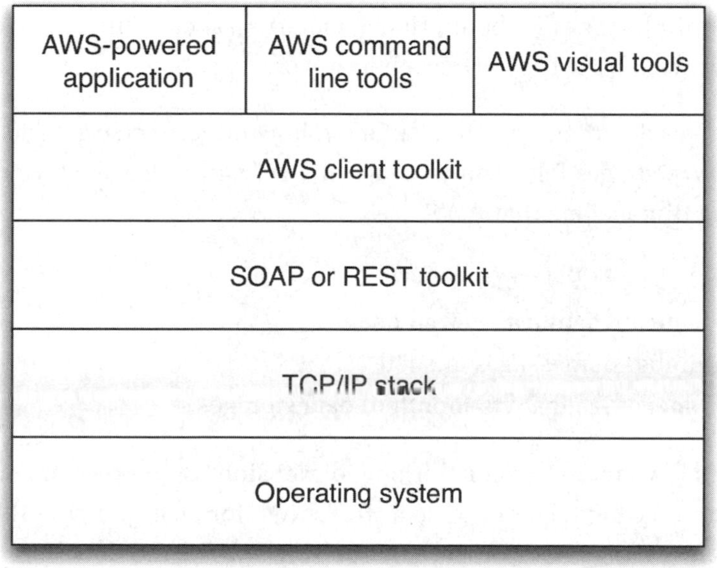

AWS-powered application	AWS command line tools	AWS visual tools
AWS client toolkit		
SOAP or REST toolkit		
TCP/IP stack		
Operating system		

Figure 2.1. Putting the pieces together

The command line tools and visual tools communicate with AWS using the open, published APIs. So, you're able to duplicate what you see any tool do in your own applications. As a consequence of this strict layering of behavior, all developers are on an equal footing.

---

[3] http://www.php.net/simplexml/

In the section called "Key Concepts" below, I'll discuss the basic functions (for example, `RunInstances`) and the associated command line tools (`ec2-run-instances`). Keep in mind that the same functionality can be accessed using visual tools supplied by Amazon or by third parties, and that you can always build your own tools using the same APIs.

Dollars and Cents

Because AWS is a pay-as-you-go web service, there's a separate cost for the use of each service. You can model your AWS costs during development time to gain a better understanding of what it will cost to operate your site at scale. With sufficient attention to detail you should be able to compute the actual cost of serving a single web page, or performing some other action initiated by one of your users. You can also use the AWS Simple Monthly Calculator[4] to estimate your costs.

With that in mind, let's talk about pricing, metering, accounting, presentment, and billing before we look at the services themselves.

Pricing involves deciding what to charge for, how often to charge, and how much to charge. AWS charges for resource usage at a very granular level. Here are some of the pricing dimensions that AWS uses:

- **Time**—an hour of CPU time.
- **Volume**—a gigabyte of transferred data.
- **Count**—number of messages queued.
- **Time and space**—a gigabyte-month of data storage.

Most services have more than one pricing dimension. If you use an Amazon EC2 (Elastic Compute Cloud) server to do a web crawl, for example, you'll be charged for the amount of time that the server is running and for the data that you fetch.

The web site detail page for each AWS service shows the cost of using the service. Each AWS service is published and visible to everyone. The pricing for many of the services reflects volume discounts based on usage; that is, the more you use the service, the less it costs per event. Pricing for the services tends to decline over time

---

[4] http://calculator.s3.amazonaws.com/calc5.html

due to the effects of Moore's Law and economies of scale.[5] Pricing also reflects the fact that operating costs can vary from country to country.

Metering refers to AWS measuring and recording information about your use of each service. This includes information about when you called the service, which service you called, and how many resources you consumed in each of the service's pricing dimensions.

Accounting means that AWS tabulates the metered information over time, adding up your usage and tracking your overall resource consumption. You can use the AWS Portal to access detailed information about your resource consumption.

Presentment involves making your AWS usage available so that you can see what you've used and the cost you've incurred. This information is also available from the AWS portal.

Billing indicates that AWS will charge your credit card at the beginning of each month for the resources you consumed in the previous month.

Does any of this seem a little familiar? Indeed, your utility supplier (phone, water, or natural gas) takes on a very similar set of duties. This similarity causes many people to correctly observe that an important aspect of cloud computing is utility pricing.

Key Concepts

Let's review some key concepts and AWS terms to prepare to talk about the services themselves. In the following sections, I include lists of some of the functions and commands that you can use to access the relevant parts of AWS mentioned below. These lists are by no means complete; my intention is to give you a better sense of the level of abstraction made possible by AWS, and also to hint at the types of functions that are available within the AWS API.

---

[5] Moore's Law refers to the long-term trend where the number of transistors placed on an integrated circuit doubles every two years. It has since been generalized to reflect technology doubling in power and halving in price every two years.

Availability Zone

An AWS **Availability Zone** represents a set of distinct locations within an AWS Region. Each Availability Zone has independent power grid and network connections so that it's protected from failures in other Availability Zones. The zones within a Region are connected to each other with inexpensive, low-latency connections. The Region name is part of the zone name. For example, us-east-1a is one of four zones in the us-east-1 Region.

The mapping of a zone name to a particular physical location is different yet consistent for each AWS account. For example, my us-east-1a is possibly different to your us-east-1a, but my us-east-1a is always in the same physical location. This per-user mapping is intentional and was designed to simplify expansion and load management.

The `DescribeAvailabilityZones` function and the `ec2-describe-availability-zones` command return the list of Availability Zones for a Region.

Region

An AWS **Region** represents a set of AWS Availability Zones that are located in one geographic area. Each AWS Region has a name that roughly indicates the area it covers, but the exact location is kept secret for security purposes. The current Regions are `us-east-1` (Northern Virginia), `us-west-1` (Northern California), `eu-west-1` (Ireland), and `ap-southeast-1` (Signapore). Over time, additional Regions will become available. The `DescribeRegions` function and the `ec2-describe-regions` command return the current list of Regions. You may choose to make use of multiple Regions for business, legal, or performance reasons.

Access Identifiers

AWS uses a number of different **access identifiers** to identify accounts. The identifiers use different forms of public key encryption and always exist in pairs. The first element of the pair is public, can be disclosed as needed, and serves to identify a single AWS account. The second element is private, should never be shared, and is used to create a signature for each request made to AWS. The signature, when transmitted as part of a request, ensures the integrity of the request and also allows AWS to verify that the request was made by the proper user. AWS can use two different sets of access identifiers. The first comprises an Access Key ID and a Secret

Access Key. The second is an X.509 certificate with public and private keys inside. You can view your access identifiers from the AWS portal.[6]

Amazon Machine Image

An **Amazon Machine Image (AMI)** is very similar to the root drive of your computer. It contains the operating system and can also include additional software and layers of your application such as database servers, middleware, web servers, and so forth. You start by booting up a prebuilt AMI, and before too long you learn how to create custom AMIs for yourself or to share, or even sell. Each AMI has a unique ID; for example, the AMI identified by `ami-bf5eb9d6` contains the Ubuntu 9.04 Jaunty server. The `DescribeImages` function and the `ec2-describe-images` command return the list of registered instances. The AWS AMI catalog[7] contains a complete list of public, registered AMIs.

Instance

An **instance** represents one running copy of an AMI. You can launch any number of copies of the same AMI. Instances are launched using `RunInstances` and the `ec2-run-instances` command. Running instances are listed using `DescribeInstances` and `ec2-describe-instances`, and terminated using the `TerminateInstances` function or the `ec2-terminate-instances` command. Before long you will also learn about the AWS Management Console, which is a visual tool for managing EC2 instances.

Elastic IP Address

AWS allows you to allocate fixed (static) IP addresses and then attach (or route) them to your instances; these are called **Elastic IP Addresses**. Each instance can have at most one such address attached. The "Elastic" part of the name indicates that you can easily allocate, attach, detach, and free the addresses as your needs change. Addresses are allocated using the `AllocateAddress` function or the `ec2-allocate-address` command, and attached to an instance using the `AssociateAddress` function or the `ec2-associate-address` command.

---

[6] http://aws.amazon.com/account
[7] http://aws.amazon.com/amis

Elastic Block Store Volume

An **Elastic Block Store** (EBS) volume is an addressable disk volume. You (or your application, working on your behalf) can create a volume and attach it to any running instance in the same Availability Zone. The volume can then be formatted, mounted, and used as if it were a local disk drive. Volumes have a lifetime independent of any particular instance; you can have disk storage that persists even when none of your instances are running. Volumes are created using the `CreateVolume` function or the `ec2-create-volume` command, and then attached to a running instance using the `AttachVolume` function or the `ec2-attach-volume` command.

Security Group

A **Security Group** defines the allowable set of inbound network connections for an instance. Each group is named and consists of a list of protocols, ports, and IP address ranges. A group can be applied to multiple instances, and a single instance can be regulated by multiple groups. Groups are created using the `CreateSecurityGroup` function and the `ec2-add-group` command. The `AuthorizeSecurityGroupIngress` function and the `ec2-authorize` command add new permissions to an existing security group.

Access Control List

An **Access Control List** (ACL) specifies permissions for an object. An ACL is a list of identity/permission pairs. The `GetObjectAccessControlPolicy` function retrieves an object's existing ACL and the `SetObjectAccessControlPolicy` function sets a new ACL on an object.

AWS Infrastructure Web Services

Now that you know the key concepts, let's look at each of the AWS infrastructure web services.

Amazon Simple Storage Service

The Amazon **Simple Storage Service (S3)** is used to store binary data objects for private or public use. The S3 implementation is fault-tolerant and assumes that hardware failures are a common occurrence.

There are multiple independent S3 locations: the United States Standard Region, Northern California Region,[8] Europe, and Asia.

S3 automatically makes multiple copies of each object to achieve high availability, as well as for durability. These objects can range in size from one byte to five gigabytes. All objects reside in buckets, in which you can have as many objects as you like. Your S3 account can accommodate up to 100 buckets or named object containers. Bucket names are drawn from a global namespace, so you'll have to exercise some care and have a sound strategy for generating bucket names. When you store an object you provide a key that must be unique to the bucket. The combination of the S3 domain name, the globally unique bucket name, and the object key form a globally unique identifier. S3 objects can be accessed using an HTTP request, making S3 a perfect place to store static web pages, style sheets, JavaScript files, images, and media files. For example, here's an S3 URL to a picture of Maggie, my Golden Retriever: http://sitepoint-aws-cloud-book.s3.amazonaws.com/maggie.jpg.

The bucket name is `sitepoint-aws-cloud-book` and the unique key is `maggie.jpg`. The S3 domain name is s3.amazonaws.com.

Each S3 object has its own ACL. By default, each newly created S3 object is private. You can use the S3 API to make it accessible to everyone or specified users, and you can grant them read and/or write permission. I set Maggie's picture to be publicly readable so that you can see her.

Other AWS services use S3 as a storage system for AMIs, access logs, and temporary files.

Amazon S3 charges accrue based on the amount of data stored, the amount of data transferred in and out of S3, and the number of requests made to S3.

Amazon CloudFront

Amazon **CloudFront** is a content distribution service designed to work in conjunction with Amazon S3. Because all Amazon S3 data is served from central locations in the US, Europe, and Asia, access from certain parts of the world can take several hundred milliseconds. CloudFront addresses this "speed of light" limitation with

---

[8] The Northern California location provides optimal performance for requests originating in California and the Southwestern United States.

a global network of edge locations (16 at press time) located near your end users in the United States, Europe, and Asia.

After you have stored your data in an S3 bucket, you can create a CloudFront Distribution. Each distribution contains a unique URL, which you use in place of the bucket name and S3 domain to achieve content distribution. Maggie's picture is available at the following location via CloudFront: http://d1iodn8r1n0x7w.cloudfront.net/maggie.jpg.

As you can see, the object's name is preserved, prefixed with a URL taken from the bucket's distribution. The HTTP, HTTPS, and RTMP protocols can be used to access content that has been made available through CloudFront.

CloudFront charges accrue based on the amount of data transferred out of CloudFront and the number of requests made to CloudFront.

Amazon Simple Queue Service

You use the **Simple Queue Service (SQS)** to build highly scalable processing pipelines using loosely coupled parts. Queues allow for flexibility, asynchrony, and fault tolerance. Each step in the pipeline retrieves work units from an instance of the queue service, processes the work unit as appropriate, and then writes completed work into another queue for further processing. Queues work well when the requirements—be it time, CPU, or I/O speed—for each processing step for a particular work unit vary widely.

Like S3, there are separate instances of SQS running in the US and in Europe.

SQS usage is charged based on the amount of data transferred and the number of requests made to SQS.

Amazon SimpleDB

Amazon **SimpleDB** supports storage and retrieval of semi-structured data. Unlike a traditional relational database, SimpleDB does not use a fixed database schema. Instead, SimpleDB adapts to changes in the "shape" of the stored data on the fly, so there's no need to update existing records when you add a new field. SimpleDB also automatically indexes all stored data so it's unnecessary to do your own profiling or query optimization.

The SimpleDB data model is flexible and straightforward. You group similar data into domains. Each domain can hold millions of items, each with a unique key. Each item, in turn, can have a number of attribute/value pairs. The attribute names can vary from item to item as needed.

Like the other services, SimpleDB was built to handle large amounts of data and high request rates. So there's no need to worry about adding additional disk drives and implementing complex data replication schemes as your database grows. You can grow your application to world-scale while keeping your code clean and your architecture straightforward.

SimpleDB charges accrue based on the amount of data stored, the amount of data transferred, and the amount of CPU time consumed by query processing.

Amazon Relational Database Service

The Amazon **Relational Database Service** (RDS) makes it easy for you to create, manage, back up, and scale MySQL database instances. RDS calls these **DB Instances**, and that's the terminology I'll be using in this book.

RDS handles the tedious and bothersome operational details associated with running MySQL so that you can focus on your application. You don't have to worry about procuring hardware, installing and configuring an operating system or database engine, or finding storage for backups. You can scale the amount of processing power up or down, and increase the storage allocation in a matter of minutes, so you can respond to changing circumstances with ease. You can back up your DB Instance to Amazon S3 with a single call or click, and create a fresh DB Instance from any of your snapshots.

RDS also has a Multi-AZ (or Multi-Availability Zone) option that allows you to run a redundant backup copy of your DB Instance for extra availability and reliability.

Amazon RDS charges accrue based on the amount of time that each DB Instance is running, and the amount of storage allocated to the instance.

Amazon Elastic Compute Cloud

The **Elastic Compute Cloud (Amazon EC2)** infrastructure gives you the ability to launch server instances running the AMI (Amazon Machine Instance) of your choice. Instance types are available with a wide range of memory, processing power, and local disk storage. You can launch instances in any EC2 Region and you can choose to specify an Availability Zone if needed. Once launched, the instances are attached to your account and should remain running until you shut them down.

Each instance is protected by a firewall which, by default, blocks all internal and external connectivity. When you launch instances you can associate any number of security groups with them. The security groups allow you to control access to your instances on a very granular basis.

The EC2 infrastructure provides instances with an IP address and a DNS entry when they're launched. The address and the entry are transient: when the instance shuts down or crashes they are disassociated from the instance. If you need an IP address that will survive a shutdown or that can be mapped to any one of a number of machines, you can use an Elastic IP Address. These addresses are effectively owned by your AWS account rather than by a particular EC2 instance. Once allocated, the addresses are yours until you decide to relinquish them.

The instances have an ample amount of local disk storage for temporary processing. Like the standard IP address and DNS name, this storage is transient and is erased and reused when you're finished with the instance.

Elastic Block Store (EBS) volumes can be used for long-term and more durable storage. You can create a number of EBS volumes, attach them to your instances, and then format the volumes with the file system of your choice. You can make snapshot backups to S3, and you can restore the snapshots to the same volume or use them to create new volumes.

EC2 charges accrue based on the number of hours the instance runs and the amount of data transferred in and out. There is no charge to transfer data to and from other AWS services in the same Region. The charges for EBS volumes are based on the size of the volume (regardless of how much data is actually stored) and there are also charges for I/O requests. To prevent hoarding, you are charged for Elastic IP addresses that you allocate but don't use.

The EC2 CloudWatch feature provides monitoring within EC2. It collects and stores information about the performance (CPU load average, disk I/O rate, and network I/O rate) of each of your EC2 instances. The data is stored for two weeks and can be retrieved for analysis or visualization.

The EC2 **Elastic Load Balancer** allows you to distribute web traffic across any number of EC2 instances. The instances can be in the same Availability Zone or they can be scattered across several zones in a Region. The elastic load balancer performs periodic health checks on the instances that it manages, and will stop sending traffic to any instances it determines to be unhealthy. The health check consists of a configurable ping to each EC2 instance.

Finally, the EC2 **Auto Scaling** feature uses the data collected by CloudWatch to help you build a system that can scale out (adding more EC2 instances) and scale in (shutting down EC2 instances) within a defined auto scaling group. Auto scaling lets you define triggers for each operation. For example, you can use Auto Scaling to scale out by 10% when the average CPU utilization across the auto scaling group exceeds 80%, and then scale in by 10% when the CPU utilization drops below 40%.

Amazon Elastic MapReduce

The Elastic **MapReduce** service gives you the ability to use a number of EC2 instances running in parallel for large-scale data processing jobs. This service uses the open source Hadoop framework,[9] an implementation of the MapReduce paradigm. Invented by Google, MapReduce isolates you from many of the issues that arise when you need to launch, monitor, load (with data), and terminate dozens or even hundreds of instances. Elastic MapReduce works just as well for pedestrian tasks, such as log file processing, as it does for esoteric scientific applications, such as gene sequencing.

Other Services

AWS gains new features and services with great regularity. To stay up to date with the latest and greatest happenings, you should check the AWS home page and the AWS Blog[10] (written by yours truly) from time to time.

---

[9] http://hadoop.apache.org/mapreduce/

[10] http://aws.typepad.com/

What We've Covered

In this chapter, we took a closer look at each of the AWS infrastructure services, reviewing their usage characteristics and pricing models. We also examined a number of key AWS concepts. In the next chapter, we'll tool up in preparation for building our first scripts that make use of all these capabilities.

Chapter

Tooling Up

Now that you're familiar with the range of Amazon Web Services and what they're capable of, you may be wondering how we start using them. Before we start coding, however, we'll need to tool up. I'll spend some time on the visual tools (user interfaces and consoles) and command line tools. I'll also discuss the level below the tools: the libraries available for a particular programming language. This book will focus on PHP, but I'll provide some general rules for library selection. This chapter will also lead you through creating of your AWS account, installing CloudFusion, and the necessary command line tools.

Technical Prerequisites

Before we go too much further, I want to ensure that my expectations regarding your programming and system management skills are correct. It's also important that you have the right hardware and software at your disposal.

Skills Expectations

Because this book is targeted at mid-level PHP programmers, I assume that you can already read and write PHP with some skill. I'll avoid using any esoteric features of PHP, but I'll also avoid explaining the `error_reporting` function or the detailed behavior of `foreach` loops. I also expect you to know the mechanics of writing, debugging, and running PHP code.

On the web technology side, I expect you to know HTML and some CSS, and a tiny bit of JavaScript.

On the systems side, I assume that you're comfortable with the Linux/Unix command line, as there's no time to explain `ls`, `scp`, or `grep`. I assume that you've mastered the ins and outs of your text editor, be it vi, emacs, Notepad, or otherwise.

These days, developers in small organizations are expected to know a thing or two about system administration. I assume that you, too, are quite the "devministrator" and that common system administration tasks, such as installing packages and examining log files, are part of your skill repertoire.

Hardware and Software Expectations

In the sections that follow, I expect you to have a Mac or a PC that is connected to the Internet. Your PC can be running Windows, or it can be running the Linux distribution of your choice.

It's often useful to run some PHP code locally. Packages like WAMP for Windows[1] or MAMP for the Mac[2] make it easy to install and configure PHP, MySQL, and an Apache web server for local development. I'll be talking about this again in the section called "Running the PHP Code in This Book".

You need a web browser. If all you have is Internet Explorer, that's fine—but some of the visual tools take the form of Firefox extensions.

You'll need a good **SSH (Secure Shell)** client. For Windows use, my personal favorite is PuTTY,[3] which is fast and reliable, and its terminal emulation is flawless. For Mac OS X and Linux, you can use the command line SSH clients that come with your operating system.

---

[1] http://www.wampserver.com/en/
[2] http://www.mamp.info/en/index.html
[3] http://www.chiark.greenend.org.uk/~sgtatham/putty/

If you work in a corporate setting and your desktop has been locked down, the cloud actually gives you a really interesting new option. You can launch an EC2 instance running Windows, access it using the Windows Remote Desktop, and use that for development while leaving your desktop machine untouched.

Optional but Recommended

My final three recommendations are that you have some spare domain names, a good DNS service, and a source code control system.

Back when I was young, domain names were expensive ($75 per year) and complex to register. These days they're cheap to acquire and registration is very simple. I recommend that you have at least one or two freely available as you work through the examples in this book.

You should also have access to a DNS provider, so that you can map your domain names to IP addresses. When I was merely middle-aged I used to run my own DNS server. Since 2004 I've been a very happy customer of ZoneEdit.[4] You can have DNS service for up to five domains at no charge.

You may want to think about a source code control system for your application as well. A source code control system hosted in the cloud will let you keep track of all the bits and pieces of your application, and will allow you to retrieve the newest code at any time. I have been using CVS Dude[5] as my CVS host since 2004. Since CVS is even more archaic than I am,[6] they also host the more modern Subversion system. Depending on the needs of your project, you may also want to consider GitHub,[7] Google Code,[8] or SourceForge.[9] Some of the free systems require you to use a specific open source license, so read the fine print first.

---

[4] http://www.zoneedit.com/

[5] http://www.cvsdude.org/

[6] In case you haven't noticed, I enjoy poking fun at myself and making a big deal of the fact that I'm not exactly a spring chicken. I hope you enjoy my peculiar brand of humor.

[7] http://github.com/

[8] http://code.google.com/hosting/

[9] http://sourceforge.net/

Tools and Libraries

Now that we've reviewed the AWS infrastructure services and made sure that you have the right skills and some technical prerequisites mastered, it's time to gear up and do some work.

In this section I will tell you about the programming libraries, command line tools, and visual tools that are available to you as an AWS developer. In each case I will provide several alternatives in order to make clear that you have a number of reasonable options. Some of the items I'll describe were created and are maintained by Amazon; others are the work of independent developers.

Tool Considerations

Here are some points to consider when choosing your tools:

Documentation
Are the tools backed by some good documentation? Does the documentation match the current release? Does the maintainer strive to create a complete product or is documentation always lagging behind the code?

Popularity and Reputation
What comes up when you do a web search for the name of the tool? Can you locate the tool's community without too much trouble?

Community Support
Check to see if the tools have a strong community behind them. Is there a discussion forum? See what other developers have to say and whether they're contributing or complaining. Also, see if the original creators or current maintainers are participating in the community, or if they're in hands-off mode. Do they enjoy interacting with their users, or has it become a chore?

Update Frequency
Take a look at the release and patch history for the tool. Are updates released in sync with new releases of AWS? Does the creator release patches on a timely basis in response to problems? Is there a fixed release schedule?

Style

> Is the tool a good fit for your working style? Are the command, function, or data structure names consistent and logical? Are your educated guesses correct more often than not?[10]

Security

> You'll be trusting these tools with your AWS public and secret keys, so caution is advised. At the very least, you should understand how and where the tool stores your keys and how it protects them from accidental disclosure or casual discovery.

Language Libraries

Language libraries occupy the space between your application and the web service calls. The libraries provide an adapter that matches the structure and style of the language, so that your application code will look and feel *native*. Some libraries provide an object oriented interface to AWS. All the libraries take care of the details involved in making a call, including handling of default parameter values, managing private and public keys, signing the requests, making the web service calls, checking for error conditions, and parsing returned values into native objects. Some libraries also provide functions to retry calls that have failed due to a transient error; others will accumulate data returned by multiple calls into a single return value.

The official Amazon libraries for PHP are very nice, but as of this writing they lack support for some of the services—S3, for example. If you have no requirement for S3 support, those libraries may fit the bill for you. You can find the EC2 libraries[11] (base EC2, CloudWatch, Auto Scaling, and Elastic Load Balancing), as well as a number of additional libraries for PHP and other languages, at the same link.

In this book we'll be using the CloudFusion library written by Ryan Parman. This library supports all the AWS services. CloudFusion supports multi-threaded access and bulk operations, and is supplied in open source form under the BSD license.[12] CloudFusion also includes a number of high-level utility functions to make AWS even easier to use.

---

[10] I could write an entire book on why I'll never use the word "intuitive" to describe this property, but I have to finish this one first.

[11] http://developer.amazonwebservices.com/connect/kbcategory.jspa?categoryID=85

[12] http://www.opensource.org/licenses/bsd-license.php

Here's some code to illustrate how you can use CloudFusion to create an S3 bucket. I'm including this code to show you that CloudFusion is clean and easy to use:

```php
#!/usr/bin/php
<?php

error_reporting(E_ALL);
require_once('cloudfusion.class.php');

$s3  = new AmazonS3();
$res = $s3->create_bucket("jeff_barr_bucket");

if ($res->isOK())
{
  print("Bucket created\n");
}
else
{
  print("Error creating bucket\n");
}
?>
```

First, we create a new `AmazonS3` object from which we can access the functions we need. Creating a bucket involves a single method call to the `create_bucket` function, supplying the new bucket's name. We can then test to ensure that there were no errors by using the `isOK` method.

No need to worry about the details right now—we'll be jumping in before too long. The CloudFusion project maintains a GitHub repository[13] and a web site.[14] We'll dive deeper into CloudFusion in the section called "Installing CloudFusion" at the end of this chapter, so it's unnecessary to download or configure it just yet.

Command Line Tools

Not so long ago, typing commands into a shell window was considered the state of the art in human-computer interaction. Although visual tools have obviated much of the need to do this on a routine basis, there are still a good number of reasons to use the command line from time to time. Command line tools are easier to use as part of a script. Routine operations that involve a sequence of commands and some

---

[13] http://github.com/cloudfusion/cloudfusion
[14] http://getcloudfusion.com/

decision-making can be automated. The output from two or more command line tools can be blended together. All things considered, these tools still serve a purpose.

Amazon supplies a number of command line tools. The first set is called API tools because there's one tool for each function in the EC2 API. For example, the `ec2-run-instances` command is a wrapper around the EC2 `RunInstances` function. The tools are written in Java; the source, however, is unavailable. The EC2 API tools are divided into four packages:

1. The Amazon EC2 API Tools[15] provide access to the core EC2 API functions.

2. The Amazon CloudWatch API Tools[16] provide access to the CloudWatch API functions.

3. The Auto Scaling API Tools[17] provide access to the Auto Scaling API functions.

4. The Elastic Load Balancing API Tools[18] provide access to the Elastic Load Balancing API functions.

Amazon also supplies a set of AMI tools.[19] More special-purpose in nature, you use these tools to create, upload, and register customized Amazon Machine Images (AMIs).

Members of the AWS developer community have created a number of command line tools. Some of these focus on providing access to a single service; others aim to be all encompassing. A good example of the latter is Tim Kay's top rated aws command.[20] This aspiring Swiss Army Knife now provides functions for EC2 services, S3, and SQS. Written in Perl, this script runs on Linux and Windows.

Visual Tools

At the top of the stack we find the visual tools. Developers have really exercised their creativity in this area and there are many tools to choose from; I'll cover a few of my favorites here. There are at least four types of tools:

---

[15] http://developer.amazonwebservices.com/connect/entry.jspa?externalID=351&categoryID=251

[16] http://developer.amazonwebservices.com/connect/entry.jspa?externalID=2534&categoryID=251

[17] http://developer.amazonwebservices.com/connect/entry.jspa?externalID=2535&categoryID=251

[18] http://developer.amazonwebservices.com/connect/entry.jspa?

[19] http://developer.amazonwebservices.com/connect/entry.jspa?externalID=368

[20] http://timkay.com/aws/

1. Dynamic Ajax-powered applications—the AWS Management Console is a good example of this type of application.
2. Browser extensions—the ElasticFox and the S3Fox are both extensions to the Firefox web browser.
3. Standalone desktop applications—CloudBerry Explorer, Bucket Explorer, and the SimpleDB Explorer are all in this category.
4. Device-specific applications—the iPhone applications from Ylastic and Direct Thought are both in this category.

AWS Management Console

The AWS Management Console[21] is effectively part of AWS. Because it's part of the AWS site, there's no configuration work required. Once you've logged in, you have full access to all EC2 services, CloudFront, and Elastic MapReduce. You can see your running instances and launch new ones. You can manage security groups, Elastic Block Store volumes, Elastic IP addresses, and identity key pairs. Figure 3.1 shows what it looks like.

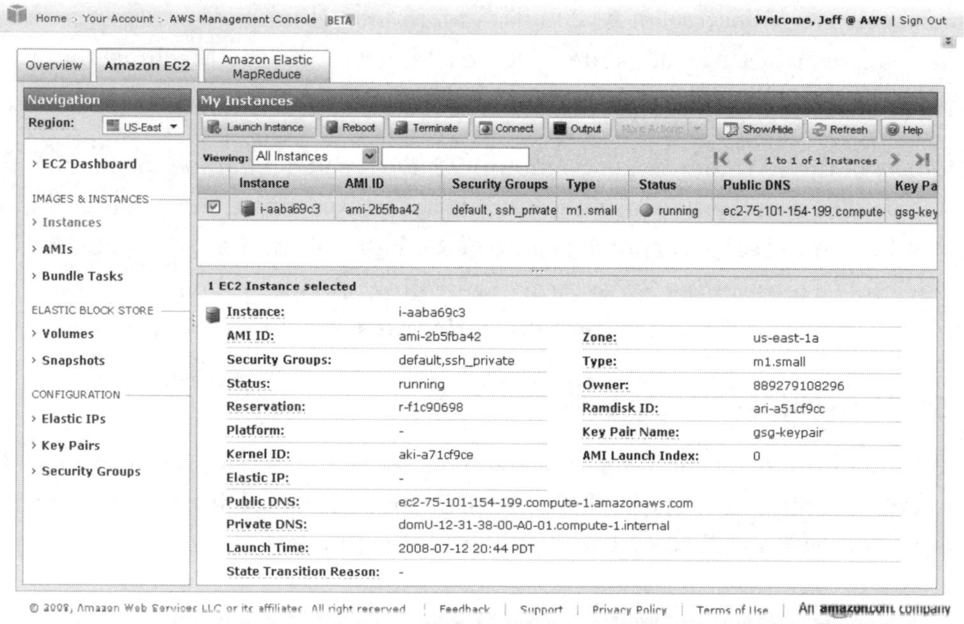

Figure 3.1. The AWS Management Console

---

[21] http://console.aws.amazon.com

ElasticFox

ElasticFox[22] is a Firefox extension available for free. After installing the extension and restarting your browser, you can access ElasticFox through the **Tools** menu. ElasticFox is an open source tool and has a SourceForge project of its very own.

Figure 3.2 shows ElasticFox listing available AMIs.

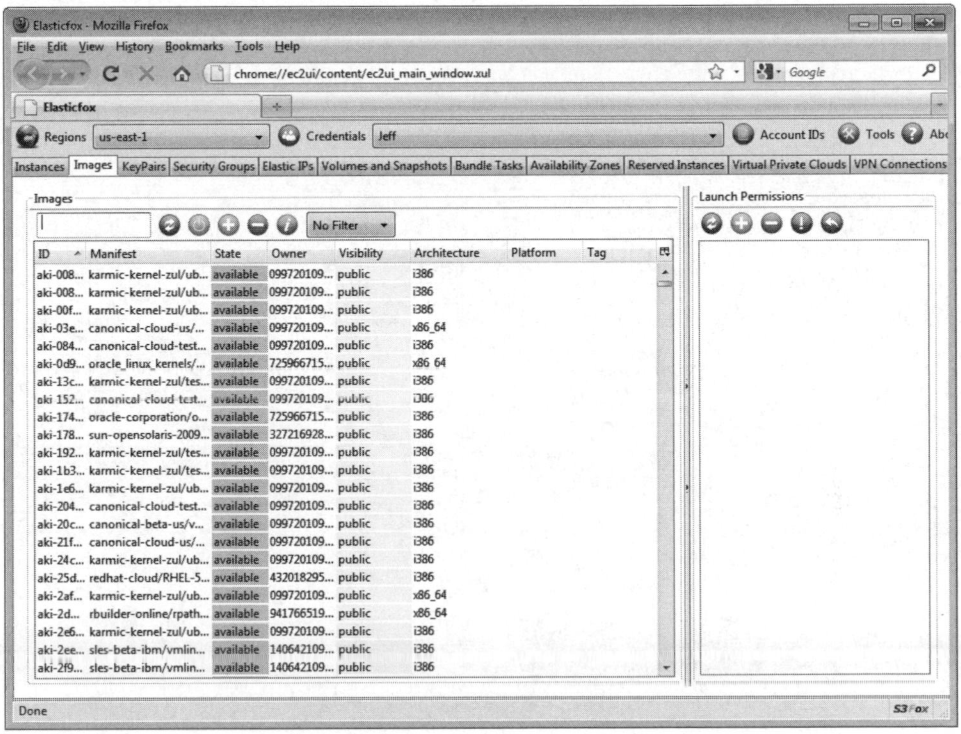

Figure 3.2. ElasticFox displaying a list of available AMIs

[22] http://developer.amazonwebservices.com/connect/entry.jspa?externalID=609

S3Fox

S3Fox[23] is a free S3 and CloudFront extension for Firefox, and a product of Suchi Software Solutions. This too makes it easy to copy files from your desktop to Amazon S3 (and vice versa) using a two-paned interface. Figure 3.3 shows what the S3Fox looks like; the local disk is in the left pane, while the S3 bucket is on the right.

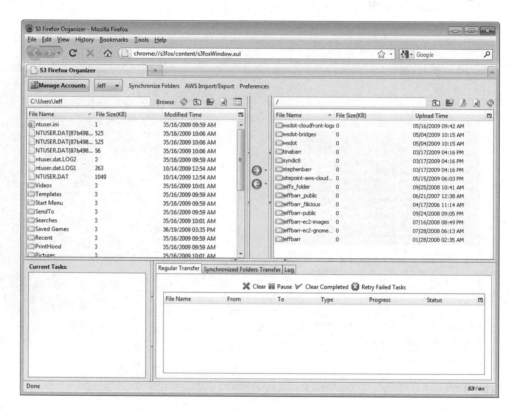

Figure 3.3. The S3Fox Organizer with its dual-paned approach

23 http://www.s3fox.net/

CloudBerry Explorer

CloudBerry Explorer[24] is a free, standalone desktop application and a product of CloudBerry Lab. You can manage your S3 buckets, copy files into and out of Amazon S3, and create CloudFront distributions. There's also a professional version that supports file encryption, data compression, and access to FTP servers. A screenshot from the free version is shown in Figure 3.4.

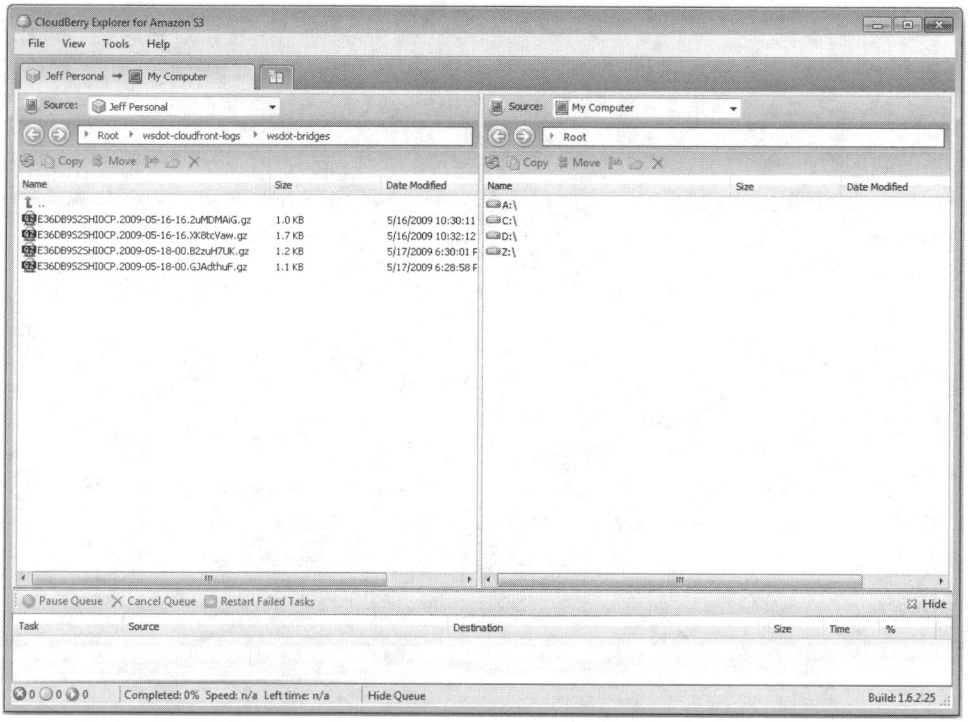

Figure 3.4. CloudBerry Explorer displaying the S3 bucket (left) and local disk (right)

---

[24] http://cloudberrylab.com/

Bucket Explorer

Bucket Explorer[25] is a commercial desktop application from Chambal.com. You can download free trial versions for Windows, Mac, and Linux. In addition to managing S3 buckets and objects, Bucket Explorer supports shared buckets, local and remote synchronization, and versioning. Figure 3.5 shows a screenshot of Bucket Explorer in action.

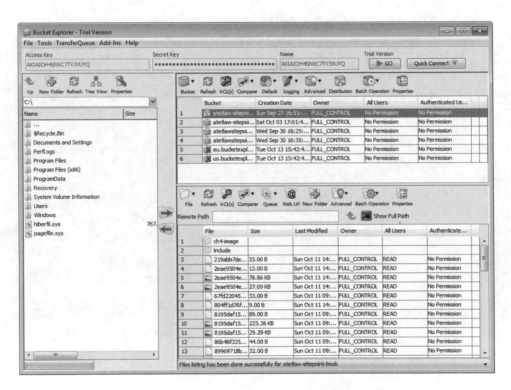

Figure 3.5. Bucket Explorer with a bucket list on top and contents at the bottom

---

[25] http://www.bucketexplorer.com/

SimpleDB Explorer

SimpleDB Explorer,[26] shown in Figure 3.6, is also produced by Chambal.com and is available in versions for Windows, Mac, and Linux. It features complete read-write access to SimpleDB domains and metadata, along with querying, sorting, and pagination through large result sets.

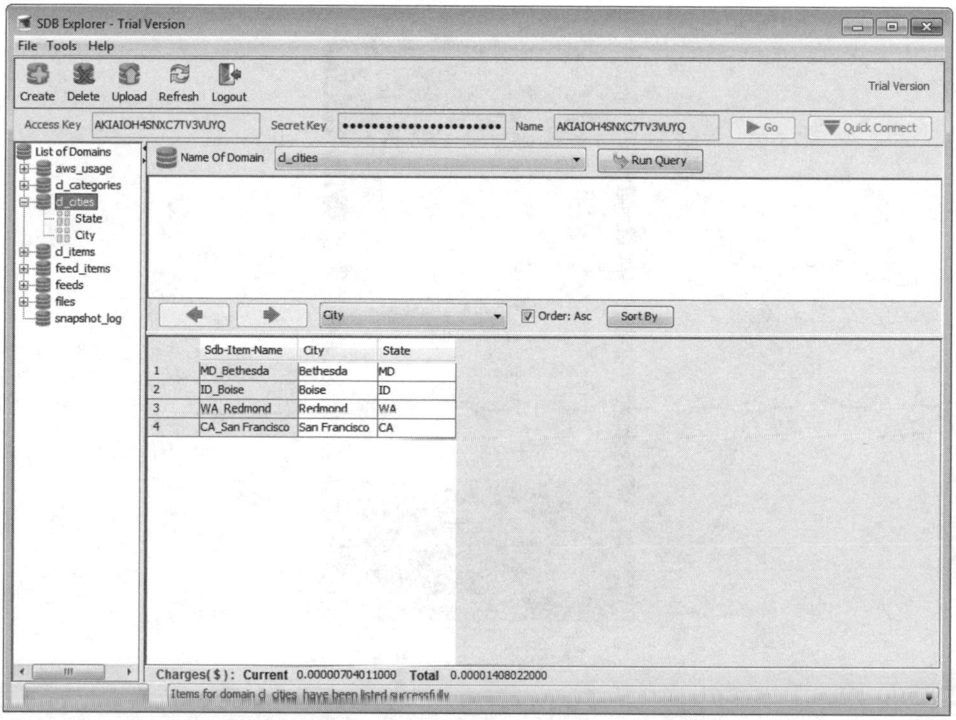

Figure 3.6. The SimpleDB Explorer interface

---

[26] http://www.sdbexplorer.com/

Ylastic

Ylastic[27] supports complete management of EC2 services, SQS, S3, CloudFront, and SimpleDB on Apple iPhone and phones based on the Google Android operating system (the latter can be seen in Figure 3.7). While it's advisable to use a more capable device as your primary AWS management tool, it can certainly be useful to have a portable management tool at hand.

Figure 3.7. Ylastic on the Android phone

DirectEC2

The Direct Thought company has created DirectEC2,[28] a native interface to EC2 services for the iPhone and the iPod Touch. The application features complete control of each aspect of EC2 functionality: AMIs, running instances, EBS volumes, EBS volume snapshots, Security Groups, IP addresses, and Keypairs. Figure 3.8 demonstrates what it looks like.

Figure 3.8. DirectEC2 on the iPhone

Creating an AWS Account

You're going to need an AWS account in order to run the code in this book. The accounts are free and you'll only be charged for the services that you actually use, but you'll need an email address and credit card in order to create your account.

You can skip this section if you already have an active AWS account.

---

[28] http://www.directthought.com/launch.html#directEC2

Start by visiting http://aws.amazon.com and click on the button labeled **Sign Up Now**, as shown in Figure 3.9.

Get Started

Sign up for a free AWS account.

Sign Up Now ▶

Figure 3.9. The Sign Up Now button

On the next page, enter your email address and select the **I am a new user** option, then click on the **Sign in using our secure server** button. Proceed to the registration page. Fill in your name, enter your email address a second time (for verification), choose a secure password, and click on the **Create account** button.

Enter your contact information (including your street address) on the next page, then scroll down a bit so that the AWS license agreement is visible. Read all the fine print and check the checkbox to indicate that you've read and agree to the terms of the license. Scroll down some more and enter the security check code, and click the **Continue** button.

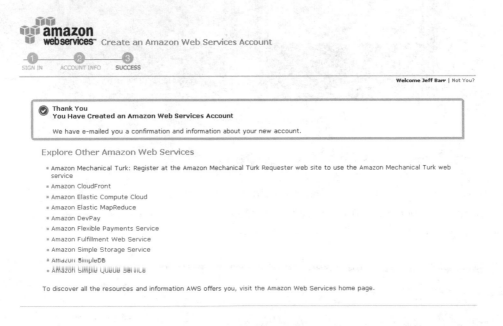

Figure 3.10. This page confirms you've successfully created your AWS account

Once you've done this, you'll see a page like the one shown in Figure 3.10, indicating that you now have an AWS account. Congratulations, and welcome to the club!

There's still a little more left to do, though. We've yet to reach the part where you enter your credit card number. The next step is to sign up for an actual AWS service. Click on the **Amazon Elastic Compute Cloud** button, and then click on the **Sign Up For Amazon EC2** button. You may need to enter your email address and password to access the next page.

The next page includes complete pricing information on EC2 services and S3; you need to use S3 to store your Amazon Machine Images, so this form covers both. Review the pricing information, then scroll down to the bottom of the page and enter your credit card information.[29] Click the **Continue** button and on the next page, select **Use This Address** if the address you already entered is also the billing address for your credit card. Otherwise, enter the appropriate address and click on the **Continue** button. Finally, scroll down to the bottom of the confirmation page and click on the **Complete Sign Up** button.

You'll see the "Thank you for signing up ..." page and a notice informing you that you'll receive a sequence of confirmation emails after the sign-up process:

1. the "Welcome to Amazon" email that indicates that you now have an Amazon account
2. the "Welcome to AWS" email that indicates that you now have an AWS account
3. the final pair of emails indicating that you've signed up for EC2 services and S3

Obtaining Your AWS Keys

Once you've created an AWS account, the next step is to access your public and private AWS keys.

Go to the AWS portal at http://aws.amazon.com and select **Security Credentials** from the **Account** menu, as shown in Figure 3.11.

---

[29] You may want to review the section on Payment Safety and Security on the Amazon web site at http://www.amazon.com/gp/help/customer/display.html?ie=UTF8&nodeId=518224&#safe.

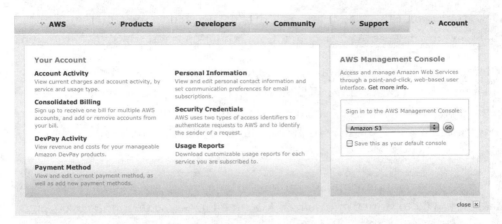

Figure 3.11. Account menu

Enter your email address and password again if necessary. You'll now see the **Security Credentials** page. Scroll down to find the section labeled **Your Access Keys**, as shown in Figure 3.12.

Your Access Keys			
Created	Access Key ID	Secret Access Key	Status
September 10, 2009	AKIAPR3EJJI36PMQQV5T	Show	Active (Make Inactive)
Create a New access Key			

Figure 3.12. Your Access Keys

You're going to need this key in the next section, so select your Access Key ID and then copy and paste it into a scratch file (Notepad or TextEdit is always good for this).

Now click on the **Show** link to see your **Secret Access Key**, like the one shown in Figure 3.13. Again, select it, copy it, and paste it to your scratch file.

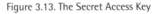

Figure 3.13. The Secret Access Key

With this information in hand, you're all set to download and install CloudFusion in the next section.

Running the PHP Code in This Book

All the code in this book is PHP code. We'll be running PHP on the command line and on a web server. Along with the book's assumption about your PHP knowledge, is the assumption that you can install and run PHP and a web server on your specific platform. However, there's just enough room in this chapter to provide a nudge in the right direction.

If you use Windows, look no further than the WampServer package[30] to have you up and running in no time at all. Similarly, MAMP[31] is a one-click installer for Mac OS X. Most Linux distributions already have Apache and PHP installed, but they're also available via your distribution's package manager. If you need more information, have a look at Chapter 1 of Kevin Yank's book *Build Your Own Database Driven Web Site Using PHP and MySQL*, freely available on sitepoint.com.[32]

GD Not Included in Mac OS X

Some of the code in the next chapter makes extensive use of PHP's GD library[33] for image manipulation. Unfortunately, while PHP is included as part of Mac OS X, the GD extension is excluded. To remedy this situation you can either use MAMP, mentioned above, or install the Mac OS X PHP package linked from the PHP web site under the heading **Binaries for other systems**.[34]

We're about to get serious with PHP, but before we do I have to mention this vital information. The PHP programs in this book that commence with a shebang (#!/usr/bin/php) are meant to be run from the command line, for example:

```
#!/usr/bin/php
<?php

: php script

?>
```

---

[30] http://www.wampserver.com/en/
[31] http://www.mamp.info/
[32] http://articles.sitepoint.com/article/php-amp-mysql-1-installation/
[33] http://www.php.net/gd/
[34] http://www.php.net/downloads.php

Running PHP scripts from the command line takes the form:

```
$ path_to_php_executable php_script_file [php_script_arguments]
```

The $ in this example represents the command prompt and is not typed in. Here's an example of running a PHP script on a Linux machine:

```
$ /usr/bin/php list_buckets.php
```

Here's another example, this time on a Mac OS X machine using MAMP:

```
$ /Applications/MAMP/bin/php5/bin/php list_buckets.php
```

Here's an example of running these scripts on a Windows machine from the Windows Command Prompt:

```
C:\> C:\PHP5\php list_buckets.php
```

Further details about running PHP from the Windows command line can be found in the PHP Manual.[35]

Running PHP as a Shell Script

If you're running these scripts on a Linux or Mac OS X machine you can run them like a shell script, but you need to make the files executable first. You can do so using the chmod command:

```
$ chmod +x list_buckets.php
```

After doing that you can run your scripts like so:

```
$ ./list_buckets.php
```

In order for this to work, the shebang line in all your scripts must indicate the location of the PHP executable on your system.

Scripts that are meant to be run on your web server will have no shebang:

---

[35] http://www.php.net/manual/en/install.windows.commandline.php

```
<?php

  : php script

?>
```

PHP 5.3.0 and Time Zones

If you're using PHP 5.3.0, there is an important change from previous versions. PHP 5.3.0 will now issue a warning-level log message whenever you use a date-related function without specifying a time zone. PHP has always defaulted to the time zone of the machine it's running on, but that behavior is now deemed to be unreliable and so the warning is emitted.

To avoid seeing the warning messages you must specify a time zone when using date functions, or else set a default time zone.[36] The easiest way to set a default time zone is to edit your **php.ini** file, specifically the following line:

```
; Defines the default timezone used by the date functions
;date.timezone =
```

Uncomment the line and add a valid time zone value. You can find a list of time zone values on the PHP web site.[37] Here's an example:

```
; Defines the default timezone used by the date functions
date.timezone = America/Los_Angeles
```

Installing CloudFusion

Many of the examples in this book can be run locally—that is, from your PHP-equipped desktop machine running Windows, Mac OS, or Linux—or remotely on a server or an EC2 instance. Wherever you plan to run them from, that's where you'll need to install CloudFusion. Here are the steps involved:

1. As at the time of writing, the latest version of CloudFusion was 2.5. You can download it from the project's web site at http://getcloudfusion.com. Unzip

---

[36] http://www.php.net/manual/en/migration52.datetime.php
[37] http://www.php.net/manual/en/timezones.php

the downloaded file archive and move the resulting **cloudfusion** directory to the location where you'd like CloudFusion to be installed.

2. Modify the PHP `include_path` setting in your **php.ini** file; this is to include the full path to the location of the CloudFusion library files.

    On a Linux system, this file is found in the **/etc** directory (as well as on Mac OS X). I put CloudFusion in the **/mnt/cloudfusion** directory, so I edited the `include_path` to look like this:

    ```
    include_path = ".:/php/includes:/mnt/cloudfusion"
    ```

    If you're on a Windows machine your **php.ini** file will be found in your PHP installation folder. If you've placed the CloudFusion files in **c:\cloudfusion**, this is what your `include_path` statement will look like:

    ```
    include_path = ".;c:\php\includes;c:\cloudfusion"
    ```

    You should also create a folder for the source code for all the examples in this book; then, download the code and append that directory name to the `include_path` as well.

3. Now turn your attention to the CloudFusion directory. Copy the file **config-sample.inc.php**, rename it **config.inc.php**, and open this new file for editing. Locate the following statements:

    ```
    define('AWS_KEY', '');
    define('AWS_SECRET_KEY', '');
    ```

    Edit the first statement so that your access key ID is between the quotes. Edit the second statement so that your secret access key is between quotes, like so:

    ```
    define('AWS_KEY', 'your_access_key_id');
    define('AWS_SECRET_KEY', 'your_secret_access_key');
    ```

    If other people can access the computer where you've stored your keys, take appropriate steps to protect both the computer and this file from disclosure.

4. Delete your scratch file.

Where We've Been

In this chapter we talked about the technical prerequisites that you'll need in order to gain the most possible value from the rest of the book. We started tooling up, reviewing a few of the many programming libraries, command line tools, and visual tools available for AWS. We stepped through the AWS registration process and obtained an account with a key to access the web services. We also installed the CloudFusion library. We're now ready to begin coding.

Chapter 4

Storing Data with Amazon S3

In this chapter, we'll dive headfirst into Amazon S3, the Simple Storage Service. After a quick overview of the most important S3 concepts, we'll spend the greater part of this chapter reviewing the code needed to manipulate buckets and objects in S3 and its content-distribution sibling, CloudFront.

S3 Overview

S3 is an Internet-scale data storage service. All data is stored redundantly to guard against problems brought on by temporary connectivity issues or permanent hardware failures. S3 can scale to handle vast amounts of data and deal with a very large number of concurrent accesses. At the time of writing, S3 held over 124 billion objects and was handling over one trillion requests per year.[1]

S3 lets you store your data in containers called **buckets**. A bucket is a named storage entity attached to a particular AWS account. You can create up to 100 buckets in your AWS account. The bucket names must be globally unique, so you'll have to choose with care and keep on trying until you find available names.

---

[1] http://aws.amazon.com/about-aws/whats-new/2009/03/30/celebrating-3-years-of-amazon-s3-with-3-months-of-transfer-in-for-3-centsgb/

Buckets are used to group any number of S3 objects. When I say *any number*, I really mean it—it is perfectly reasonable to store millions or tens of millions of objects in a single S3 bucket. Depending on your needs, you may choose to use a number of buckets for a single application, or you may choose to use a single bucket for each application.

You can store any type of data you like in S3. It could be text files such as HTML pages, CSS style sheets, or C source code, or binary files such as JPEG images, tar backup files, or even encrypted data (you can encrypt sensitive data before storing it in S3, if you'd like). S3 is ideal for storing web data. Each S3 object has its own URL and S3 can handle a very high request rate.

S3 can store objects of up to 5GB in size. This is a limit that you'll probably never approach in practice, due to various factors. Depending on the speed of your internet connection, it could take hours or even days to upload an object of this size. If the connection was interrupted, you'd have to restart the upload from the beginning. Also, some of the S3 tool kits attempt to read the entire object into memory before uploading it.

Every S3 object has a unique URL formed by concatenating these components:

- protocol (`http://` or `https://`)
- bucket name ending with "."
- S3 endpoint (`s3.amazonaws.com`)
- object key starting with "/"

The object key can itself contain "/" characters. These characters are simply part of the object's name and have no special meaning to S3. S3 is not a hierarchical file system and has no concept of a subfolder. The S3 tools listed in Chapter 3 maintain the polite fiction that the "/" is special and allows the user to traverse of the contents of an S3 bucket as if it contained actual subfolders.

S3 can be accessed using either one of two APIs. The SOAP API contains functions such as `ListAllMyBuckets`, `CreateBucket`, and `DeleteBucket`. The HTTP API uses the standard HTTP verbs (`GET`, `PUT`, `HEAD`, and `DELETE`) as the basis for all operations. The `GET` operation retrieves the contents of a bucket or an object, the `PUT` operation creates a new bucket or object, the `DELETE` operation removes a bucket or an object, and the `HEAD` operation retrieves information about an object.

You can attach metadata in the form of key-value pairs when you create a new S3 object. The metadata is returned in the form of HTTP headers when the object is retrieved using an HTTP GET request.

Access to each S3 bucket and object is regulated by an **ACL** or Access Control List. An ACL contains a series of up to 100 **grants**, with each grant consisting of a grantee and a permission. Using the ACL, you can grant access to specific users or to groups of users.

Specific users represent an individual AWS account. The account can be specified using an email address or a canonical user ID, but it is always returned as a CanonicalUser object—the email address is simply a convenience.

Groups represent predefined classes of users, any AWS user, or anonymous users (anyone at all).

The permission component of a grant in an ACL specifies the access given to the related grantee. You can grant permissions to buckets or to objects—but be aware that the semantics are slightly different for each, as described in Table 4.1.

Table 4.1. S3 Permission Grants When Applied to Buckets and Objects

Permission	When applied to a bucket	When applied to an object
READ	Permission to list the contents of the bucket	Permission to read the object or its metadata
WRITE	Permission to create, replace, or delete any object in the bucket	Unsupported for objects
READ_ACP	Permission to read the bucket's ACL	Permission to read the object's ACL
WRITE_ACP	Permission to overwrite the bucket's ACL	Permission to overwrite the object's ACL
FULL_CONTROL	All of the above	All of the above

The owner of a bucket or an object always has implicit READ_ACP permission; you can always access the ACL of your own objects. Similarly, the owner also has implicit WRITE_ACP permission, so you can always change the ACL of your own object too. The FULL_CONTROL permission is provided for convenience and has the same effect as applying the READ, WRITE, READ_ACP, and WRITE_ACP permissions.

Permissions on buckets and objects are distinct. The bucket's permissions have no influence on the permissions of newly uploaded objects; ACLs must be set separately for each new object.

The S3 Pricing Model

Your S3 usage is charged in three dimensions:

- amount of data stored
- amount of data transferred in and out of S3
- the number of requests made to S3

Let's examine each of these dimensions in detail.

Your S3 storage charges are based on a unit known as a **gigabyte-month**. If you store exactly one gigabyte for exactly one month, you'll be charged for one gigabyte-month, which is $0.15 (fifteen cents).[2] Time and space can be traded for one another, so you could also store two gigabytes for half of a month for $0.15, or even 30 gigabytes for one day if you'd like. Internally, S3 uses a more fine-grained billing unit, a **byte-hour**. This allows AWS to measure your usage with a very high degree of accuracy and to bill you accordingly.

Your data transfer charges are based on the amount of data transferred in (uploaded) and out (downloaded) from S3. Data transferred in to S3 is charged at a rate of $0.10 per gigabyte. Once again, this amount is prorated. Data transferred out of S3 is charged on a sliding scale starting at $0.17 per gigabyte and decreasing based on volume, reaching $0.10 per gigabyte for all outgoing data transfer in excess of 150 terabytes per month. As an important special case, there is no charge to transfer data between S3 and an Amazon EC2 instance in the same Region.

There are also nominal (yet important) charges for each request made to S3. HTTP GET requests are charged at the rate of $0.01 for every 10,000 requests. PUT, COPY, LIST, and POST requests are charged at the rate of $0.01 for every 1,000 requests.

Putting it all together, this pricing model means that you can probably prototype and then run your S3 powered application for next to nothing, paying for more storage and more data transfer only as your application becomes popular.

---

[2] All AWS prices are subject to change. The latest prices for S3 can be found at http://aws.amazon.com/s3.

> ### Watch That Meter!
>
> You need to keep in mind that the meter is always running! If you write a program to poll one of your S3 buckets every second (a LIST request) you'll be spending 86 cents every day, whether there's anything new in the bucket or otherwise. You should also check your loop terminating conditions with extreme care. It's better to avoid writing an infinite loop which costs you money with every iteration.

You can (and should) check your S3 usage at any point during the month to verify that it's in accord with your expectations. You can do this by logging into the AWS portal and selecting the **Account Activity** option from the **Your Account** menu.

CloudFront Overview

CloudFront is a web service for content delivery, allowing you to distribute web content at high speed with low latency. CloudFront integrates with S3, making it very easy to distribute any public S3 object to CloudFront's network of 14 global edge locations.[3] As of this writing, the edge locations are spread through the United States, Europe, and Asia, as shown in Table 4.2.

Table 4.2. Edge Locations in the CloudFront Network

United States	Europe	Asia
Ashburn, Virginia	Amsterdam	Hong Kong
Dallas/Fort Worth, Texas	Dublin	Singapore
Los Angeles, California	Frankfurt	Tokyo
Miami, Florida	London	
Newark, New Jersey		
New York, New York		
Palo Alto, California		
Seattle, Washington		
St. Louis, Missouri		

CloudFront is very easy to use. You simply create a distribution for any of your S3 buckets and CloudFront does the rest.

---

[3] The number of edge locations, and the locations themselves, may change over time.

The CloudFront Pricing Model

Your CloudFront usage is charged in two dimensions:

- data transfer
- the number of requests made to CloudFront

Data transferred in and out of CloudFront is charged on a sliding scale. Starting at a rate of $0.17 per gigabyte, it decreases according to volume, reaching $0.05 per gigabyte for all outgoing data transfer in excess of 1,000 terabytes per month. You're also charged for the data transfer from S3 to CloudFront. The latest prices for CloudFront can be found at http://aws.amazon.com/cloudfront.

There's a charge of $0.013 for every 10,000 HTTP GET requests processed by CloudFront.

Programming S3 and CloudFront

With the preliminaries out of the way, it's time to start on the fun part—the code! In this section, you'll learn how to list your buckets, create new buckets, and list the objects in a bucket in several different ways. We'll also cover how to process the contents of a bucket (performing some simple image processing along the way), and how to distribute your content using CloudFront.

Running the Code

As we mentioned in the section called "Running the PHP Code in This Book" in Chapter 3, the programs in this section that start with a shebang (`#!/usr/bin/php`) are meant to be run from the command line. The others are meant to be run via a web server.

Creating an S3 Bucket

Moving right along, let's go ahead and create a new bucket. Before we begin, though, we'll create a new PHP file and call it **book.inc.php**. This will contain a lot of common definitions and functions we'll be using throughout this book. I've placed it in a subfolder called **include**.

The first definition we'll add to our **book.inc.php** file is the name of our S3 bucket:

```
                                   chapter_04/include/book.inc.php (excerpt)
<?php

define('BOOK_BUCKET', 'sitepoint-aws-cloud-book');

?>
```

Here we've created a new constant named BOOK_BUCKET and given it the value
sitepoint-aws-cloud-book. Of course, you'll need to decide on your own distinct
bucket name; as I mentioned earlier bucket names must be globally unique, and
I've already nabbed this one!

Here's the code for creating a new S3 bucket:

```
                                    chapter_04/create_bucket.php (excerpt)
#!/usr/bin/php
<?php

error_reporting(E_ALL); ❶

require_once('cloudfusion.class.php'); ❷
require_once('include/book.inc.php');

$s3  = new AmazonS3(); ❸
$res = $s3->create_bucket(BOOK_BUCKET);

if ($res->isOK()) ❹
{
  print("'${bucket}' bucket created\n");
}
else
{
  print("Error creating bucket '${bucket}'\n");
}
?>
```

Let's examine the code statement by statement:

We begin by setting the error reporting level. This statement instructs PHP to report all errors and potential errors. This important programming discipline lets you know about problems sooner rather than later. You'll win in the long term because most of the potential bugs will have been shaken out earlier in the piece.

 Next we include the required files. The first statement pulls the **cloudfusion.class.php** file into memory. This file contains the CloudFusion library used throughout this book. The second statement pulls the **book.inc.php** file into memory.

❸ Now we come to the main part of our script. First, we create a new AmazonS3 object and then call the create_bucket method—the key statement in this script—to create a new bucket. If you've customized the definition of BOOK_BUCKET in **book.inc.php**, it will create a bucket just for you (assuming that the bucket doesn't already exist).

One point you should be aware of, is that the CloudFusion library is using your AWS key ID and secret key to access the web service. We configured these values back in the section called "Installing CloudFusion" in Chapter 3.

❹ The last statement checks that the call was made to S3, and that S3 returned a status code indicating that the operation was processed successfully. If the bucket exists and you own it, the create_bucket call will succeed. If the bucket exists but it belongs to another user, the create_bucket call will fail and the isOK method will return FALSE. Our statement prints an appropriate status message to indicate success or failure.

We can make this script a little bit more useful by allowing the specification of a bucket name on the command line, like so:

chapter_04/create_bucket.php *(excerpt)*

```php
#!/usr/bin/php
<?php

error_reporting(E_ALL);

require_once('cloudfusion.class.php');
require_once('include/book.inc.php');

if ($argc != 2) ❶
{
  exit("Usage: " . $argv[0] . " bucket name\n");
}

$bucket = ($argv[1] == '-') ? BOOK_BUCKET : $argv[1]; ❷

$s3  = new AmazonS3();
$res = $s3->create_bucket($bucket);

if ($res->isOK())
{
  print("'${bucket}' bucket created\n");
}
else
{
  print("Error creating bucket '${bucket}'\n");
}

?>
```

❶   First, we check to see how many arguments are supplied. If there are not exactly two, we exit the script and display a helpful usage message.

❷   This program expects the first argument to be a bucket name. If the bucket name is a dash character (-), the default bucket (BOOK_BUCKET) is used instead.

Running this script with the default bucket's name gives the following output:

```
$php create_bucket.php -
'sitepoint-aws-cloud-book' bucket created
```

Listing Your S3 Buckets

Here's how to list your S3 buckets:

```
chapter_04/list_buckets.php (excerpt)

#!/usr/bin/php
<?php

error_reporting(E_ALL);

require_once('cloudfusion.class.php');

$s3 = new AmazonS3();
$buckets = $s3->get_bucket_list();
```

```

foreach ($buckets as $bucket)
```

```
{
  print($bucket . "\n");
}

exit(0);
?>
```

The above code should be relatively easy to understand:

   This is the key statement that retrieves the list of buckets associated with your account. The method returns an array with one string element for each bucket.

   Once we have the list, we can loop through the array and print the name of each bucket using the `print` statement. If you're running this for the first time, you may only see one name: the name of the bucket you created in the last section.

Here's what I see when I run this program from my personal AWS account:

```
$php list_buckets.php
andybarr
aws-dev-relations
biancabarr
carmenbarr

: many more buckets
```

```
sitepoint-aws-cloud-book
sitepoint-aws-cloud-book-thumbs
```

This is a simple yet powerful piece of code. In a few statements we established a connection to S3, retrieved a list of buckets, iterated over the result, and printed the name of each bucket on a line of its own. If all this makes sense, you're well on your way to mastering S3.

Bucket Listing as a Web Page

Since this is a book about web programming, let's get a bit fancier and output the list of buckets as a web page. This version of the script is very similar to the previous **list_buckets.php** script, as we're still using the `get_bucket_list` method:

chapter_04/list_buckets_page.php (excerpt)

```php
<?php

error_reporting(E_ALL);

require_once('cloudfusion.class.php');

$s3 = new AmazonS3();
$buckets = $s3->get_bucket_list();

$output_title = 'Chapter 3 Sample - List of S3 Buckets';
$output_message = 'A simple HTML list of your S3 Buckets';
include 'include/list_buckets.html.php';

exit(0);
?>
```

The last three statements are new. We set two variables, `$output_title` and `$output_message` with informative content that will be appearing on the web page. The final `include` statement includes the HTML template for our bucket list:

chapter_04/include/list_buckets.html.php *(excerpt)*

```
<!DOCTYPE html PUBLIC "-//W3C//DTD XHTML 1.0 Strict//EN"
  "http://www.w3.org/TR/xhtml1/DTD/xhtml1-strict.dtd">
<html xmlns="http://www.w3.org/1999/xhtml" xml:lang="en" lang="en">
<head>
  <title><?php echo $output_title ?></title>
</head>
<body>
  <h1><?php echo $output_title ?></h1>
  <p><?php echo $output_message ?></p>
  <ul>
    <?php foreach($buckets as $bucket): ?>
      <li><?php echo $bucket ?></li>
    <?php endforeach ?>
  </ul>
</body>
</html>
```

In the code above, `$output_title` becomes the page title and top-level heading, while `$output_message` is output as an informative note at the top of the page within a HTML paragraph. The list of buckets in the `$buckets` array is output as an HTML unordered list, as shown in Figure 4.1, with the help of a `foreach` loop.

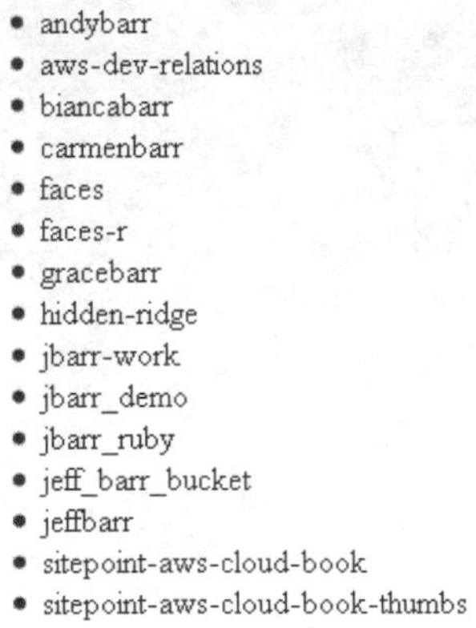

- andybarr
- aws-dev-relations
- biancabarr
- carmenbarr
- faces
- faces-r
- gracebarr
- hidden-ridge
- jbarr-work
- jbarr_demo
- jbarr_ruby
- jeff_barr_bucket
- jeffbarr
- sitepoint-aws-cloud-book
- sitepoint-aws-cloud-book-thumbs

Figure 4.1. A simple list of S3 buckets

Listing Objects in a Bucket

Now that you know how to create buckets and list these buckets from the command line and from a web page, let's look at the contents of a particular bucket. In this script we list all the objects within the first bucket we created (using the constant BOOK_BUCKET):

chapter_04/list_bucket_objects.php *(excerpt)*

```php
#!/usr/bin/php

error_reporting(E_ALL);

require_once('cloudfusion.class.php');
require_once('book.inc.php');

$s3     = new AmazonS3();
$objects = $s3->get_object_list(BOOK_BUCKET);

if($objects) {
  foreach ($objects as $object)
  {
    print($object . "\n");
  }
} else {
  print("No objects found in " . BOOK_BUCKET . "\n");
}

exit(0);
?>
```

Here's the key statement in the above example:

```php
$objects = $s3->get_object_list(BOOK_BUCKET);
```

The get_object_list method is a simple shortcut method. When given no extra parameters, it will return a list of the first (alphabetically speaking) 1,000 object keys in a bucket. Optional parameters can be used to start returning keys alphabetically after a given key or to filter the list of keys after they've been retrieved from S3. Like get_bucket_list, this method returns an array with one key in string form per element.

You're probably wondering why this function returns just 1,000 keys. Remember that buckets can contain millions of objects, but returning such a long list all at once would be problematic on several levels—simply transmitting the lists would take a long time. As we'll see in the next section, a web-scale system like S3 must provide a way to access long lists in chunks of a reasonable size.

Of course, your newly created bucket has no objects in it at this time, so this script will do little more than alert you to that fact. To give it a more complete test run, you can either add some objects to your bucket using one of the tools we saw in the section called "Visual Tools" in Chapter 3 (such as S3Fox or CloudBerry Explorer), or skip ahead to the section called "Uploading Files to S3" later in this chapter.

Finally, here's a challenge: based on the **create_bucket.php** script we developed above, it should be fairly easy for you to change the **list_bucket_objects.php** script, so that you can specify a bucket name on the command line.

Processing Complex CloudFusion Data Structures

It's time to take a little detour.

The CloudFusion functions that I have told you about thus far all return simple data structures—arrays of strings. However, the functions that I will use later in this chapter return a more complex data structure called a `ResponseCore`. S3 returns its results in the form of an XML document; CloudFusion parses the XML using PHP's SimpleXML package and includes the parsed objects in the response where they can be referenced by name.[4]

The following code calls S3 to list the first 1,000 objects in the bucket `BOOK_BUCKET`, and then calls PHP's handy `print_r` function to display the resulting object tree:

chapter_04/list_bucket_objects_raw.php (excerpt)

```php
#!/usr/bin/php
<?php

error_reporting(E_ALL);

require_once('cloudfusion.class.php');
require_once('include/book.inc.php');

$s3 = new AmazonS3();
$res = $s3->list_objects(BOOK_BUCKET);
```

---

[4] Complete documentation for SimpleXML can be found at http://www.php.net/simplexml.

```
print_r($res);
exit(0);
?>
```

The resulting output is far too long to display in its entirety (465 lines for my buckets). Let's look at some excerpts instead. Here's the first part:

```
$php list_bucket_objects_raw.php
ResponseCore Object
[header] => Array
(
  [x-amz-id-2] => Ya7yAuUClv7HgR6+JJpzOsYDM1m4/Zy+dORmk5cSAu+qV+v+6
➥9gLSHlytlD77wAn
  [x-amz-request-id] => 14AA13F3F0B76032
  [date] => Thu, 28 May 2009 06:51:26 GMT
  [content-type] => application/xml
  [transfer-encoding] => chunked
  [connection] => close
  [server] => AmazonS3
  [_info] => Array
  (
    [url] => https://sitepoint-aws-cloud-book.s3.amazonaws.com/
    [content_type] => application/xml
    ⋮
```

The first line indicates that the data is of type `ResponseCore`. Further on, we find some standard PHP arrays. If we need to, we can access the data like this:

```
$res->header['transfer-encoding']
$res->header['_info']['url']
```

`$res` is an object and `header` is one of the object's instance variables, so it's accessed using the `->` operator. The `header` instance variable is a PHP array, so its members are accessed using the array syntax.

In the second line the `_info` member of `header` is itself an array, so a second set of brackets are used to access the `url` value inside.

A little bit further down in the output, we find the following:

```
[body] => SimpleXMLElement Object
(
  [Name] => sitepoint-aws-cloud-book
  ⋮
```

The body instance variable is of type `SimpleXMLElement`. It starts out with a `Name` instance variable, which can be accessed as `$res->body->Name`.

Even further down we finally find what we came here for—the list of objects in the bucket:

```
[Contents] => Array
(
  [0] => SimpleXMLElement Object
  (
    [Key] => images/2008_shiller_housing_projection.jpg
    [LastModified] => 2009-05-22T23:44:58.000Z
    [ETag] => "e2d335683226059e7cd6e450795f3485"
    [Size] => 236535
    [Owner] => SimpleXMLElement Object
    (
      [ID] => 7769a42be4e57a034eeb322aa8450b3536b6ca56037c06ef19b1e1
➥eabfeaab9c
      [DisplayName] => jeffbarr
    )
    [StorageClass] => STANDARD
  )
  ⋮
```

You can see that `body` contains an instance variable called `Contents`, which is another array containing all the files in the bucket. Each file in the bucket is represented by a `SimpleXMLElement` object; each has `Key`, `ETag`, `Size`, `Owner`, and `StorageClass` members, accessed like this:

```
$res->body->Contents[0]->Key
$res->body->Contents[0]->ETag
$res->body->Contents[0]->Size
$res->body->Contents[0]->Owner->ID
$res->body->Contents[0]->Owner->DisplayName
$res->body->Contents[0]->StorageClass
```

Of course, you're free to use intermediate variables to make this code shorter or more efficient.

You may be wondering where the object names (`Contents`, `Key`, `Size`, and so forth) come from. The `list_objects` method makes an HTTP `GET` request to S3 to fetch a list of the first 1,000 objects in the bucket. The request returns an XML document, and CloudFusion parses and returns it as the `body` object. The object names are taken directly from the XML tags in the document.

If we were to modify the previous script to print out some of these values, it may look like this example:

```php
#!/usr/bin/php
<?php

error_reporting(E_ALL);

require_once('cloudfusion.class.php');
require_once('include/book.inc.php');

$s3 = new AmazonS3();
$res = $s3->list_objects(BOOK_BUCKET);

print("Bucket Url: " . $res->header['_info']['url'] . "\n");
print("Bucket Name: " . $res->body->Name    . "\n");
print("First Key:   " . $res->body->Contents[0]->Key . "\n");
print("Second Key: " , $res->body->Contents[1]->Key . "\n");
exit(0);
?>
```

In the above example we output the bucket's URL and name, followed by the keys of the first two items in the bucket.

We have now come to the end of the detour. I hope that the ride was scenic, yet educational. Next, we will use this newfound knowledge to create a very handy utility function.

Listing Objects in a Bucket as a Web Page

Before we can write a script that outputs a list of all the objects in a bucket within a web page, we first have to write a rather complex function. We'll add this function to our **book.inc.php** file and call it `getBucketObjects`:

chapter_04/include/book.inc.php *(excerpt)*

```php
function getBucketObjects($s3, $bucket, $prefix = '') ❶
{
  $objects = array();
  $next = '';

  do ❷
  {
    $res = $s3->list_objects($bucket,
        array('marker' => urlencode($next),
            'prefix' => $prefix)
      ); ❸

    if (!$res->isOK()) ❹
    {
      return null;
    }

    $contents = $res->body->Contents; ❺
    foreach ($contents as $object)
    {
      $objects[] = $object;
    }

    $isTruncated = $res->body->IsTruncated == 'true'; ❻

    if ($isTruncated)
    {
      $next = $objects[count($objects) - 1]->Key; ❼
    }
  }
  while ($isTruncated);

  return $objects; ❽
}
```

This function is more complex than anything you've seen so far, but there's no need to worry. Earlier in this chapter I told you that one "list bucket" request to S3 will return at most 1,000 keys, regardless of how many keys are in the bucket. Our getBucketObjects function simply calls list_objects again and again until S3 says that there are no more objects to return:

1 Our function accepts three arguments: an `AmazonS3` object, an S3 bucket, and a prefix value that defaults to an empty string.

2 We use a `do … while` loop, so that the body of the loop always runs at least once.

3 Each time I call `list_objects`, I pass in a value called `$next`. The first time through the loop, `$next` is an empty string, and `list_objects` starts at the beginning (alphabetically speaking) of the bucket. On subsequent loop iterations, `$next` is set to the final key returned on the previous iteration. This tells S3 to start retrieving keys alphabetically following the previous iteration's final key.

4 If the `list_objects` call fails, the function returns `null`.

5 We retrieve the `Contents` array from the body of the response returned to our `list_objects` call, then loop through the values storing each one in the `$objects` array. This array will eventually be our return value.

6 The data returned by a call to `list_objects` includes an element named `IsTruncated`. If this value is the string `"true"`, the listing is incomplete and there are more objects to be found. This condition is also used to control the loop.

7 If the list is incomplete, we set the `$next` value ready to begin the next iteration.

8 When the loop terminates, the `$objects` array is returned.

Put it together and this function fetches all the objects in the bucket, puts them all into one array, and returns the array.

 Avoid Going Loopy

I will freely admit that I failed to correctly state the termination condition when I first wrote this code. I knew that this would be tricky, so I used a print statement at the top to ensure that I avoided creating a non-terminating loop that would spin out of control and run up my S3 bill. I advise you to do the same when you're building and testing any code that costs you money to execute.

With this function in hand, creating a list of the objects in the bucket becomes easy. Here's all we have to do:

chapter_04/list_bucket_objects_page.php *(excerpt)*

```php
<?php

error_reporting(E_ALL);

require_once('cloudfusion.class.php');
require_once('include/book.inc.php');

$bucket = IsSet($_GET['bucket']) ? $_GET['bucket'] : BOOK_BUCKET; ❶

$s3 = new AmazonS3();

$objects = getBucketObjects($s3, $bucket); ❷

$fileList = array();

foreach ($objects as $object) ❸
{
  $key = $object->Key;
  $url = $s3->get_object_url($bucket, $key);
  $fileList[] = array('url' => $url, 'name' => $key,
                      'size' => number_format((int)$object->Size)); ❹
}

$output_title = "Chapter 3 Sample - List of S3 Objects in Bucket' .
    '${bucket}'";
$output_message = "A simple HTML table displaying of all the' .
    ' objects in the '${bucket}' bucket.";
include 'include/list_bucket_objects.html.php'; ❺

exit(0);
?>
```

This code generates a web page and can accept an optional `bucket` argument in the URL query string. Let's rip this one apart and see how it works:

 This code checks to see if the `bucket` argument was supplied. If it was, then it's used as the value of `$bucket`. Otherwise, the default value, the `BOOK_BUCKET` constant, is used.

 Here we call our custom `getBucketObjects` function that fetches the list of objects in the given bucket and stores them in the `$objects` array.

The next step is to iterate over the array and process each one.

We store three values for each object in the $fileList array: the object's URL, key (which we store as name), and size (converted to an integer and formatted like a number).

We include our HTML template to output the values in the $fileList array.

Here's what the **list_bucket_objects.html.php** HTML template looks like:

chapter_04/include/list_bucket_objects.html.php *(excerpt)*

```
<!DOCTYPE html PUBLIC "-//W3C//DTD XHTML 1.0 Strict//EN"
  "http://www.w3.org/TR/xhtml1/DTD/xhtml1-strict.dtd">
<html xmlns="http://www.w3.org/1999/xhtml" xml:lang="en" lang="en">
<head>
  <title><?php echo $output_title ?></title>
</head>
<body>
  <h1><?php echo $output_title ?></h1>
  <p><?php echo $output_message ?></p>
  <table>
    <thead>
      <tr><th>File</th><th>Size</th></tr>
    </thead>
    <tbody>
    <?php foreach($fileList as $file): ?>
      <tr>
        <td><a href="<?php echo $file['url'] ?>">
            <?php echo $file['name'] ?></a>
        </td>
        <td><?php echo $file['size'] ?></td>
      </tr>
    <?php endforeach ?>
    </tbody>
  </table>
</body>
</html>
```

The template iterates over the $fileList array and creates a table row for each file, placing a link to the file in the first column and the file size in the second column.

Figure 4.2 shows what it looks like (I had already uploaded some files to my bucket).

images/2008_shiller_housing_projection.jpg	236,535
images/3DoorScion.jpg	61,918
images/AndyBass.jpg	73,388
images/AndyWorkstation.jpg	80,841
images/Jeffbase.gif	37,561
images/Jeffbase.psd	545,419
images/Jeffbasebright.gif	37,452
images/Jeffbasebright.psd	532,308
images/STP65708.JPG	1,716,926
images/Scion XB Stretch.jpg	66,598
images/Scion XB.jpg	70,882

Figure 4.2. Listing objects in an S3 bucket

You may have spotted the fact that we now have all the parts needed to make a simple S3 file browser. I'll leave that as a challenge to you. With just a little bit of work you should be able to connect **list_buckets_page.php** and **list_bucket_objects_page.php**.

Uploading Files to S3

Now that we know how to obtain information about buckets and their objects from S3, let's figure out how to put new objects into S3. This is quite easy; we just need two more utility functions that we'll add to our **book.inc.php** file.

The first function is called uploadObject:

```
                                    chapter_04/include/book.inc.php (excerpt)
function uploadObject($s3, $bucket, $key, $data,
    $acl = S3_ACL_PRIVATE, $contentType = "text/plain")
{
  $res = $s3->create_object($bucket,
      array(
        'filename'    => $key,
        'body'        => $data,
        'acl'         => $acl,
```

```
        'contentType' => $contentType
    ));
  return $res->isOK();
}
```

The `uploadObject` function accepts between four and six parameters. The first four specify the S3 access object, the destination bucket, the desired object key, and the data to be stored in the object. The final two specify a non-default ACL and a content type for the stored object.

Web browsers use the object's content type to figure out how to display the object. For example, a content type of `image/png` tells the browser that the object is an image and that it is in PNG format.

As you can see, the `uploadObject` function simply calls the `create_object` method and checks the returned value to ensure that the object was actually stored in S3.

If S3 is unable to store the object, it will return an `HTTP 500` (internal server error) code. This is almost always a recoverable condition; the proper response is to make several attempts with increasing time delays between attempts (sometimes known as **exponential backoff**). Here's a more sophisticated version of the `uploadObject` function, this one with a retry mechanism:

```
function uploadObject($s3, $bucket, $key, $data,
    $acl = S3_ACL_PRIVATE, $contentType = "text/plain")
{
  $try = 1;
  $sleep = 1;
  do
  {
    $res = $s3->create_object($bucket,
        array(
          'filename'    => $key,
          'body'        => $data,
          'acl'         => $acl,
          'contentType' => $contentType
        ));

    if ($res->isOK()) {
      return true;
    }
```

```
    sleep($sleep);
    $sleep *= 2;
  }
  while(++$try < 6);
  return false;
}
```

This version of our function will try up to six times to create a new object in a bucket. Each time it tries, the length of the pause (before the next try) doubles.

Our next function helps us determine a file's content type:

chapter_04/include/book.inc.php *(excerpt)*

```php
function guessType($file)
{
  $info = pathinfo($file, PATHINFO_EXTENSION);
  switch (strtolower($info))
  {
    case "jpg":
    case "jpeg":
      return "image/jpg";

    case "png":
      return "image/png";

    case "gif":
      return "image/gif";

    case "htm":
    case "html":
      return "text/html";

    case "txt":
      return "text/plain";

    default:
      return "text/plain";
  }
}
```

Given a filename, this function uses the file's extension to make a very simple guess as to the content type of the file. There's no inspection of the file's content at all, and the function expects the file extension to accurately reflect the contents. To serve its purpose for this chapter the function handles just a few types.

Putting it all together with some argument processing, looping, and error checking, we have a handy command to upload one or more files to S3:

chapter_04/upload_file.php *(excerpt)*

```php
#!/usr/bin/php
<?php

error_reporting(E_ALL);

require_once('cloudfusion.class.php');
require_once('include/book.inc.php');

if ($argc < 3) ❶
{
  exit("Usage: " . $argv[0] . " bucket files...\n");
}

$bucket = ($argv[1] == '-') ? BOOK_BUCKET : $argv[1]; ❷

$s3  = new AmazonS3();

for ($i = 2; $i < $argc; $i++) ❸
{
  $file        = $argv[$i];
  $data        = file_get_contents($file);
  $contentType = guessType($file);

  if (uploadObject($s3, $bucket, $file, $data, ❹
      S3_ACL_PUBLIC, $contentType))
  {
    print("Uploaded file '${file}' to bucket '{$bucket}'\n");
  }
  else
  {
    exit("Could not upload file '${file}'" .
        " to bucket '{$bucket}'\n");
  }
}
```

```
exit(0);
?>
```

This script is designed to be run from the command line like so:

```
$php upload_file.php bucket_name file_name [...]
```

Let's take a closer look:

 First, we check to see if there are any arguments supplied; if there are none we display a helpful usage message and exit the script.

 This program expects the first argument to be a bucket name. If the bucket name is a dash character (-), the default bucket (BOOK_BUCKET) is used instead.

❸ The remaining arguments are considered to be the files to upload. We then loop through all the inputted filenames.

❹ Within each loop we call our uploadObject function. I chose to use the path name to each object exactly as supplied, to enable usage of key names with embedded slash characters.

Here's what this program looks like in action:

```
$php upload_file.php - images/catatonia_album.jpg
Uploaded file 'images/catatonia_album.jpg' to bucket
➥'sitepoint-aws-cloud-book'
```

We have really covered quite a bit of ground in just a few pages. You should now understand how to upload images to an S3 bucket, browse the bucket, and then view the images by clicking on a link. In the next section, you will learn how to generate thumbnail versions of all the images in a bucket.

Creating and Storing Thumbnail Images

Our next utility function will take an in-memory image, figure out the appropriate height and width for a thumbnail, and then create the thumbnail.

Firstly, in our **book.inc.php** file, we need to create two constants; one to store the desired thumbnail size, and one to store the default name for the bucket that will store our thumbnails. I want the thumbnail images to be 200 pixels on the longest side, and I want to define a suffix to add to my default bucket name in order to create the thumbnail bucket name, so I'll add the following:

chapter_04/include/book.inc.php (excerpt)

```
define('THUMB_SIZE', 200);
define('THUMB_BUCKET_SUFFIX', '-thumbs');
```

Of course, before we can use the thumbnail bucket we have to make sure it exists! You can use the **create_bucket.php** script we developed earlier to do that.

Here's the code for the thumbnailImage function; once again, this goes into our **book.inc.php** file:

chapter_04/include/book.inc.php (excerpt)

```
function thumbnailImage($imageBitsIn, $contentType)
{

  $imageIn = ImageCreateFromString($imageBitsIn);
  $inX = ImageSx($imageIn);
  $inY = ImageSy($imageIn);

  if ($inX > $inY)
  {
    $outX = THUMB_SIZE;
    $outY = (int) (THUMB_SIZE * ((float) $inY / $inX));
  }
  else
  {
    $outX = (int) (THUMB_SIZE * ((float) $inX / $inY));
    $outY = THUMB_SIZE;
  }

  $imageOut = ImageCreateTrueColor($outX, $outY);
  ImageFill($imageOut, 0, 0,
      ImageColorAllocate($imageOut, 255, 255, 255));
  ImageCopyResized($imageOut, $imageIn,
        0, 0, 0, 0,
        $outX, $outY, $inX, $inY);
```

```
$fileOut = tempnam("/tmp", "aws") . ".aws";

switch ($contentType)
{
  case "image/jpg":
    $ret = ImageJPEG($imageOut, $fileOut, 100);
    break;

  case "image/png":
    $ret = ImagePNG($imageOut, $fileOut, 0);
    break;

  case "image/gif":
    $ret = ImageGIF($imageOut, $fileOut);
    break;

  default:
    unlink($fileOut);
    return false;
}

if (!$ret)
{
  unlink($fileOut);
  return false;
}

$imageBitsOut = file_get_contents($fileOut);
unlink($fileOut);
return $imageBitsOut;
}
```

I'll refrain from going through this code in detail—this chapter focuses on S3, rather than graphics programming. The code makes extensive use of PHP's GD library.[5] Put simply, it creates a copy of an image and resizes it so that its longest dimension is equal to the number of pixels specified in the THUMB_SIZE constant, while preserving the width-height ratio of the image.

Generating the thumbnail for a good-sized image can take a substantial fraction of a second due to the number of pixels to be moved around; also, the ThumbNailImage

---

[5] http://www.php.net/gd

function must write the new image to a temporary file and then read it back into memory.

With this code in hand it's now a simple matter to do some argument processing and thumbnail each image in the given bucket. Here's how to do it:

```php
#!/usr/bin/php
<?php

error_reporting(E_ALL);

require_once('cloudfusion.class.php');
require_once('include/book.inc.php');

if ($argc != 3) ❶
{
  exit("Usage: " . $argv[0] . "in-bucket out-bucket\n");
}

$bucketIn  = ($argv[1] == '-') ❷
               ? BOOK_BUCKET
               : $argv[1];

$bucketOut = ($argv[2] == '-') ❸
          ? $bucketIn . THUMB_BUCKET_SUFFIX
               : $argv[2];

print("Thumbnailing '${bucketIn}' to '${bucketOut}'\n");

$s3  = new AmazonS3();
$objectsIn = getBucketObjects($s3, $bucketIn); ❹

foreach ($objectsIn as $objectIn)
{
  $key = $objectIn->Key;
  print("Processing item '${key}':\n");

  if (substr(guessType($key), 0, 6) == "image/") ❺
  {
    $startTime   = microtime(true); ❻
    $dataIn      = $s3->get_object($bucketIn, $key); ❼
    $endTime     = microtime(true);
    $contentType = guessType($key);
```

```
      printf("\tDownloaded from S3 in %.2f seconds.\n",
        ($endTime - $startTime));

      $startTime = microtime(true);
      $dataOut   = thumbnailImage($dataIn->body, $contentType);
      $endTime   = microtime(true);

      printf("\tGenerated thumbnail in %.2f seconds.\n",
        ($endTime - $startTime));

      $startTime = microtime(true);
      if (uploadObject($s3, $bucketOut, $key, $dataOut,
          S3_ACL_PUBLIC, $contentType))
      {
        $endTime = microtime(true);

        printf("\tUploaded thumbnail to S3 in %.2f seconds.\n",
          ($endTime - $startTime));
      }
      else
      {
        print("\tCould not upload thumbnail.\n");
      }
    }
    else
    {
      print("\tSkipping - not an image\n");
    }
    print("\n");
  }
exit(0);
?>
```

Let's go through this code step by step:

 First, we need to ensure that we have the minimum requirement of three arguments: the name of the script, the image bucket name, and the thumbnail
bucket name.

❷ Much like the previous example, this code allows the input and output buckets
to be set to default values by using the "-" character for the first two command
line arguments.

The default bucket name for our thumbnail bucket will be our default bucket name plus the suffix we defined earlier.

 Here we use our `getBucketObjects` function to retrieve all the objects in our bucket.

 We'll make use of our `guessType` function to ensure we only process objects that have a content type beginning with "`image/`".

 This code might look a bit cluttered because I've wrapped each major operation in timing code like this:

```
$startTime   = microtime(true);
: code operation
$endTime     = microtime(true);
```

This allows us to print useful time-related information as our script runs. Subtracting `$startTime` from `$endTime` will provide us with the elapsed time that we can format for output:

```
printf("Completed in %.2f seconds.\n", ($endTime - $startTime));
```

 There's just one new S3 call here:

```
$dataIn = $s3->get_object($bucketIn, $key);
```

The `get_object` method downloads the object from S3 and returns its data as a string.

 Here our `thumbnailImage` function generates a thumbnail and stores it in `$dataOut`.

 Our `uploadObject` function uploads the generated thumbnail to our thumbnail bucket.

Here's an example of the output produced when a single file is "thumbnailed":

```
$php thumbnail_bucket.php - -
Processing item 'images/a380_factory.jpg':
  Downloaded from S3 in 0.78 seconds.
  Generated thumbnail in 0.19 seconds.
  Uploaded thumbnail to S3 in 0.09 seconds.
```

The combination of S3, PHP, and GD lets you do some powerful graphics processing without a whole lot of work. You could easily modify the thumbnail code to reduce the quality of the image, paint a watermark over it, or map colors to grayscale values.

Creating a CloudFront Distribution

Before we can work with CloudFront Distributions, you have to make sure you've activated the feature in your AWS account. Visit http://aws.amazon.com/cloudfront/ and then click the **Sign Up for Amazon CloudFront** button, activation is only one more click away.

Although it's possible to write code to create a CloudFront distribution for an S3 bucket (and you're welcome to, of course), I'm choosing to sidestep it. Instead, it's easier to just use a graphical interface to create your distribution. You will be able to do this in any of the tools mentioned in the section called "Visual Tools" in Chapter 3. The AWS Management Console[6] makes it very simple; select the **Amazon CloudFront** tab and click the **Create Distribution** button, as shown in Figure 4.3.

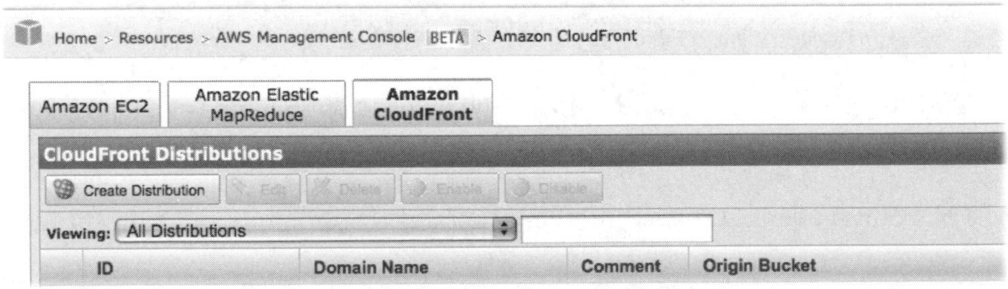

Figure 4.3. Click the Create **Distribution** button

Once set up, you'll have to wait several minutes while the CloudFront distribution is created.

---

[6] http://console.aws.amazon.com

Let's wrap up this chapter by making an image browser. We'll use CloudFront for efficient global distribution of the original and thumbnailed images.

Listing CloudFront Distributions

Here's a simple script to list all of your CloudFront distributions:

chapter_04/list_distributions.php (excerpt)

```php
#!/usr/bin/php
<?php

error_reporting(E_ALL);

require_once('cloudfusion.class.php');
require_once('include/book.inc.php');

$cf = new AmazonCloudFront();
$res = $cf->list_distributions();

if (!$res->isOK())
{
  exit("Could not retrieve list of CloudFront distributions\n");
}

$distributions = $res->body->DistributionSummary;

printf("%-16s %-32s %-40s\n", "ID", "Domain Name", "Origin");
printf("%'=-16s %'=-32s %'=40s\n", "", "", "");

foreach ($distributions as $distribution)
{
  $id         = $distribution->Id;
  $domainName = $distribution->DomainName;
  $origin     = $distribution->Origin;

  printf("%-16s %-32s %-40s\n", $id, $domainName, $origin);
}
exit(0);
?>
```

The code structure should be familiar to you by now. The `list_distributions` method returns an array of objects, which are then iterated over and printed. Notice, though, that we instantiate a new `AmazonCloudFront` object instead of an `AmazonS3` object like the previous scripts, and the `list_distributions` method to retrieve the details of the distributions.

The response object can be queried in the same way as our previous S3 scripts. In the response returned to the `list_distributions` method, the `$res->body->DistributionSummary` property will contain an array of `SimpleXMLElement` objects, one for each CloudFront distribution. The script above simply iterates over this array and extracts the `Id`, `DomainName`, and `Origin` property of each for display in the output, formatted into a table similar to the following:

```
$php list_distributions.php
Id                 Domain Name                        Origin
================= ================================= ===============
➡===========================
nnnnnnnnnnnnnn    nnnnnnnnnnnnnn.cloudfront.net     sitepoint-aws-
➡cloud-book.s3.amazonaws.com
```

When you run this script with your AWS account, the `ID` and `Domain Name` columns will show your unique values.

Listing S3 Files with Thumbnails

Okay, time for the last script in this chapter! We first need one more utility function to make this work: the `findDistributionForBucket` function that will return the CloudFront distribution for a given S3 bucket. You guessed it, we'll put this one in our **book.inc.php** file:

chapter_04/include/book.inc.php (excerpt)

```php
function findDistributionForBucket($cf, $bucket)
{
  $res = $cf->list_distributions();

  if (!$res->isOK())
  {
    return null;
  }

  $needle = $bucket . ".";
  $distributions = $res->body->DistributionSummary;
```

```
  foreach ($distributions as $distribution)
  {
    if (substr($distribution->Origin, 0, strlen($needle)) ==
        $needle)
    {
      return $distribution;
    }
  }

  return null;
}
```

This function accepts a CloudFront access object and the name of a bucket. It fetches the list of CloudFront distributions and attempts to match each one to the supplied bucket name. If a match is made, the distribution object is returned.

The code below is an enhanced version of **list_bucket_objects_page.php**, as seen earlier in this chapter. It adds a thumbnail to the table for all the image objects in the bucket that also have a corresponding image in the thumbnail bucket. It also uses the CloudFront URL if available:

chapter_04/list_bucket_objects_page_thumbs.php *(excerpt)*

```php
<?php

error_reporting(E_ALL);

require_once('cloudfusion.class.php');
require_once('include/book.inc.php');

$bucket = IsSet($_GET['bucket']) ? $_GET['bucket'] : BOOK_BUCKET;
$bucketThumbs = $bucket . THUMB_BUCKET_SUFFIX;

$s3 = new AmazonS3(); ❶
$cf = new AmazonCloudFront();

$dist = findDistributionForBucket($cf, $bucket); ❷
$thumbsDist = findDistributionForBucket($cf, $bucketThumbs);

$objects = getBucketObjects($s3, $bucket); ❸
$objectThumbs = getBucketObjects($s3, $bucketThumbs);

$thumbs = array(); ❹
```

```
foreach ($objectThumbs as $objectThumb)
{
  $key = (string) $objectThumb->Key;

  if ($thumbsDist != null) ❺
  {
    $thumbs[$key] = 'http://' . $thumbsDist->DomainName
        . "/" . $key;
  }
  else
  {
    $thumbs[$key] = $s3->get_object_url($bucketThumbs, $key);
  }
}

$fileList = array(); ❻
foreach ($objects as $object)
{
  $key = (string) $object->Key;

  if ($dist != null)
  {
    $url = 'http://' . $dist->DomainName . "/" . $key;
  }
  else
  {
    $url = $s3->get_object_url($bucket, $key);
  }

  $thumbURL = IsSet($thumbs[$key]) ? $thumbs[$key] : ''; ❼
  $fileList[] = array('thumb' => $thumbURL, 'url' => $url,
      'name' => $key, 'size' => number_format((int)$object->Size));
}

$output_title = "Chapter 3 Sample - List of S3 Objects in Bucket"
    . " '${bucket}'";
$output_message = "A simple HTML table displaying of all the objects"
    . "in the '${bucket}' bucket with thumbnails.";

include 'include/list_bucket_objects_thumbs.html.php';

exit(0);
?>
```

Let's take a look at this code:

 First, we instantiate new AmazonS3 and AmazonCloudFront objects.

 Here we determine whether there's a CloudFront distribution for each of our buckets.

❸ Once again we use our getBucketObjects function to retrieve all the objects from our two buckets.

 We iterate through all the objects in our thumb bucket, and populate the $thumbs array using the object keys as array keys and storing their URLs.

❺ If there's a CloudFront distribution for our thumbnails, we use its URL; otherwise, we use the standard S3 URL.

❻ We do the same operation for all the objects in the specified bucket; this is stored in the $fileList array and will be used in the HTML output.

❼ This is a new addition from the **list_bucket_objects_page.php** script to the $fileList array. The thumbnail URL is saved if there's a matching thumbnail, otherwise an empty string is stored.

Here's the HTML template that generates the output:

chapter_04/list_bucket_objects_thumbs.html.php (excerpt)

```
<!DOCTYPE html PUBLIC "-//W3C//DTD XHTML 1.0 Strict//EN"
  "http://www.w3.org/TR/xhtml1/DTD/xhtml1-strict.dtd">
<html xmlns="http://www.w3.org/1999/xhtml" xml:lang="en" lang="en">
<head>
  <title><?php echo $output_title ?></title>
</head>
<body>
  <h1><?php echo $output_title ?></h1>
  <p><?php echo $output_message ?></p>
  <table>
    <thead>
      <tr><th>File</th><th>Size</th></tr>
    </thead>
    <tbody>
    <?php foreach($fileList as $file): ?> ❶
      <tr>
        <td>
          <?php if($file['thumb'] != ''): ?> ❷
          <a href="<?php echo $file['url'] ?>">
              <img src="<?php echo $file['thumb'] ?>"/></a>
          <?php endif ?>
        </td>
        <td><a href="<?php echo $file['url'] ?>">
          <?php echo $file['name'] ?></a>
        </td>
        <td><?php echo $file['size'] ?></td>
      </tr>
    <?php endforeach ?>
    </tbody>
  </table>
</body>
</html>
```

There's a couple of interesting points in the code above:

❶   This template iterates over the `$fileList` array, adding a table row for each
     element of the array, and a table cell for the thumbnail image, the filename,
     and file size.

❷   The contents of the thumbnail table cell are only added if there's a thumbnail
     URL specified for that file, otherwise the cell is left empty.

Figure 4.4 shows what the output looks like.

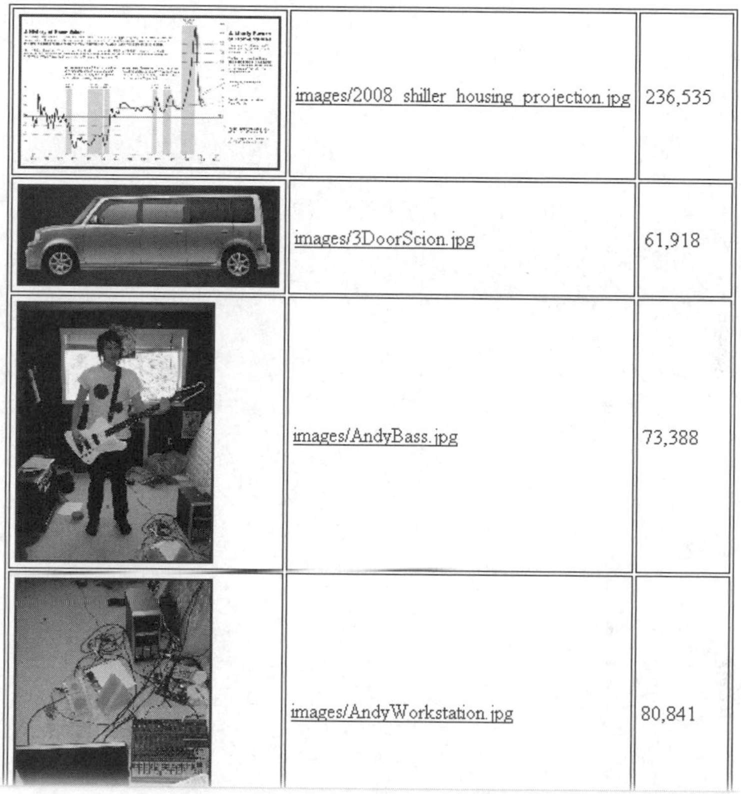

Figure 4.4. Object listing with thumbnails

Finally

This has been a long and code-heavy chapter. Starting from scratch you've learned how to create S3 buckets, list your buckets, and upload files to S3. You have discovered how to process the contents of one bucket into another, and how to use CloudFront for efficient content distribution. With all these new skills in hand, you should be ready to create some intriguing S3 applications of your very own.

Web Hosting with Amazon EC2

In this chapter, you will learn all about the Amazon Elastic Compute Cloud (Amazon EC2) infrastructure. We'll take one more look at the concept of the programmable data center, and then we'll review the key Amazon EC2 concepts, including the pricing model. We'll use the AWS Management Console to do the setup work needed to actually launch an EC2 instance, and then we'll launch one and get it all set up. After that we will talk about the Amazon Machine Image (AMI) in depth, and we will even create one of our own. We'll wrap up by writing a short (but very cool) program to manipulate Amazon EC2 resources using the API.

The Programmable Data Center

In Chapter 1, I described the concept of a programmable data center as central to cloud computing. Manual labor and hands-on system building are replaced by automated provisioning, dynamic resource allocation, and a model where every function of the data center is accessible through an API call.

To illustrate the difference between a traditional, human-powered internet hosting provider and a modern, programmable data center, let's list the steps needed for a single server to be up and running:

1. locate or acquire suitable server hardware
2. acquire and attach adequate disk storage
3. ensure adequate rack space, power, and cooling
4. arrange for internet connectivity
5. procure and set up networking gear such as switches, routers, and load balancers
6. install the hardware
7. boot the server
8. install the operating system
9. configure necessary applications
10. allocate and route IP addresses
11. make firewall entries for access and protection
12. configure monitoring to verify that the system is functional
13. scale all of the above components in response to increasing traffic

Each of these steps is time-consuming and the labor involved expensive when done by hand. A programmable data center replaces each step with equivalent API calls and shrinks the time needed to complete each step from hours, days, or weeks to seconds. This rapid-response, mass production model is a key aspect of cloud computing.

Programmable configuration control also simplifies growth and evolution, since additional resources are readily available.

Amazon EC2 Overview

The Amazon EC2 infrastructure exhibits all the concepts of the programmable data center that I listed above. In fact, Amazon EC2 services provide access to multiple data centers (Availability Zones) in multiple geographic regions and are really a collection of programmable data centers. You simply make web service requests "to the cloud" and Amazon EC2 capabilities do the rest. Servers, operating system images, firewall entries, load balancers, IP addresses, and disk storage volumes are all available in a matter of seconds. In this section, we'll address the difference between persistent and ephemeral resources, cover the key Amazon EC2 concepts, review the pricing model, and discuss the ways the EC2 infrastructure works with other AWS infrastructure services.

Persistent and Ephemeral Resources

Amazon EC2 resources can be grouped into two classes—persistent and ephemeral —and it's important that you understand the differences between the two.

Persistent resources, once allocated to your account, can be expected to remain operational in the face of transient or permanent hardware or software failures. The Amazon implementation of a persistent resource makes uses of redundancy, auto-mated failover, and automatic recovery to provide you with stable resources. The following EC2 resources are persistent:

- Elastic IP Addresses
- Elastic Block Storage (EBS) Volumes
- Elastic Load Balancers
- Security Groups
- Amazon Machine Images (AMIs) stored in Amazon S3 or as Amazon EBS snap-shots

Ephemeral resources, on the other hand, are without built-in redundancy and will eventually fail. When they fail, stored data and state information is generally lost. Therefore, you're expected to use other EC2 facilities to implement your own re-dundancy, failover, and recovery. The following EC2 resources are ephemeral:

- Amazon EC2 Instances

At this point you may be thinking, "What? The instances can crash at any point and take my local data with them?" This is true, but, as developers often say, this is a feature, rather than a bug. One of the most important architectural aspects of a large-scale internet site (Amazon.com is a great example, of course) is that you can think of the individual servers as if they were all transient and extremely unreliable, and that you can use software to build a reliable system from unreliable parts.

Practically speaking, Amazon EC2 servers are actually fairly durable. One of my personal EC2 instances has been running without a hitch for 742 days. When it ul-timately fails, I'll simply boot up another copy of my custom AMI, restore my data from S3, and keep going.

Once you start to think of all your servers as fundamentally unreliable (Amazon EC2 or otherwise), which sounds a lot worse than it actually is, you start to realize that you can build a system in such a way that loss of a particular server is really no big deal. The cloud also makes it easy for you to simulate a number of failure scenarios so that you can ensure that your recovery logic works as expected. Once you've been through a few of these exercises you can sleep better at night, confident that recovery from a system failure is easy, and in some cases even automatic.

Speaking from experience, I can tell you that making the mental shift from "I'm scared, it could go away at any time" to "I'm confident that it could go away at any time and nothing bad will happen" is when you know that your thinking has become truly cloud-friendly.

Amazon EC2 Terminology

The most important EC2 concept is the instance. Using a **virtualization** technique, the EC2 infrastructure runs machine instances on behalf of several EC2 users on the same physical hardware. The virtualization software ensures that each logical instance receives a guaranteed share of memory space and CPU time, and makes sure that instances running on the same hardware avoid interfering with each other in any way.

An instance can be running any one of a number of operating systems, including Linux (multiple distributions are available), Windows Server, or OpenSolaris.

When you start up an Amazon EC2 instance you must specify the **instance type**. There are currently nine EC2 instance types, as shown in Table 5.1.[1]

The costs listed in Table 5.1 are current as of publication time and reflect the charges for Linux or OpenSolaris instances running in the United States. Prices for instances running in Europe or Asia, for Windows instances, and for Windows instances running in Europe or Asia, are higher.

The speed of each core is measured in terms of EC2 Compute Units; each unit is roughly the equivalent of a 1.0 to 1.2 GHz 2007-era AMD Opteron or Intel Xeon processor.

All instance types besides the **Small** have more than one **virtual core**. The virtual cores are independent processing units that run concurrently. You can take advantage

---

[1] The set of instance types is expected to grow and change over time. You can always find the latest list of instance types on the EC2 home page at http://aws.amazon.com/ec2.

of this power by running more than one CPU-bound program at once, or by writing your programs with its multi-core capabilities in mind. The latter method, though, is an advanced topic, and beyond the scope of this book.

Table 5.1. Amazon EC2 Instance Types

Name	CPU Word Size	CPU Virtual Cores	CPU Core Speed (EC2 Compute Units)	RAM	Local Disk	Cost/Hour
Small	32-bit	1	1	1.7GB	160GB	$0.085
Large	64-bit	2	2	7.5GB	850GB	$0.34
Extra Large	64-bit	4	2	15GB	1,690GB	$0.68
High-CPU Medium	32-bit	2	2.5	1.7GB	350GB	$0.17
High-CPU Extra Large	64-bit	8	2.5	7GB	1,690GB	$0.68
High Memory Extra Large	64-bit	2	3.25	17.1GB	420GB	$0.50
High Memory Double Extra Large	64-bit	2	3.25	34.2GB	850GB	$1.20
High Memory Quadruple Extra Large	64-bit	8	3.25	68.4GB	1,690GB	$2.40
Cluster Compute	64-bit	8 (two processors, each with 4 cores)	2.5	23GB	1,690GB	$1.60

As you can see from the table, the larger instance types have faster cores and more of them.

You need to consider a number of factors when you choose the EC2 instance types for your application. First, you'll need to make sure that your application is compatible with the CPU word size. A number of high-end database products run only on 64-bit hardware. Once you've built an AMI, it's specific to the CPU word size; it's impossible to run AMIs built for a 32-bit instance type on a 64-bit instance type, or vice versa. Next, you'll need to think about the resource demands of your application. Applications that need a lot of processing power relative to the amount of memory may run best on the High-CPU instances. Within the 32-bit and 64-bit product lines, there is plenty of room to move up and down to optimize your resource usage. Experienced EC2 users generally benchmark their application on two or three different instance types and then choose the one that provides the best price/performance level. Finally, you'll need to decide whether you want to have lots of small instances or fewer large ones. This scale-out versus scale-up decision is, once again, very specific to your application's needs. Complex, multi-tier applications will often use multiple instance types. For example:

- Small instances for the web tier
- Extra Large instances for the relational database tier
- High-CPU Extra Large instances for a CPU-intensive application tier

Using a larger number of smaller instances also gives you the flexibility to distribute them across two or more Availability Zones for better fault tolerance. Extremely large-scale applications can even span more than one EC2 region, running some instances in the United States, some in Europe, and others in Asia. It's actually quite easy to create these complex, multi-homed topologies using EC2 capabilities. When you build an application that literally spans the world, cloud computing will become even more compelling. You can build "follow-the-sun" applications, adding resources when and where your users are busiest and removing them when they're asleep. You can add functional redundancy and geographic dispersion without having to deal with additional data center or bandwidth suppliers.

When you launch an instance you always run a particular AMI (Amazon Machine Image). As we discussed in Chapter 2, the AMI contains your operating system and can also contain other layers and parts of your application. You can choose from a number of predefined AMIs or you can build your own. You have a lot of flexibility in how you configure and customize your AMIs. You can build a set of distinct AMIs for each tier of your application, or you can create a generic AMI that self-customizes at startup time according to its role. AMIs can be stored in Amazon S3 or as Elastic Block Storage snapshots. The newer, snapshot-based model is faster and more flexible. Instances that have been booted from an EBS snapshot can be shut down and then restarted at will, on the same instance type or on another one with different specifications; however, you can't migrate between instance types with different word sizes without rebuilding the AMI.

Each of your EC2 instances can be included in any number of EC2 security groups when the instance is launched. The security groups are part of your AWS account and can be applied to any number of instances. Each group defines a set of allowable inbound connections using rules that contain a protocol, a port, and an IP address range. Once an instance is launched, the set of groups attached to it cannot be changed. However, the group itself can be changed (rules added or deleted) and the changes will take effect immediately. Groups can be used to implement fine-grained access control logic for multi-tier applications. For instance, Table 5.2 describes one way to set up your security groups.

Table 5.2. Sample Security Groups

Group Name	Rules
web_access	▪ allow HTTP access (port 80) from anywhere ▪ allow SSH access (port 22) from corporate network
db_access	▪ allow access to MySQL database (port 3306) ▪ allow SSH access (port 22) from corporate network
app_access	▪ allow access to application server (port 5000) ▪ allow SSH access (port 22) from corporate network

The security groups would then be applied to the instances as listed in Table 5.3.

Table 5.3. Instances and Security Groups

Instance Role	Security Group
web server	web_access
database server	db_access
application server	app_access

With a clean and properly factored set of groups as a base, it becomes possible to think about making changes dynamically. For example, a scheduling utility built around the `AuthorizeSecurityGroupIngress` and `RevokeSecurityGroupIngress` AWS functions could make periodic changes to the `app_access` group to implement rotating, remote access by backup system administrators for emergency access. Or, the rules in the `db_access` group could be made more selective by dynamically adding permissions based on the IP addresses of the servers in the web tier.

Instances within a single security group can communicate freely with each other. Therefore, it would be imprudent to use, for example, a single `ssh_access` group to allow SSH access to instances in more than one tier of the previous example.

A public IP address is assigned to each instance as part of the launch process. However, because the instances are ephemeral, the IP address will have the same lifetime as the instance. The EC2 Elastic IP address feature supports allocation of public IP addresses that are stable and that have a lifetime independent of any particular EC2 instance. The addresses are allocated to your AWS account. Once allocated they remain under your control until relinquished, regardless of whether you use them or not. You can attach (route) any of your IP addresses to any of your EC2 instances.

As noted earlier in this section, the local disk storage included with each EC2 instance is ephemeral. The storage will remain intact if a running instance is rebooted, but it's scrubbed and then reused after the instance has been terminated. The EC2 Elastic Block Store (EBS) provides persistent storage with high reliability and availability. You can create an EBS volume and then attach it to any of your instances in the same Availability Zone. You can create point-in-time snapshot backups to Amazon S3 and then restore the backups to the same volume, or you can use them to create a fresh volume. EBS volumes can be formatted and used to store files, or they can be used as unformatted "raw" storage.

The Amazon DevPay system lets you use Amazon's subscription and billing infrastructure for your own EC2-based applications. DevPay gives you the ability to create your own payment plan with any combination of up-front, recurring, and usage-based fees. Once you've attached the payment plan to an AMI of your creation, your customers can sign up for it and launch one or more copies of the AMI. They'll pay for usage via their Amazon account.

All Together Now

Amazon EC2 functionality becomes even more powerful when it's used in conjunction with the other AWS infrastructure services. We've already talked about the use of Amazon S3 for storage of AMIs and EBS snapshots. And, as we saw in the last chapter, you can call the S3 APIs using PHP code running on an EC2 instance. S3 is ideal for storage of any amount of unstructured application data—binary or string.

In a similar fashion, code running on an EC2 instance can use Amazon SimpleDB for structured data store, the Relational Database Service for storage of relational data, and the Amazon Simple Queue Service as a scalable inter-instance or inter-process buffer. Elastic MapReduce runs on EC2 services and can be used to process large amounts of data.

Adding to the appeal of this architectural model is the fact that latency between EC2 services and these services is very low, since they're running in the same Region.

The Amazon EC2 Pricing Model

Your Amazon EC2 usage is charged in a number of dimensions that include instance use, data transfer, AMI storage, IP address reservations, EBS data storage, and EBS I/O. These prices will change over time, so you should consult the Amazon EC2 home page[2] for the latest information.

Instance Use

Hourly (on-demand) pricing for each of the EC2 instance types is shown earlier in Table 5.1. Instance usage begins when the instance starts running, and is billed in whole-hour increments. These are base prices, and several factors can affect the final price:

- It's more expensive to run EC2 instances in the Europe and Asia Pacific Regions.
- It costs more to run Windows than it does to run Linux or OpenSolaris.
- AMIs accessed via DevPay are charged at the rates set by the AMI's creator.
- You can arrange for a lower hourly rate by purchasing reserved instances.

---

[2] http://aws.amazon.com/ec2

Taking all these factors into consideration, you should plan on watching your AWS account with care during the first hours and weeks of operation.

If you plan to keep a number of EC2 instances running over time, you should also investigate the reserved instance option. With this option you pay an up-front fee to reserve an instance for a period of one or three years, and then pay a smaller per-hour charge when you're actually using the instance. The final per-hour cost is lower than it would be for on-demand usage. At current rates, a three-year reserved instance is less expensive than an on-demand instance if the instance is used at least 19% of the time. Purchase of a reserved instance will also ensure that you can allocate an EC2 instance when you need it.

Data Transfer

Your data transfer charges are based on the amount of data transferred in and out of your EC2 instances. Data transferred into your instances is charged at a rate of $0.10 per gigabyte. Once again, this amount is prorated. Data transferred out of your instances is charged on a sliding scale that starts at $0.17 per gigabyte and decreases according to volume, reaching $0.10 per gigabyte for all outgoing data transfer in excess of 150 terabytes per month.

There are some important special cases for data transfer:

- There's no charge for data transfers within an AWS Availability Zone.
- Data transferred between regions is charged at internet rates as described at the beginning of this section. You'll be charged for both sides of the transfer (out of one region and into the other).
- Data transferred between Availability Zones in the same region is charged at the rate of $0.01 per gigabyte.
- No charges apply to transfer data back and forth between EC2 and other AWS services in the same region.

AMI Storage

The AMIs that you create are stored directly in Amazon S3 or as EBS snapshots (which are also stored in S3), and you pay the usual S3 rates for doing so. My own customized Linux AMIs typically consume 500 to 700 megabytes of space. Windows AMIs are generally larger, often weighing in at more than five gigabytes. If you create and retain multiple versions of your AMIs, or if you create separate AMIs for each tier of your application, it'd be wise to pay attention to your storage costs.

IP Address Reservations

You can allocate Elastic IP addresses and attach them to an EC2 instance at no charge. However, if you allocate an address but fail to attach it to an instance, you'll be charged $0.01 per hour for it. You can do up to 100 remap (attach or detach) operations per month at no charge. After that you will pay $0.10 for each remap.

Elastic Block Store

The storage consumed by your Elastic Block Store volumes is charged at the rate of $0.10 per gigabyte per month. Because this is raw storage that you can use in any desired way, you're charged based on how much you allocate, rather than on how much you use.

You're also charged $0.10 for each million I/O requests you make to EBS. Like all other AWS charges, this amount will be prorated based on actual usage, so you'd pay $0.05 for 500,000 I/O requests.

Launching Your First Amazon EC2 Instance

Now that we've taken care of the concepts and the pricing, it's time to actually use EC2 functionality. We'll prepare our SSH keys, become familiar with the AWS Management Console, then launch an instance. Once the instance is running we'll allocate and attach an IP address to it, and then we'll create, attach, and format an EBS volume. We'll rev up Apache and put some code into place, then we'll shut it all down.

Creating and Preparing an SSH Key

We'll need to be able to connect to our instances using SSH, but before we can do that we need to create one or more Amazon EC2 key pairs. This is a way to prove our identity to the Amazon EC2 instance when we connect.

Point your browser at http://console.aws.amazon.com and log in if necessary. Click on the Amazon EC2 tab. If you've yet to sign up for EC2 services you'll need to do that, supplying a credit card to take care of your charges.

If you're in Europe or Asia, you may prefer to use the local EC2 region for this exercise. You can do this by selecting it from the **Region** menu shown in Figure 5.1.

Region: [US West ▼]
US East (N. Virginia)
US West (N. California)
EU West (Ireland)

Figure 5.1. The AWS Management Console's Region menu

EC2 Regions in CloudFusion

At the time of writing, the current version of CloudFusion (2.5) has limited support for EC2 Regions other than the default (us-east-1). Should you experience problems running any of the code in the book, it's worth trying it again using instances in the us-east-1 Region. CloudFusion 2.6 is expected to fix many of these issues, and it should be released in the near future. If it's already available by the time you read this, then some of the code may require modification to take advantage of these new features; this should be easy to do with a quick pass through the documentation pertaining to the methods in question.

Once the AWS Management Console is visible, click on **Key Pairs** and then press the **Create Key Pair** button. This will display the dialog shown in Figure 5.2.

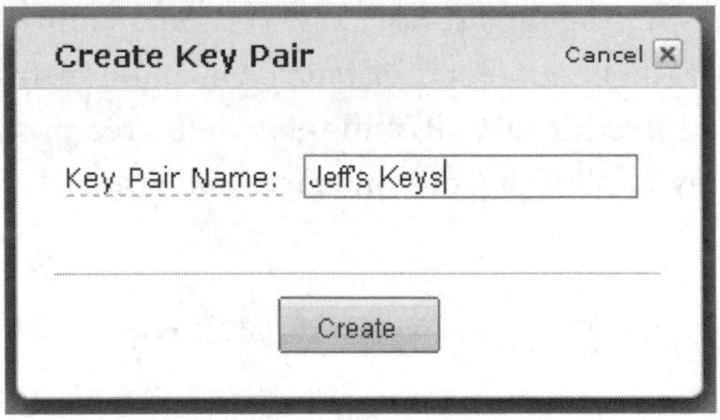

Create Key Pair   Cancel ✕

Key Pair Name: [Jeff's Keys]

[Create]

Figure 5.2. Creating and naming a new key pair

Enter a name for your key pair (I chose "Jeff's Keys") and press the **Create** button. After you press the button, the AWS Management Console will initiate a file download. Depending on your browser settings, you'll either be prompted to save a file or the file will be saved to your local disk.

Save the **.pem** to a safe and secure place. Why safe? If you lose the file you'll have to regenerate it. Once you do so you'll no longer have SSH access to your existing EC2 instances. Why secure? If an unauthorized person finds the file, they'll have access to your running instances.

Preparing PuTTY on Windows

As I mentioned in the section called "Hardware and Software Expectations" in Chapter 3, I highly recommend the PuTTY SSH client. Before we can use it to connect, though, we need to convert the private key into a format that PuTTY can use. If you've yet to do so, obtain a copy of PuTTY and the associated PuTTYgen utility.[3] You can download the self-contained executable files or the handy installer. You'll be using PuTTY a lot so consider creating a desktop shortcut for it.

Launch PuTTYgen, click on the **Conversions** menu, and choose **Import key**. Locate the **.pem** file you saved earlier and open it. You can add a passphrase (a local password) to make the key more secure if you'd like, as I'm doing in Figure 5.3. You'll have to supply the passphrase each time you use the key. Go to PuTTYgen's **File** menu and choose **Save private key**. Once again, put this key in a safe and secure location on your local desktop.

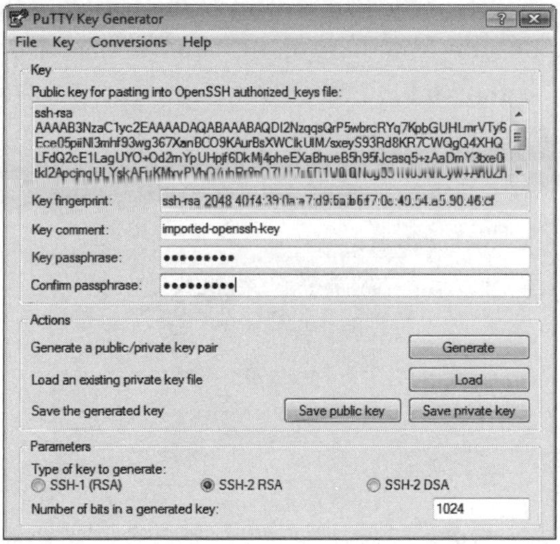

Figure 5.3. Adding a passphrase during key conversion

---

[3] http://www.chiark.greenend.org.uk/~sgtatham/putty/

Preparing Your Key Pair on Mac OS X or Linux

Open a terminal window in the directory where you saved your key pair file. Our first important task is to set the correct file permissions, otherwise we'll be unable to use it to connect; we'll receive a big `WARNING: UNPROTECTED PRIVATE KEY FILE!` error message. Use the `chmod` command to restrict read and write permissions to the file owner (replace *your_key_file.pem* with the name of your file):

```
$ chmod 600 your_key_file.pem
```

If you like, you can also set up a passphrase by using the following command:

```
$ ssh-keygen -p
```

You'll be prompted for the location of your key pair file, and asked to enter in the passphrase twice for confirmation.

Touring the AWS Management Console

You already have the AWS Management Console open in your browser, so take a few minutes to explore the **Navigation** pane under the Amazon EC2 tab. As you can see, there are links for each of the EC2 resources described in this chapter. We'll be using the console quite a bit from here on in. You can also use the **Help** button in the top-right corner, as shown in Figure 5.4, to learn more about each feature of the console.

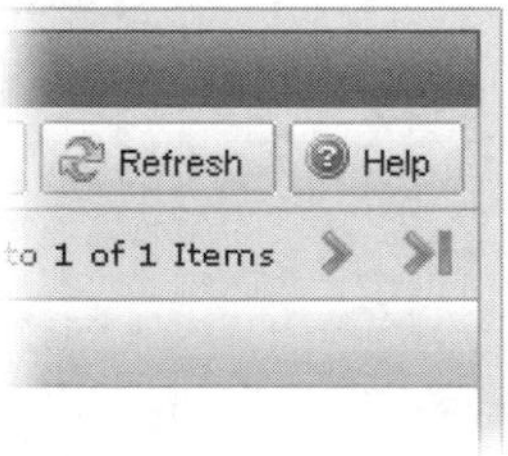

Figure 5.4. The AWS Management Console's Help Button

Launching Your First Instance

At this point you're all revved up and are at the starting line. It's time to actually launch an instance. For this exercise we'll launch the LAMP Web Starter. This AMI incorporates the Fedora Core 8 Linux distribution, along with PHP, Apache, and MySQL.

Click on **Instances** in the **Navigation** pane, and then press the **Launch Instances** button. The **Request Instances Wizard** will be displayed, as Figure 5.5 illustrates.

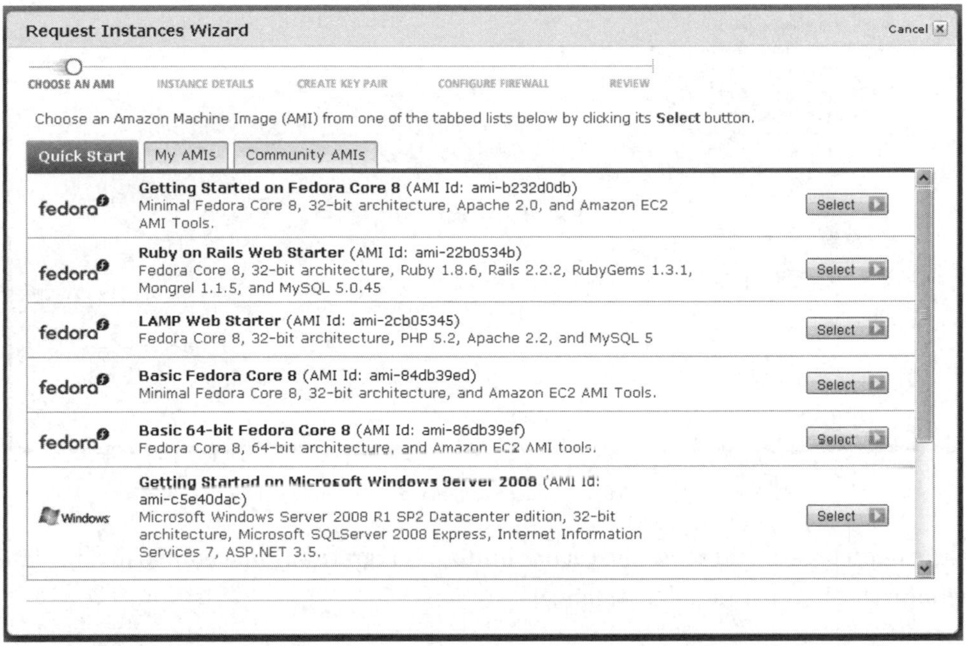

Figure 5.5. The Request Instances Wizard

Click the **Select** button next to the **LAMP Web Starter** AMI. The second page, **Instance Details**, we can leave as is, so click the **Continue** button. On the third page of the wizard (**Create Keypair**), choose your key pair from the menu and click the **Continue** button. On the wizard's fourth page (**Configure Firewall**), make sure that the default security group is selected and click the **Continue** button.

On the fifth and final page of the wizard (**Launch**), review your settings, as shown in Figure 5.6.

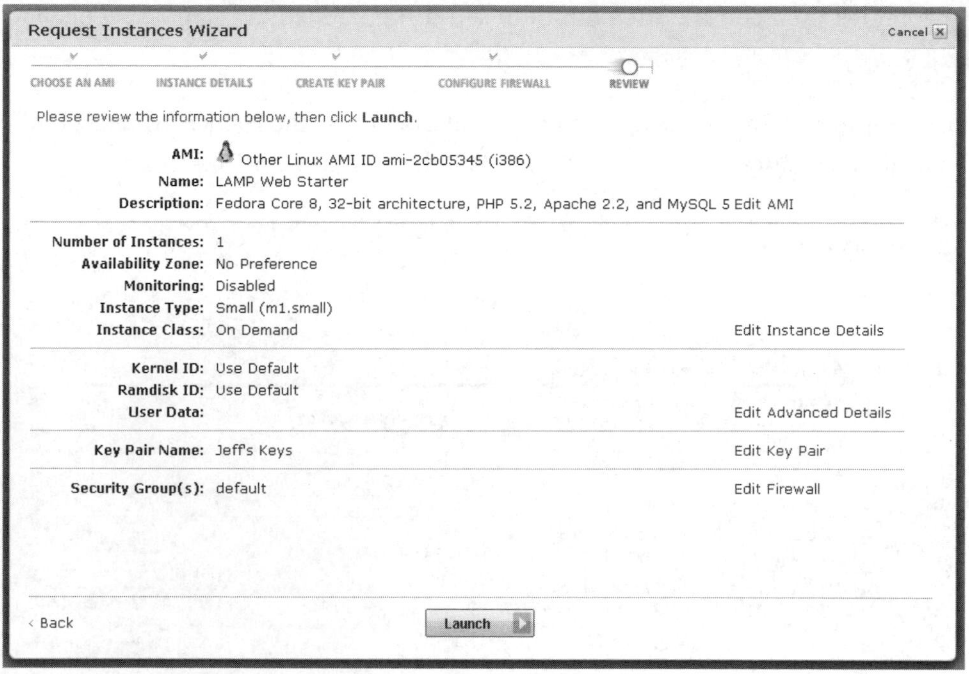

Figure 5.6. Take a deep breath and press **Launch**

Take a deep breath and press the **Launch** button. Congratulations, you've just initiated the launch of your first EC2 instance!

Close the final page of the wizard, and keep an eye on the **My Instances** list. Behind the scenes the EC2 infrastructure is preparing your instance for use, which involves:

1. finding an available server
2. copying the AMI to the boot disk of the server for an S3-backed instance, or creating an EBS volume from the AMI for an EBS-backed instance
3. booting the server
4. applying security settings
5. starting the metering process to track your usage

Linux and OpenSolaris instances typically launch in a minute or two. Windows instances can take a bit longer, sometimes up to five minutes.

When your instance changes to a **running** status, it's ready for use. In Figure 5.7 I have two instances running, so there are two rows and two status indicators.

Figure 5.7. The instances are running

Enabling SSH Access

Before connecting to the new instance, you need to make sure that the EC2 security group named `default` allows SSH (port 22) access and HTTP (port 80) access. Older AWS accounts allowed access on these ports by default, so there's no need for concern if you check your group and it's already there.

Click on **Security Groups**, then on the group named default, and take a look at the list of **Allowed Connections**. Make sure that the list includes **SSH** in the **Connection Method** column with **From Port** and **To Port** set to 22. If there's no entry like this, change the **Custom...** select menu on the bottom row to **SSH** and press the **Save** button (the other fields will fill in automatically). If you know the IP address of your desktop computer, you can use it as the **Source IP**, along with a "/32" suffix.[4]

Do the same for HTTP on port 80 if it's missing from the list. Figure 5.8 illustrates adding a new entry for HTTP, after already adding an entry for SSH.

Figure 5.8. Adding connection methods to the default security group

---

[4] If you choose to do this, be sure to update the group if the IP address of your desktop computer changes. You could also add multiple SSH rules to enable access from more than one IP address.

Connecting to the Instance

There's a lot of useful information in the **My Instances** list. Of particular interest is the column labeled **Public DNS**, as shown in Figure 5.9.

Public DNS
ec2-72-44-33-237.compute-1.amazonaws.com
ec2-75-101-154-199.compute-1.amazonaws.com

Figure 5.9. The console showing the Public DNS name of each running instance

Copy the public DNS name for your instance, as you'll need it to connect via SSH.

Connecting with PuTTY on Windows

Launch PuTTY and paste the Public DNS name into the **Host Name** field, as shown in Figure 5.10.

Figure 5.10. Configuring PuTTY for Windows

Now click the **Auth** tree item (nested inside of the **SSH** item) shown in Figure 5.11 and use the **Browse...** button to locate the private key that you saved from PuTTYgen.

Figure 5.11. Configuring SSH authentication on PuTTY

Click the **Open** button and PuTTY will connect to your instance, authenticating itself using the public portion of your private key. PuTTY will then ask you to confirm your request to use the key, as depicted in Figure 5.12.

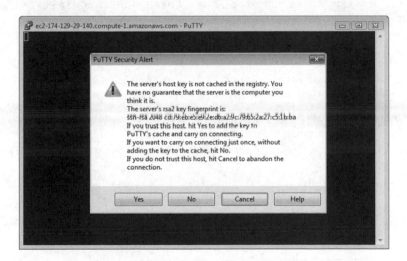

Figure 5.12. PuTTY confirming use of new key

Click **Yes**, and then enter **root** when your instance prompts you to log in. Since you've already identified yourself using your key, a password is unnecessary for the root account. However, if you've set up a passphrase for your key you'll be prompted for it. Figure 5.13 shows a successful login.

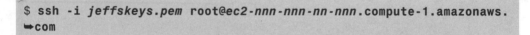

Figure 5.13. Successful login to a fresh EC2 instance

Connecting with the Mac OS X or Linux Terminal

Open a new terminal window and enter the following command:

```
$ ssh -i jeffskeys.pem root@ec2-nnn-nnn-nn-nnn.compute-1.amazonaws.
➥com
```

Replace *jeffskeys.pem* with your own key pair file and *ec2-nnn-nnn-nn-nnn* with
the public DNS name of your instance. You'll receive the following response:

```
The authenticity of host 'ec2-nnn-nnn-nnn-nnn.compute-1.amazonaws.
➥com (nnn.nnn.nnn.nnn)' can't be established.
RSA key fingerprint is cd:79:eb:e3:e9:2e:d6:b2:9c:79:65:2a:27:c5:
➥1b:ba.
Are you sure you want to continue connecting (yes/no)?
```

Of course, the host information and RSA key fingerprint details will be different to
those above. If you enter **yes** to the question above, you will be logged in and will
receive the following output:

```
Warning: Permanently added 'ec2-nnn-nnn-nnn-nnn.compute-1.amazonaws
➥com,nnn.nnn.nnn.nnn' (RSA) to the list of known hosts.

     _|  _|_  )   Fedora 8
     _| (    /    32-bit
```

```
        __|\__|__|

 Welcome to an EC2 Public Image
                  :-)

    Base

 --[ see /etc/ec2/release-notes ]--

[root@domU-12-31-38-00-2E-18 ~]#
```

If you had set a passphrase on your key pair file, you'll be prompted to enter it as well. Again, the host and prompt information will differ to those above.

Now We're Connected

Congratulations, you now have full control of your very own EC2 instance! If you plan to start up more than one EC2 instance, you should make sure that you can tell them apart by making the shell prompt more distinct. Here's how to set the shell prompt to the string "<dev>: " to indicate that the shell is on a development (as opposed to production) server:

```
[root@domU-12-31-38-00-2E-18 ~]# export PS1="<dev>: "
```

Run the following command to see which packages have already been installed:

```
<dev>: yum list | grep installed
```

You should see a long list. Feel free to spend some time exploring your new EC2 instance. Try out your favorite Linux commands and verify that they work as you expect them to. You can install new packages using the yum command. If you prefer emacs to vim, install it like this:

```
<dev>: yum -y install emacs
```

If you decide to pause at this point, remember that your instance is now running and that you're paying for it by the hour. If there's no need to keep it running, return to the AWS Management Console, select the instance, and choose **Terminate** from the **Instance Actions** menu. When you do this, all data stored on the instance will be lost.

If you launched an EBS-backed AMI, you have an additional option. You can choose **Stop** from the **Instance Actions** menu. The operating system will be cleanly shut down, and the status of the instance will change to **stopped**. Later, you can choose to start the instance again and it will boot up with all the files on the root file system remaining intact. This additional flexibility is among one of the many reasons to prefer EBS-backed AMIs over their older S3-backed cousins.

Assigning an IP Address

Let's give this instance a permanent IP address of its own. Close your SSH session with the `exit` command, and then return to the AWS Management Console. Click on **Elastic IPs** in the **Navigation** pane and press the **Allocate New Address** button. Press the **Yes, Allocate** button in the dialog to confirm your wish to allocate a new IP address. After a very brief pause, your newly allocated address will be listed in the **Addresses** list.

At this point the address is yours, but is still unassociated with any particular EC2 instance. Let's remedy that. Click on the address in the list to select it, and then press the **Associate** button, which will bring up the dialog shown in Figure 5.14.

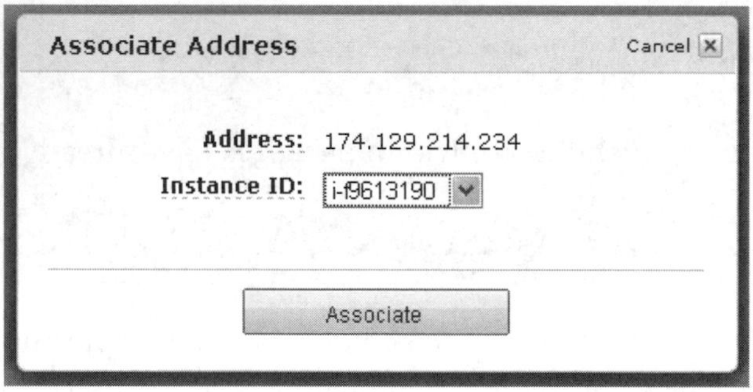

Figure 5.14. Associating an Elastic IP Address with an EC2 instance

Select the appropriate instance ID in the menu, and press the **Associate** button in the dialog. Now create a new SSH session using the Elastic IP address instead of the host name. If you happen to have a spare domain name and a DNS provider, you can map the domain name to the public IP address.

Recall that you're charged for allocated but unmapped IP addresses. If you decide to terminate your instance and have no need for the IP address anymore, be sure to release it using the AWS Management Console.

Creating an EBS Volume

Now that you have an instance and an IP address, let's create, attach, and format a storage volume.

Once created, you can attach an EBS volume to any of the instances that are in the same Availability Zone as the volume. Since our instance is already running, let's figure out which zone it's running in. Return to the AWS Management Console, and select the **Instances** view. Click on the row of your instance and inspect the detailed instance properties displayed at the bottom, as shown in Figure 5.15.

Zone:	us-east-1a
Type:	m1.small
Owner:	889279108296
Ramdisk ID:	ari-a51cf9cc
Key Pair Name:	Jeff's Keys
AMI Launch Index:	0

Figure 5.15. Finding the instance's Availability Zone

My instance is in zone us-east-1a. Click on **Volumes** in the **Navigation** pane, press the **Create Volume** button, and you will be presented with the dialog box shown in Figure 5.16.

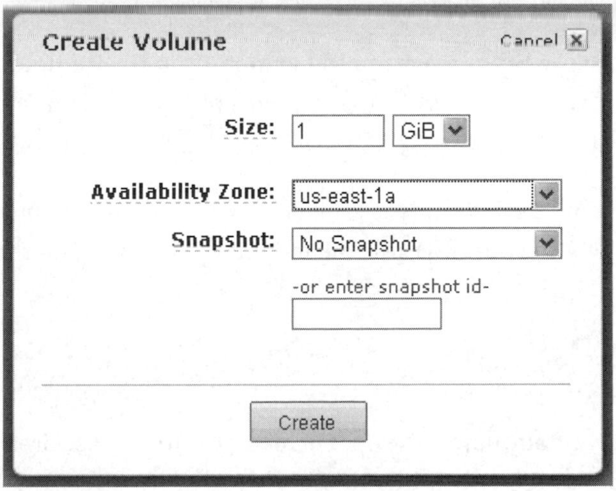

Figure 5.16. Creating an EBS Volume

The dialog form accepts values in units of **gibibytes** (GiB) and **Tebibytes** (TiB). These are the power-of-two analogs of the more familiar gigabytes (GB) and terabytes (TB), both of which represent powers of ten. One gibibyte is 1,073,741,824 bytes, whereas one gigabyte is 1,000,000,000 bytes.

Enter the desired volume size (10GiB is a good value) and select the Availability Zone of your instance. Leave the other fields as they are and press the **Create** button. The new volume will appear in the EBS Volumes list, with a **creating** status. Wait a few seconds, press the **Refresh** button, and the status should change to **available**.

Now select the volume and press the **Attach** button (or right-click on it and choose **Attach Volume**) to reveal the Attach Volume dialog shown in Figure 5.17.

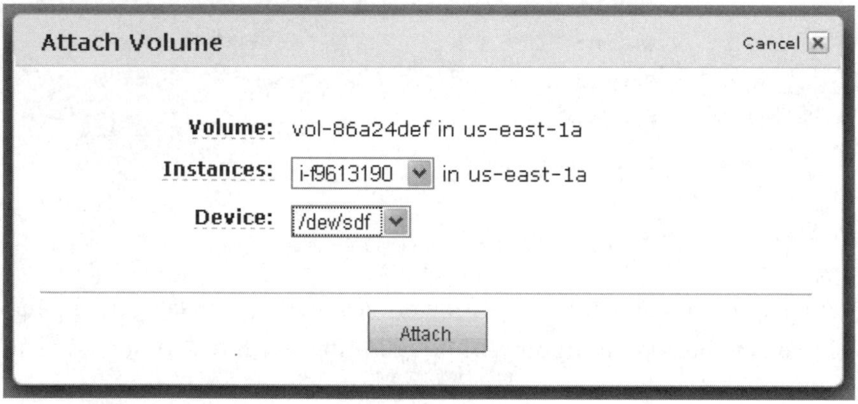

Figure 5.17. Attaching an EBS Volume to an Amazon EC2 instance

Select your instance, keep a record of the value in the **Device** field, and press the **Attach** button. Refresh the EBS Volumes list until the **Attachment Information** column contains the word "attached."

At this point the new EBS volume is attached to your instance, but not yet ready to store files. Head over to your SSH session and put a file system on the newly attached volume:

```
<dev>: mkfs -F /dev/sdf
```

After this command completes, **/dev/sdf** is ready to store files. Create a mount point and mount the file system on it like this:

```
<dev>: mkdir /data
<dev>: mount /dev/sdf /data
```

You now have a persistent, high-performance disk volume running on EBS. Keep in mind that you'll be charged for the storage allocated to the EBS volume whether you put files on it or not.

Testing Apache

The Apache web server The Apache web server is already installed, configured, and running on the LAMP Web Starter AMI. Take your IP address, put an `http://` prefix on it, and visit the resulting URL in your browser. Figure 5.18 shows what you'll see.

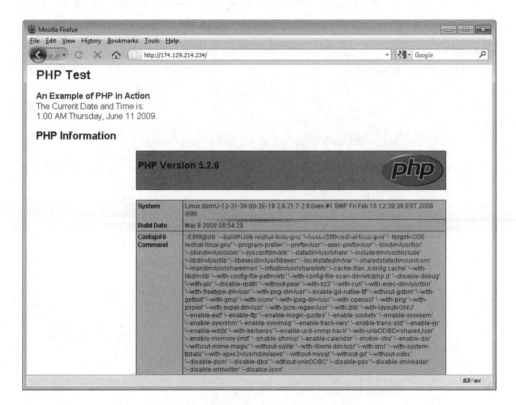

Figure 5.18. Apache and PHP up and running

You'll probably recognize this as the output of the PHP `phpinfo` function.

Running Some Code

The default home page is stored at **/home/webuser/helloworld/htdocs/index.php**. You can make some simple changes to it now if you'd like; the text editors vim[5] and nano[6] are available by default, or if you installed emacs[7] previously you can use that. For example, change the first <h1> tag:

```
<h1>Jeff's PHP Test</h1>
```

Insert your own name, if you'd like. Refresh the page and confirm that the page changes accordingly.

The new EC2 instance needs a little bit of tweaking before it can run the PHP code from the previous chapter. Create a directory on the EBS volume:

```
<dev>: mkdir /data/src
<dev>: cd /data/src
```

We need to install the Git version control system:

You Can Install More than One Package at a Time

You can use yum to install several packages concurrently. This can be handy when you're preparing a new AMI from scratch, as it's more efficient than installing them individually. For example, I use the command **yum -y install emacs cvs svn** to install emacs, CVS, and Subversion in one fell swoop.

Now that we can download and unzip the CloudFusion library:

```
<dev>: wget http://tarzan-aws.googlecode.com/files/
↪cloudfusion_2.5.zip
--2010-07-26 00:57:02--  http://tarzan-aws.googlecode.com/files/
↪cloudfusion_2.5.zip
Resolving tarzan-aws.googlecode.com... 72.14.254.82
Connecting to tarzan-aws.googlecode.com|72.14.254.82|:80...
↪connected.
```

---

[5] http://vim.sourceforge.net/

[6] http://www.nano-editor.org/

[7] http://www.gnu.org/software/emacs/

```
HTTP request sent, awaiting response... 200 OK
Length: 184441 (180K) [application/x-zip]
Saving to: `cloudfusion_2.5.zip'

100%[=======================================>] 184,441
➥89.7K/s   in 2.0s

2010-07-26 00:57:05 (89.7 KB/s) - `cloudfusion_2.5.zip'
➥saved [184441/184441]

<dev>: unzip cloudfusion_2.5.zip
Archive:  cloudfusion_2.5.zip
   creating: cloudfusion/
  inflating: cloudfusion/_utilities.class.php
  inflating: cloudfusion/cloudfront.class.php
    ⋮
  inflating: cloudfusion/sqsqueue.class.php
<dev>: rm -f cloudfusion_2.5.zip
```

This will install CloudFusion in directory **/data/src/cloudfusion**.

Now you'll need to follow the same procedure we went through in the section called "Installing CloudFusion" in Chapter 3. The PHP include_path setting needs to be updated to include the path **/data/src/cloudfusion**. The **php.ini** file can be found at **/etc/php.ini**. And the **/data/src/cloudfusion/config-sample.inc.php** file needs to be copied to **config.inc.php**, and your AWS account key information added.

Create a new directory **/data/src/book** and create a new PHP file called **index.php** with the following contents:

```php
<?php
error_reporting(E_ALL);

require_once('tarzan.class.php');

$s3 = new AmazonS3();
$buckets = $s3->get_bucket_list();
?>
<html>
  <head>
    <title>S3 Buckets</title>
  </head>
  <body>
```

```
   <h1>S3 Buckets</h1>
   <ul>
   <?php foreach($buckets as $bucket): ?>
     <li><?php echo $bucket ?></li>
   <?php endforeach ?>
   </ul>
  </body>
</html>
```

Make sure that the **index.php** file is world-readable:

```
<dev>: chmod 644 index.php
```

Now create a symbolic link from Apache's **htdocs** directory to the **/data/src/book** directory where our **index.php** file resides:

```
<dev>: cd /home/webuser/helloworld/htdocs
<dev>: ln -s /data/src/book book
```

Append /book to the URL that you used at the start of this section and visit the resulting address in your browser. You should see a list of the S3 buckets you set up in Chapter 4. Otherwise, make sure you've edited the **php.ini** file and added the correct include_path, and edited the CloudFusion **config.inc.php** file with your AWS key ID and secret key values. You might also try editing the **php.ini** file and setting display_errors to On; then examine the PHP error message, and try to diagnose your problem from there.

Shutting Down

You can leave the instance running as long as you'd like, or you can shut it down now. As we discussed earlier, you can also stop an EBS-backed instance and then start it up again at a later time.

If you plan to shut down the instance but want to keep the EBS volume around for later, be sure to sync and unmount it so that no data is lost and the file system remains uncorrupted. Here's what you need to do.

```
<dev>: sync
<dev>: umount /dev/sdf
```

You can shut the instance down from the AWS Management Console, or you can simply halt it from within:

```
<dev>: halt
```

You Did It!

Well, now you know how to launch an EC2 instance, set it up with an Elastic IP address, and create, attach, and format an Elastic Block Store volume. As you can probably see for yourself, it is actually quite easy to start and configure a basic EC2 instance.

All about AMIs

Now we're going to learn more about Amazon Machine Images (AMIs). We'll take a look at the AMI catalog and discuss the origins of the AMIs found there. We'll talk about the factors to consider when choosing an AMI, and then spend some time learning how to create a new AMI.

The AMI Catalog

The EC2 AMI catalog[8] is shown in Figure 5.19.

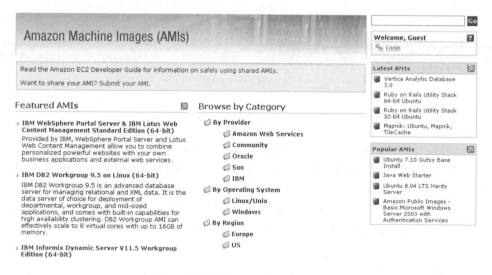

Figure 5.19. The Amazon EC2 AMI Catalog

---

[8] http://aws.amazon.com/amis

The AMI catalog lists and categorizes all the public EC2 AMIs. The center column, **Browse by Category**, allows you to view AMIs based on provider, operating system, or region. The last category is present because AMIs are local to a particular EC2 region. The first category, **Amazon Web Services**, contains the AMIs provided by Amazon. The second category, **Community**, contains AMIs built by members of the AWS developer community. The remaining categories list AMIs provided by companies such as Oracle, Sun, and IBM.

Click on a category to see a list of AMIs, and then click on an item in the list to learn more about a particular AMI. Figure 5.20 illustrates the amount of information available for the Ubuntu 9.04 Jaunty Server AMI Listing.

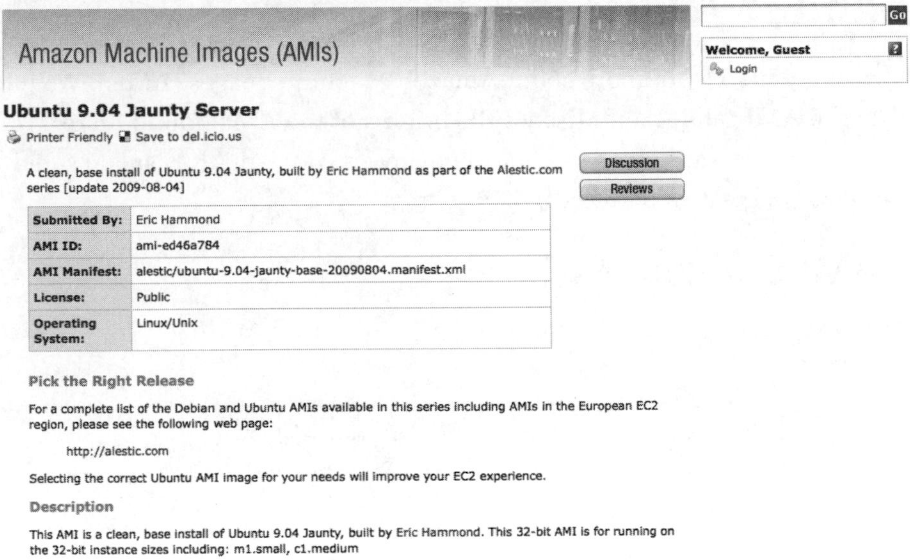

Figure 5.20. The Ubuntu 9.04 Jaunty Server AMI Listing

The AMI listing contains essential information about the AMI, including the AMI ID for each region where it's available, the AMI's provenance—who created it and what is inside—along with reviews, ratings, and discussion. Some of this information can also be obtained programmatically through the `DescribeImages` function or from the command line with the `ec2-describe-images` command.

Choosing an AMI

You should consider a number of factors before choosing an AMI for a project. The AMI model provides you with lots of choices and plenty of flexibility. It's up to you to make responsible and productive use of this important aspect of Amazon EC2. You must choose a CPU word size, an operating system, and (in some instances) an operating system distribution.

In most cases you need to work backwards, starting with your application layer and making choices that ensure compatibility. In a complex architecture you may find that the best solution is heterogeneous, incorporating instances with more than one CPU word size, operating system, or operating system distribution.

EC2 AMIs are available with a very wide variety of Linux distributions, including Fedora, Debian, Ubuntu, openSUSE, Red Hat Enterprise Linux, Oracle Enterprise Linux, and Gentoo. Choosing the *right* distribution is a complex topic and beyond the scope of this section. Factors to consider include:

- compatibility with existing systems
- reputation of the distribution
- features specific to each distribution, such as package management
- availability of commercial support
- support for specific applications

Because it is so simple to start up EC2 instances, you can do compatibility and performance testing quite easily. You can explore the features of each distribution and make sure that it will meet your needs without spending much money.

Creating a Custom AMI

Why would you want to create an AMI of your own? You might want to freeze your system configuration so that you can launch additional instances that are identical to the first. You may like to share the configuration with your partners or customers, or share it with the entire EC2 community.

Before we describe the AMI creation process, let's take a quick look at some of the alternatives. Far from dissuading you from creating an AMI, I do want you to be aware that there are other ways to customize your EC2 instances. Here are some of the alternatives:

- *No Configuration*—Perhaps you can do your work with a totally stock AMI. If you're doing short-term experimental development, a predefined AMI may include everything you need. You can store your source code in an external source code control system or on an EBS volume. You can launch an instance when you arrive at the office, mount the volume, spend your day coding, and then unmount the volume and terminate the instance at the end of the day.

- *Manual Configuration*—If there's no need for you to launch multiple copies of the same AMI and if the configuration procedure is short and simple, perhaps you can take a basic approach and manually configure your AMI after you start it. On Linux systems you can install all required packages with a single command. You can even create a shell script, store it in Amazon S3, and simply download and run it each time. Because you can stop and later restart an EBS-backed instance, manual configuration is sufficient in many situations.

- *Automated Configuration*—You have the ability to pass a string (up to about 10,000 characters) of user data to each EC2 instance when you launch it. This data could be a reference to a script stored in Amazon S3, or it could be the script itself.[9] The script can perform the final customization of the instance, including retrieval of other scripts and configuration data from a source code repository.

- *Automated Role-based Configuration*—If your system incorporates multiple tiers with distinct system configurations for each tier, you can extend the Automated Configuration model to customize each tier—installing different packages and making other changes based on a parameter that describes the role of the instance. The roles are arbitrary and will depend on the application. For example, a three-tier application could have "web server," "database master," "database slave," and "application server" roles.

If none of the above options meet your needs, go ahead and make your own AMI. The process is quick and simple, and you'll walk away with an even better appreciation of the power of cloud computing and AWS.

The AMI creation process has become significantly simpler with the introduction of EBS-backed AMIs, and that's what we'll describe in this section. If you need to create an S3-backed AMI, you'll need to study the EC2 documentation to learn more about the bundling, uploading, and registration steps.

---

[9] You can pass up to 16,384 bytes of data to an EC2 instance in this way.

Here are the steps involved in creating an AMI:

1. Planning—deciding what you want to do.
2. Image preparation—creating a reusable image.
3. Image creation—creating an EBS snapshot of the image.
4. Reusing—launching multiple copies of the AMI.
5. Sharing—making the AMI accessible to others.

Planning

In this step you need to identify the purpose and content of your AMI, starting with the base operating system. From there you can load additional packages. You can also pre-populate the AMI with any special code or data that you'd like to make available to the users of your AMI.

For the purposes of this example I'll use the **Basic Fedora Core 8** AMI augmented with Apache, MySQL, CVS, Subversion, and emacs. The result will be a web development AMI that's ready to use.

If you'll be making your AMI available to other users of EC2 , you should take care to document the contents so that potential users know exactly what's inside.

If you aspire to be a prolific builder of public AMIs, you should think about ways to automate the production process to reduce manual labor and give you the ability to regenerate an AMI on demand. As a builder, you also need to stay abreast of system updates and patches, so that you can provide your user base with fresh AMIs on a timely basis. A script and an accompanying checklist can make this process simple, efficient, and reliable.

Make Lists!

I've been a list maker for a very long time. I find that writing things down keeps my mind free of clutter and ensures that I remember any obvious steps. The system rebuild process for one of my older web projects is 29 steps long. Even though I last rebuilt the system four or five years ago, I'm confident that I have enough information in my checklist to do it with ease.

Image Preparation

The image is simply the set of files that you want to package up in the AMI. You can prepare this set of files on a local (non-EC2) machine, or you can prepare them on an EC2 instance. If you're using an EC2 instance, you can use the root file system of the running machine as the basis for your image, or you can create a large but empty file and do a system installation inside it. I will use the root file system of the running machine.

The image creation process scoops up all the files on the root file system. It excludes files on other file systems (local or EBS) and it does not capture any state information external to the running instance—in particular, information about elastic IP addresses or EBS volumes. If your AMI requires this information in order to be fully functional, you'll need to arrange for addresses to be assigned and/or volumes to be attached and mounted as part of the startup process.

Let's prepare an image! Start by booting up a fresh copy of the Basic Fedora Core 8 AMI and make sure to reference your Key Pair. Log in to the instance in the usual way and install all required packages:

```
<dev>: yum -y install httpd mysql cvs svn emacs
```

There'll be a delay while all these are downloaded. Make any other desired changes. For example, make arrangements to start Apache when the system boots up. Go to the **/etc/rc4.d** directory and create a symbolic link to the proper init script:

```
<dev>: cd /etc/rc4.d
<dev>: ln -s ../init.d/httpd S15httpd
```

Once you have the system set up the way you'd like it, reboot it to make sure that it comes up in the desired state. Simply right-click on the instance in the AWS Management Console and choose the **Reboot** option, as shown in Figure 5.21.

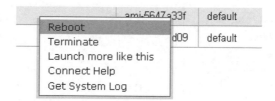

Figure 5.21. Rebooting the EC2 instance

You can also run the `reboot` command from the command prompt if you're logged in as `root`.

Verify that all desired services are running, and make further changes or customizations until you have the image working the way you want it. If you change low-level aspects of the boot process you may find that you've created an unbootable image. Just as is the case with a system running on real hardware, there's no way to recover from this. You may want to start up a pair of instances and make each preferred change on the test instance, rebooting after each change. After a successful reboot you can apply the same change to the instance that you'll use to create the reusable image. You can also bundle and upload snapshot versions of the image during the process. If you create an unbootable AMI you can back up a step or two, figure out what went wrong, and proceed from there. As I noted earlier, a good checklist will be of tremendous value here.

Resist the urge to go hog-wild and install every package that you might need some day. Larger AMIs take longer to create and to boot. Adding extraneous packages to your system also increases its **attack surface**—anything that can be accessed by an unauthenticated user in an attempt to locate a security flaw. Install what you need and no more.

Image Scrubbing

The image creation process copies all the files from the root file system, so you need to think about the files that you don't want to include. You'd probably want to exclude log files, shell history files, and your AWS keys. Once again, a good checklist can avoid embarrassment and potential security issues.

Shut down any unneeded services, remove shell history files such as **.bash_history**, empty out log files, and make sure that your AWS keys are stored elsewhere than the root file system. Here's an example:

```
<dev>: rm ~/.bash_history
rm: remove regular file `/root/.bash_history'? y
<dev>: cd /var/log
<dev>: > cron
<dev>: > maillog
<dev>: > secure
<dev>: > spooler
<dev>: > yum.log
<dev>: > httpd/error_log
<dev>: > httpd/access_log
```

Image Creation

The next step is to upload the bundle to Amazon S3. To do this you'll need your AWS access key ID, your secret access key, and an available S3 bucket.

After you have scrubbed your root file system, you can create an image by right-clicking on the instance in the AWS Management Console and choosing the option labeled **Create Image (EBS AMI)**. The **Create Image** dialog will be displayed, as shown in Figure 5.22.

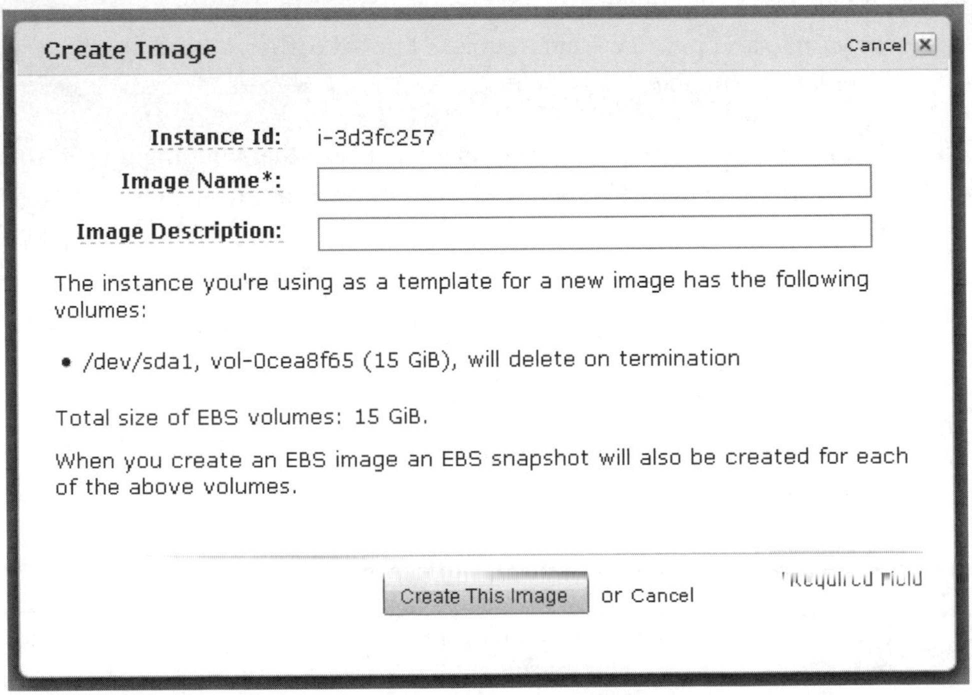

Create Image   Cancel ☒

                Instance Id: i-3d3fc257

              Image Name*:   [_____]

          Image Description: [_____]

The instance you're using as a template for a new image has the following volumes:

- /dev/sda1, vol-0cea8f65 (15 GiB), will delete on termination

Total size of EBS volumes: 15 GiB.

When you create an EBS image an EBS snapshot will also be created for each of the above volumes.

            [Create This Image]   or Cancel   *Required Field

---

Figure 5.22. The **Create Image** dialog

Give your instance a name and a description, and click the **Create This Image** button. Your instance will be rebooted as part of the image creation process, so don't be alarmed when you lose touch with it. The time that the image creation process takes is proportional to the size of your instance's root file system. The instance's state will be displayed as **available** during the creation process, but you won't be able to log in until the process has concluded.

Reusing and Sharing the AMI

Now that you've created your AMI, you can use the **My AMIs** tab of the **Launch Instance Wizard** to find and launch instances of it. Until you give the say-so, you're the only one with permission to do this; the AMI's visibility is set to **Private**.

You can choose to share your new AMI with selected AWS users or with the entire AWS community. If you elect to share with selected users you'll need their AWS account numbers.

Right-click on your AMI in the console's **AMIs** view, then choose the **Edit Permissions** option to launch the dialog shown in Figure 5.23.

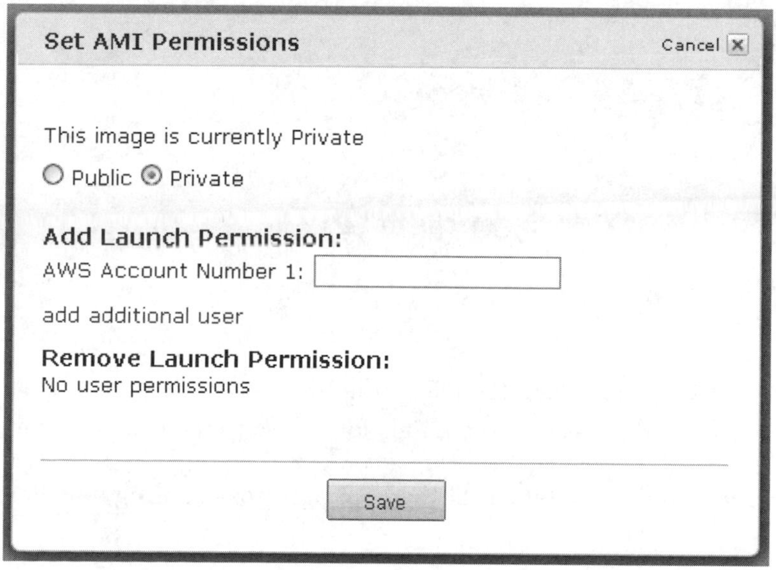

Figure 5.23. Launching the **Set AMI Permissions** dialog box

Under **Add Launch Permission**, enter the account number of a particular AWS user to share it with them. Click the **add additional user** link each time you need to enter

another account number. You can select **Public** to share the AMI with the entire
AWS community.

Using the EC2 API

Key to the concept of the programmable data center is the fact that every resource
can be manipulated by an external program. In this section we'll take a look at a
program that does exactly that. In just over 100 lines (including comments and error
checking) the program does the following:

1. launches an EC2 instance
2. waits for the instance to transition to the "running" state
3. allocates a public IP address
4. attaches the IP address to the EC2 instance
5. allocates a pair of 1GB EBS volumes
6. attaches the volumes to the EC2 instance

The program starts out in the usual way:

chapter_05/ec2_setup.php (excerpt)

```php
#!/usr/bin/php
<?php

error_reporting(E_ALL);

require_once('cloudfusion.class.php');
require_once('include/book.inc.php');

$ec2 = new AmazonEC2();
```

Like the S3 and CloudFront access objects that we used in Chapter 4, the EC2 access
object provides a complete set of methods for access to the EC2 functionality.

Launching an instance is a lot easier than buying and installing new hardware:

chapter_05/ec2_setup.php (excerpt)

```php
$options = array('KeyName' => "Jeff's Keys",
    'InstanceType' => "m1.small");

$res = $ec2->run_instances("ami-48aa4921", 1, 1, $options);
```

```
if (!$res->isOK())
{
  exit("Could not launch instance: "          .
       $res->body->Errors->Error->Message . "\n");
}
```

After forming an options array to specify the key pair and desired instance type, this code simply calls the run_instance method and checks for errors.

We'll need the instance ID and the instance's Availability Zone, so let's fetch and print them:

chapter_05/ec2_setup.php (excerpt)

```
$instances        = $res->body->instancesSet;
$instanceId       = (string)$instances->item->instanceId;
$availabilityZone = (string)$instances->item->placement->
➥availabilityZone;

print("Launched instance ${instanceId} " .
      "in availability zone ${availabilityZone}.\n");
```

The next step is to poll the instance state every ten seconds until it's actually up and running. EC2 services will stop an EBS volume from being attached to an instance while the instance is still in the process of booting up. A simple loop does the trick:

chapter_05/ec2_setup.php (excerpt)

```
do
{
  $options   = array('InstanceId.1' => $instanceId);
  $res       = $ec2->describe_instances($options);
  $instances = $res->body->reservationSet->item->instancesSet;
  $state     = $instances->item->instanceState->name;
  $running   = ($state == 'running');

  if (!$running)
  {
    print("Instance is currently in " .
    "state ${state}, waiting 10 seconds\n");
    sleep(10);
```

```
    }
}
while (!$running);
```

The `describe_instances` method returns the state of the instance passed in via the `$options` array. The actual instance state is deeply nested within the returned result, so a pair of statements are used to fetch it. The loop iterates until the instance state is the string "running".

Okay, now we need an Elastic IP address. Let's allocate it and display it like this:

chapter_05/ec2_setup.php *(excerpt)*

```php
$res = $ec2->allocate_address();
if (!$res->isOK())
{
  exit("Could not allocate public IP address.\n");
}

$publicIP = (string)$res->body->publicIp;
print("Assigned IP address ${publicIP}.\n");
```

The `allocate_address` method does the heavy lifting, and the assigned address is extracted from the returned result in the usual way.

With the address in hand it's time to attach it to the instance, like so:

chapter_05/ec2_setup.php *(excerpt)*

```php
$res = $ec2->associate_address($instanceId, $publicIP);
if (!$res->IsOK())
{
  exit("Could not associate IP address ${publicIP} " .
      "with instance ${instanceId}.\n");
}

print("Associated IP address ${publicIP} " .
      "with instance ${instanceId}.\n");
```

So far, so good! Now we can create a pair of 1GB EBS volumes and display their IDs:

chapter_05/ec2_setup.php *(excerpt)*

```php
$res1 = $ec2->create_volume(1, $availabilityZone);
$res2 = $ec2->create_volume(1, $availabilityZone);

if (!$res1->isOK() || !$res2->isOK())
{
  exit("Could not create EBS volumes.\n");
}

$volumeId1 = (string)$res1->body->volumeId;
$volumeId2 = (string)$res2->body->volumeId;

print("Created EBS volumes ${volumeId1} and ${volumeId2}.\n");
```

Notice that the volumes are created in the instance's Availability Zone, as is required.

The final step is to attach the volumes to the instance, and that's fairly easy using the attach_volume method:

chapter_05/ec2_setup.php *(excerpt)*

```php
$res1 = $ec2->attach_volume($volumeId1, $instanceId, '/dev/sdf');
$res2 = $ec2->attach_volume($volumeId2, $instanceId, '/dev/sdg');

if (!$res1->isOK() || !$res2->isOK())
{
  exit("Could not attach EBS volumes " .
       "${volumeId1} and ${volumeId2} " .
       "to instance ${instanceId}.\n");
}

print("Attached EBS volumes ${volumeId1} and ${volumeId2} " .
      "to instance ${instanceId}.\n");

?>
```

And there you have it. We just instantiated a Linux server with an Elastic IP address and a pair of disk volumes attached, with just eight calls to the EC2 API.

Closing Thoughts

We've learned a lot in this chapter. We've learned about persistent and ephemeral EC2 resources, security groups, and the EC2 pricing model. We then prepared our keys and launched our very first EC2 instance. We gave it a public IP address and created an EBS volume, then verified that the Apache web server was running as expected. From there we downloaded and installed CloudFusion and ran a test script. We learned all about AMIs—where to find them, how to choose them, and how to create them from scratch. Along the way we became familiar with many aspects of the AWS Management Console, and we learned how to allocate and manipulate EC2 resources using the actual EC2 APIs.

Before wrapping up this chapter I would like to leave you with a few closing thoughts.

The ease with which you can start, configure, and terminate instances should make you start to think about them in a different way. Instead of looking at your server as a one-off, very precious piece of hardware, you can see it as an expendable, temporary resource. If you need a second server to test a new version of your code, just go ahead and launch it. If you want to see how your code performs with a different Linux distribution or with a newer version of MySQL, again, just go ahead and launch an instance.

I'm fairly sure that you'll have gained an appreciation for the richness and power embodied in the AWS Management Console. As you saw in the code sample presented at the end of this chapter, all this power is available through the EC2 APIs as well.

Chapter

6

Building a Scalable Architecture with Amazon SQS

In this chapter you'll learn all about Amazon SQS. We'll start by addressing the concept of asynchronous messaging in the context of large-scale system architecture, and then we'll take a look at Amazon SQS and the associated programming model. Next we'll examine some of the instances where Amazon SQS can be used as a central component of a highly scalable system architecture, considering some important design patterns along the way. Then we'll put our knowledge to good use by using Amazon SQS to construct a simple image crawler and processor.

Why Asynchronous Messaging?

Asynchronous messaging refers to an architectural style dictating that applications should be built in a modular fashion. The application is composed of two or more processing steps, often arranged in a processing pipeline. The steps are loosely coupled to each other, passing work through the pipeline by sending messages from step to step. Adjacent processing steps might run on the same server, on different servers in the same local area network, or on servers owned and operated by separate organizations.

There are many advantages to this style of architecture:

- Each step runs at its own speed. Temporary slowdowns at one stage of the pipeline simply result in work piling up, instead of stalling the entire pipeline.

- No work is lost if a particular step locks up, crashes, or is temporarily overloaded. Once again, work simply piles up until processing resources are available.

- The independent nature of the steps allow them to be allocated to more than one server if necessary.

- Running steps on separate servers means that it's possible to scale the system to accommodate an increased load by simply adding more servers.

- Decomposition of complex applications into independent steps results in opportunities for reuse, and can also simplify testing, maintenance, and enhancement.

- Steps can be allocated to servers in such a way so that demands on resources such as CPU cycles, I/O bandwidth, and memory are balanced.

Each step in a processing pipeline resembles a worker on a factory assembly line. The steps simply await the arrival of a work item, process it, and then pass the work along to the next step. Here's some pseudocode for the central loop of a step in a processing pipeline:

```
while (true)
{
  M = ReceiveMessage(INPUT_QUEUE);
  P = ProcessMessage(M);
  SendMessage(P);
}
```

This particular example shows a 1:1 relationship between input and output messages, but there can be variations on this. Processing one message could result in zero, one, or many messages being sent. However, the other case, receiving multiple messages and then sending just one, is relatively rare. This is because the messages in the input queue are independent of each other and can generally be processed in any order. We'll consider other models in the next section.

Asynchronous Messaging Patterns

In this section, we'll take a look at some effective ways to decompose a complex processing system by using a series of processes connected to each other with message queues.

The first pattern is the linear processing pipeline. The first process passes work onto the second using a single queue, as depicted in Figure 6.1.

Figure 6.1. A linear processing pipeline

This pattern decouples Process 1 and Process 2, so that they can make progress independently. If Process 1 produces more results than Process 2 can absorb, they simple accumulate in Queue 1. If Process 2 has no work to do it simply idles, checking the queue for new work from time to time. This is a good starting point, but what if there is so much work to do that Process 2 is unable to keep up, and the size of the queue keeps on growing? The easiest solution is to simply start an additional copy of Process 2, as shown in Figure 6.2.

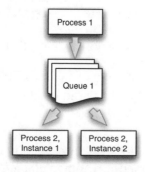

Figure 6.2. A scalable linear processing pipeline

This is a very scalable model. You can start additional instances of Process 2 to cope with the load, adjusting the number of processes to balance overall throughput, cost per hour (assuming that the processes are running on an EC2 instance), and customer satisfaction.

The scalable linear pipeline is the most common pattern and can be used in many different types of applications. Each stage of the pipeline typically performs work of a particular type, such as transforming an image, checking a data record for consistency, or changing the format of a data file.

The next pattern lets us route different types of messages to different queues. Routing could be based on the type of the message. A web crawler could have separate queues for HTML pages and for PDF documents. Alternatively, multiple queues could be used to provide better service for premium customers. This can be done in two distinct ways. A separate (and presumably lightly loaded) instance can handle the premium work, or a single instance can check and process the premium queue before handling any work in the regular one.

In any case, the first process makes some type of decision and routes the message accordingly, leading to the pattern shown in Figure 6.3.

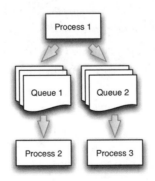

Figure 6.3. Routing work to multiple queues

Of course, you can run more than one instance of Process 2 or Process 3 to handle the workload. Because the processes are connected only by queues, you can easily add resources to cope with demand.

Several processes can write to the same queue. Perhaps they're taking data derived from different sources and extracting common elements. Figure 6.4 depicts the flow.

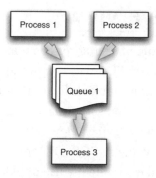

Figure 6.4. Two processes feeding a single queue

The patterns we've examined thus far have been linear, proceeding from beginning to end. However, some kinds of applications may actually need to route original data (or, more likely, other information derived from the original data) back to the beginning. This pattern is often found in web crawlers, which examine web pages for links that are then themselves crawled. Used in this way, the queues are effectively implementing a recursive processing pattern, as can be seen in Figure 6.5.

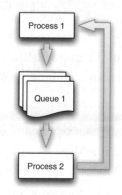

Figure 6.5. Feeding work back to earlier stages

You can combine these patterns as needed in order to implement arbitrarily complex workflows. Once you become accustomed to thinking of your application in terms of loosely coupled, autonomous work units, you'll see many different ways to put queues to work. Your applications will be modular and more flexible, and you'll be able to adapt to changing conditions more quickly.

Amazon SQS Overview

Reflecting the fundamental role of asynchronous messaging in the construction of highly scalable systems, Amazon SQS was one of the first Amazon infrastructure services to be released. Let's take a look at the terminology, operations, and pricing model in this section. As you'll soon see, Amazon SQS is fairly simple when compared to the other Amazon Web Services; however, refrain from thinking that such simplicity means there's less value in SQS. On the contrary, many of the most successful AWS applications make very heavy use of SQS.

Terminology and Concepts

You can create any number of SQS queues within the scope of your AWS account; however, Amazon does reserve the right to delete queues if no messages have been posted or retrieved for 30 consecutive days.

Each queue has a name, which must be unique within a particular instance of SQS (there are currently instances of SQS in the US and in Europe). Queue names can be up to 80 characters long and can contain alphanumeric characters, dashes, and underscores.

Every queue is identified by a unique queue URL. The URL is assigned when the queue is created. All the operations on a queue require the specification of a queue URL.

Queues are used to store messages. Messages can be up to 8,192 bytes long. Due to this low limit, messages should generally be used to pass pointers (for example, URLs) to data stored elsewhere. Amazon S3 is often a good place to store data while it's being passed through a complex processing pipeline.

Instead of being automatically deleted, a message retrieved from SQS becomes temporarily invisible so that it's unable to be retrieved a second time. Once your code retrieves a message, you have a certain amount of time—the visibility timeout—to process and then delete the message. If the message is retained (or if your application crashes while processing it) the message becomes visible once again. This model allows you to build applications that avoid data loss as a result of an application failure. The default value for the visibility timeout is 30 seconds and the maximum value is 12 hours.

When you retrieve a message from SQS, you also gain a receipt handle. You need to hold on to this handle in order to delete the message after you've processed it. You can also use the handle to change message attributes such as its visibility timeout.

Queues have a time limit: unprocessed messages will be silently deleted from the queue after four days.

You can choose to allow other applications and developers to access your queues by using an access policy. The access policy gives you very granular control over access to each aspect of SQS.

Watch Out For ...

SQS is implemented as a distributed queue and runs on multiple servers. There are a few very interesting consequences when using this design with respect to message order, message delivery, and message sampling. Let's review these consequences now so that you're fully aware of them when you've built your application.

Message Order

> Because the queue is distributed, there's no guarantee that SQS will return the messages in the same order that they were sent. Your application logic must be written so that it avoids relying on receiving messages in any particular order.

Message Delivery

> Under very rare circumstances, SQS can return the same message more than once. Your application can either treat messages as idempotent (so that processing the same one more than once has no ill affect), or it can store a state indicator in another location, such as Amazon SimpleDB.

Message Sampling

> When your application asks SQS to return a message from a queue, SQS checks a subset of the actual set of servers used to store the queue. If a queue contains less than 1,000 items, the first retrieval may return no items but a second one will.

Be sure to keep all these in mind as you develop and debug your application.

Operations

As you'll soon see, the SQS programming model is very simple. You can:

- create and delete queues from your account, and list your queues
- send, receive, and delete messages, and change message attributes such as the visibility timeout
- control a queue's access permissions on a very fine-grained basis

Stay tuned, we'll write some code in a little while.

Pricing Model

Your SQS usage is charged in two dimensions: requests and bandwidth.

You pay $0.01 (one cent) for every 10,000 SQS requests that you make. This is equivalent to a price of $0.000001 per request. Although the per-request price is very low, you still need to be careful. In particular, your application should avoid polling an SQS queue for new messages in a tight loop. Instead, you should use a time delay and consider a back-off scheme.

Your data transfer charges are based on the amount of data transferred in and out of SQS. Data transferred into SQS is charged at a rate of $0.10 per gigabyte. Once again, this amount is prorated. Data transferred out of SQS is charged on a sliding scale starting at $0.17 per gigabyte and decreasing with volume, reaching $0.10 per gigabyte for all outgoing data transfer in excess of 150 terabytes per month.

There's no charge for data transferred within a Region. For example, you can transfer data from an EC2 instance in the us-east Region to an SQS queue in the same Region at no charge.

Programming Amazon SQS

Okay, time for some code. Before we can begin, though, you'll need to make sure you've enabled the service on your AWS account. Visit the SQS home page at http://aws.amazon.com/sqs/ and click the **Sign Up For Amazon SQS** button. After signing in you can view the pricing and credit card information on the next screen, and then click the **Complete Sign Up** button to enable the service.

Like the code samples in the previous chapters, the programs that start with the shebang (#!/usr/bin/php) are meant to be run from the command line.

Creating a Queue

Let's start by creating some queues using this code:

chapter_06/create_queues.php (excerpt)

```php
#!/usr/bin/php
<?php

error_reporting(E_ALL);

require_once('cloudfusion.class.php');

if (count($argv) < 2)
{
  exit("Usage: " . $argv[0] . " QUEUE...\n");
}

$sqs = new AmazonSQS();

for ($i = 1; $i < count($argv); $i++)
{
  $queue = $argv[$i];

  $res = $sqs->create_queue($queue);

  if ($res->isOK())
  {
    print("Created queue '${queue}'\n");
  }
  else
  {
    $error = (string) $res->body->Error->Message;
    print("Could not create queue '${queue}': ${error}.\n");
  }
}

exit(0);
?>
```

This script accepts queue names on the command line, creates a new `AmazonSQS` object, calls the `create_queue` method for each queue name, and prints some helpful messages. Here's an example of the output:

```
$ php create_queues.php A B C
Created queue 'A'
Created queue 'B'
Created queue 'C'
```

If the queue is unable to be created, the error message is extracted from the returned data and then printed.

Creating a queue that already exists does not raise an error and will have no effect on the queue in any way.

Listing Queues

That was quite easy, so let's go ahead and list our queues:

chapter_06/list_queues.php *(excerpt)*

```php
#!/usr/bin/php
<?php

error_reporting(E_ALL);

require_once('cloudfusion.class.php');

$sqs = new AmazonSQS();

$res = $sqs->list_queues();

if ($res->isOK())
{
  $queues = $res->body->ListQueuesResult->QueueUrl;
  for ($i = 0; $i < count($queues); $i++)
  {
    print($queues[$i] . "\n");
  }
}
else
{
  print("Could not retrieve list of SQS queues\n");
```

```
}
exit(0);
?>
```

This program calls the `list_queues` method and then displays the resulting array.

If you have more than 1,000 queues, it's impossible to list them all using this or any other SQS function. Instead, you must supply a prefix argument to `list_queues`, processing the results in chunks delimited by the prefix. Realistically, applications that need more than 1,000 queues are few and far between, so this restriction should be harmless in practice.

Inserting Items into Queues

The next step is to load some items into the queue. Here's a program to insert one or more items into a queue; both the queue URL and the items are specified on the command line:

chapter_06/post_queue.php *(excerpt)*

```php
#!/usr/bin/php
<?php

error_reporting(E_ALL);

require_once('cloudfusion.class.php');

if ($argc < 3)
{
  exit("Usage: " . $argv[0] . " QUEUE_NAME ITEM...\n");
}

$sqs = new AmazonSQS();
$queueName = $argv[1];

for ($i = 2; $i < $argc; $i++)
{
  $message = $argv[$i];

  $res = $sqs->send_message($queueName, $message);

  if ($res->isOK())
```

```
  {
    print("Posted '${message}' to queue '${queueName}'\n");
  }
  else
  {
    $error = $res->body->Error->Message;
    print("Could not post message to queue: ${error}\n");
  }
}

exit(0);
?>
```

As you can see, this is fairly easy—the `send_message` method does all the work; all
we need to do is supply the queue name and the message to insert into the queue.
Here's how to run the script, and some example output:

```
$ php post_queue.php queue_name A B C
Posted 'A' to queue queue_name
Posted 'B' to queue queue_name
Posted 'C' to queue queue_name
```

Extracting Items from Queues

Now let's see how to pull items from the queue. The next script will poll for new
items, waiting one second and trying again when the `receive_message` method
fails to return any messages:

chapter_06/pull_queue.php *(excerpt)*

```
#!/usr/bin/php

error_reporting(E_ALL);

require_once('cloudfusion.class.php');

if ($argc != 2)
{
    exit("Usage: " . $argv[0] . " QUEUE_NAME\n");
}

$sqs = new AmazonSQS();
$queueName = $argv[1];
```

```
while (true)
{
  $res = $sqs->receive_message($queueName);

  if ($res->isOK())
  {
    if (isset($res->body->ReceiveMessageResult->Message))
    {
      $message       = $res->body->ReceiveMessageResult->Message;
      $messageBody   = $message->Body;
      $receiptHandle = (string)$message->ReceiptHandle;

      print("Message: '${messageBody}'\n");

      $sqs->delete_message($queueName, $receiptHandle);
    }
    else
    {
      sleep(1);
    }
  }
  else
  {
    $error = $res->body->Error->Message;
    print("Could not pull message from queue: ${error}\n");
  }
}

exit(0);
?>
```

Using an infinite `while` loop the script calls the `receive_message` method repeatedly. After calling the `receive_message` method, the code checks to see if it returned a message:

```
if (IsSet($res->body->ReceiveMessageResult->Message))
```

The `sleep(1)` function call makes the script pause for a second, keeping it from making excessive and wasteful calls to SQS. Even with this call in place, you should be aware that polling SQS just once per second will cost you about 8.5 cents per day, around $2.60 per month. That's a tiny amount of cash and you probably spend more than that each day at your local coffee shop; the important point to realize is that these calls do cost money.

As we discussed earlier in this chapter, it's possible for a single `receive_message` call to SQS to indicate by return value that no messages are present, even when they are. This is only occasional in practice but it's worth looking out for.

Let's test our suite of queue manipulation scripts. For best results, open up a second terminal or PuTTY window so that you can have your choice of two separate shell prompts. In the first window, create a queue with this command:

```
$ php create_queues.php my_queue
```

In the second window, start polling for messages from the new queue:

```
$ php pull_queue.php my_queue
```

The queue is empty, so the program will just loop quietly. Now go back to your first window and put some messages in the queue:

```
$ php post_queue.php my_queue 1 2 3 4 5
```

Return to the second window and you'll see your messages arrive:

```
Message: '3'
Message: '4'
Message: '1'
Message: '5'
Message: '2'
```

Odds are that the messages will show up in a different order to what you posted. This is to be expected, and is a consequence of the distributed implementation of SQS (as we discussed earlier).

Experiment until you gain a sense of how the sender and receiver work together. For example, you could pass '*' to **post_queue.php** to post the names of all the files in the current directory to the queue. Once you've finished playing with your new toy, be sure to kill the first process by typing **Ctrl+c** in the terminal window.

This handful of simple calls forms the foundation on which we can build very complex system architectures. We'll take a look at some of the most common patterns in the next section. But first, let's take a short detour and learn about a new and very useful data format known as JSON.

Introducing JSON

Later in this chapter you'll learn how to build message-based systems using Amazon SQS. Each process will pull a message from an SQS queue, process it, and quite possibly write it to another queue for further processing. We will want to be able to pass complex, structured data from process to process, so it makes sense to decide on a common data format. This format should be compact, simple to generate, and easy to process. Ideally, it would also be human-readable to simplify debugging.

Two good candidates are XML and JSON. We've already discussed XML, so you should know what it is and what it looks like.

Designed for lightweight data interchange, **JSON (JavaScript Object Notation)** is a relatively new format. JSON is a text format, and it's very clean and easy to read. Implementations of JSON are available for virtually every programming language, from ASP to Visual FoxPro.[1]

PHP has had JSON support built in since version 5.2.0. The json_encode function returns the JSON representation of any PHP value. The json_decode function accepts this JSON representation and returns the PHP value.

The JSON encoding for integers and strings is trivial, and the encoding for arrays is nice and compact. For example, let's create a multidimensional array in PHP and then print the JSON representation like so:

```
$values = array(1,"one",
  array(1, 2, 3),
  array(1, 2, array('a' => 'Uno', 'b' => 'Dos'))
);
print(json_encode($values) . "\n");
```

The above code will produce the following output:

[1] You can find more information on JSON at http://www.json.org/.

```
[1,"one",[1,2,3],[1,2,{"a":"Uno","b":"Dos"}]]
```

To create the PHP array from the JSON data is just as simple:

```
$decoded = json_decode(
    '[1,"one",[1,2,3],[1,2,{"a":"Uno","b":"Dos"}]]', true);
```

As you can see, the JSON format is easy to use, readable, and also compact. We'll use these functions later in the chapter.

Building an Image Crawler

Now it's time to put what we've learned to use, and build an actual application. The application will be an image crawler. Given the URL of a web page, the crawler will download the page and store it in Amazon S3. It will then parse the page, looking for HTML image tags, downloading all the images on the page to S3, and scaling them to a common size. After all the images on the page have been downloaded, they'll be used to draw a single, composite image. The composite image will contain all the scaled images from the original page.

Figure 6.6 illustrates the processing flow.

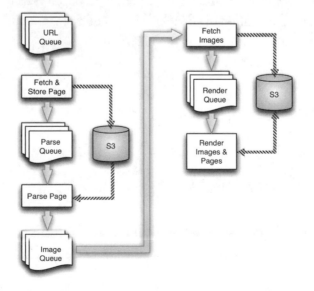

Figure 6.6. The pipeline for the image crawler

This may look complex and even a bit scary, but there's no need to worry. As you'll soon see, it's easy to build complex systems like this in modular fashion. We learned how to access Amazon S3 in Chapter 3 and we'll make use of that knowledge as we put this application together. We know how to create and work with queues, so all we need to do is write four scripts. Let's take it step by step.

Hosting the Image Crawler

You'll probably want to run the image crawler pipeline on an AMI instance. After Chapter 5, you should have no trouble getting one up and running. If you've kept the EBS volume from that chapter, you should be able to mount it again and have the CloudFusion library files available in **/data/src/cloudfusion**. Be careful to avoid running the mkfs command, because you'll erase the existing file system.

Create a new directory named **/data/src/crawler** for our image crawler files to reside in. Also create a **/data/src/include** directory in which to put our **book.inc.php**.

By the way, if you're using the LAMP Web Starter AMI you may notice an error when running the image processing scripts, due to the fact that the PHP GD library is absent. A quick command will fix that problem for you:

```
<dev>: yum -y install php-gd
```

We'll be writing some utility commands and some pipeline function scripts shortly. The utility commands can be run locally, because they shun the hard labor—they only query the queues. The commands can also be executed at any time because they only function for a limited period before they terminate. The pipeline function scripts should be run on the AMI, because they will be doing a lot of crawling, downloading, and uploading, as well as storing files in and retrieving files from S3, and some image processing.

Definitions and Utility Functions

Because each queue will be referenced by several processes, let's define some symbolic names for them in our **book.inc.php** file:

chapter_06/include/book.inc.php *(excerpt)*

```php
define('URL_QUEUE', 'c_url');
define('PARSE_QUEUE', 'c_parse');
define('IMAGE_QUEUE', 'c_image');
define('RENDER_QUEUE', 'c_render');
```

Now let's create a utility function to pull the next message from a queue without deleting it:

chapter_06/include/book.inc.php *(excerpt)*

```php
function pullMessage($sqs, $queue)
{
  while (true)
  {
    $res = $sqs->receive_message($queue);

    if ($res->isOk())
    {
      if (IsSet($res->body->ReceiveMessageResult->Message))
      {
        $message = $res->body->ReceiveMessageResult->Message;
        $messageBody = $message->Body;
        $messageDetail = json_decode($messageBody, true);
        $receiptHandle = (string)$message->ReceiptHandle;

        return array(
          'QueueURL'      => $queue,
          'Timestamp'     => date('c'),
          'Message'       => $message,
          'MessageBody'   => $messageBody,
          'MessageDetail' => $messageDetail,
          'ReceiptHandle' => $receiptHandle
        );
      }
      else
      {
        sleep(1);
      }
    }
    else
    {
      print("Could not pull message from queue '${queue}': " .
      $res->body->Error->Message . "\n");
```

```
        return null;
    }
  }
}
```

This function pauses (sleeps) for one second if no message is returned from the `receive_message` method. As we've already discussed, this could happen even if a message is available; there'll be no problems for our application, however, since it will undoubtedly be returned a second or two later.

The function returns an array with all sorts of interesting information: the queue URL that produced the message, the raw message, the message body, the decoded message body, a timestamp, and the all-important receipt handle. We'll need the receipt handle in order to delete the message after it has been processed.

A more elaborate implementation of this function could execute a more complex polling strategy, but I'll leave that up to you.

Crawl Queue Status Command

We need to have some visibility into the status of our system. Here's a small utility that shows how many items are in each queue:

chapter_06/crawl_queue_status.php *(excerpt)*

```php
#!/usr/bin/php
<?php

error_reporting(E_ALL);

require_once('cloudfusion.class.php');
require_once('include/book.inc.php');

$sqs = new AmazonSQS();
$queues = array(URL_QUEUE, PARSE_QUEUE, IMAGE_QUEUE, RENDER_QUEUE);

$underlines = '';
foreach ($queues as $queue)
{
  printf("%-12s  ", $queue);
  $underlines .= str_repeat('-', strlen($queue)) .
                 str_repeat(' ', 12 - strlen($queue)) . "  ";
```

```
}
print("\n");
print($underlines . "\n");

foreach ($queues as $queue)
{
  $res = $sqs->create_queue($queue);
  if ($res->isOK())
  {
    $size       = $sqs->get_queue_size($queue);
    printf("%-12s  ", number_format($size));
  }
}
print("\n");

exit(0);
?>
```

This script iterates over the array of our queue names and retrieves the queue size. This number is documented as being *approximate* (once more, the distributed nature of SQS is the cause of this lack of accuracy here).

Most of the remaining code is simply there to make the output look decent. Here's the output that this script produces:

```
$ php crawl_queue_status.php
c_url        c_parse        c_image        c_render
-----        -------        -------        --------
0            18             0              0
```

This indicates that there are 18 items in the c_parse queue but none in the other three queues.

Crawl Loader Command

We need a way to load a URL into the first stage of the pipeline. Here's a command line tool to do just that:

chapter_06/load_crawl_urls.php *(excerpt)*

```php
#!/usr/bin/php
<?php

error_reporting(E_ALL);

require_once('cloudfusion.class.php');
require_once('include/book.inc.php');

if ($argc < 2)
{
  exit('Usage: ' . $argv[0] . " URL...\n");
}

$sqs = new AmazonSQS();

for ($i = 1; $i < $argc; $i++)
{

  $histItem = array('Posted by ' . $argv[0] . ' at ' . date('c'));
  $message  = json_encode(array('Action' => 'FetchPage',
        'Origin' => $argv[0],
        'Data'   => $argv[$i],
        'History' => $histItem));
  $res = $sqs->send_message(URL_QUEUE, $message);

  if ($res->isOK())
  {
    print("Posted '${message}' to queue " . URL_QUEUE . "\n");
  }
  else
  {
    $error = $res->body->Error->Message;
    print("Could not post message to queue: ${error}\n");
  }
}
?>
```

The URL and some additional information are bundled as an array. We then call the json_encode function to convert the array into a JSON value—the message stored in the variable $message—and the send_message method to post it to the URL_QUEUE queue. Here's how to use this tool:

```
$ php load_crawl_urls.php http://www.sitepoint.com
```

The Feed Processing Pipeline

Now we have the tools needed to implement the four stages of our processing pipeline:

1. fetch the HTML

2. parse the HTML and extract the image URLs

3. fetch the images and create thumbnails

4. render the final mosaic image

Stage 1: Fetching the HTML

This stage is fairly simple. It pulls a URL from the URL_QUEUE queue and fetches the HTML at the URL. It stores the HTML in Amazon S3 and then passes the work along to the next stage in the pipeline by writing a message to the PARSE_QUEUE queue.

Let's review the code section by section. We start out by locating the input and output queues with our findQueueURL utility function:

chapter_06/fetch_page.php (excerpt)

```php
#!/usr/bin/php
<?php

error_reporting(E_ALL);

require_once('cloudfusion.class.php');
require_once('include/book.inc.php');

$sqs = new AmazonSQS();
$s3  = new AmazonS3();
```

Then we create a loop, processing messages as they become available. Here's the loop outline, with the most interesting part replaced by ":":

```
                                    chapter_06/fetch_page.php (excerpt)

while (true)
{
  $message = pullMessage($sqs, URL_QUEUE);

  if ($message != null)
  {
    : the interesting bit…
  }
}
?>
```

Okay, so what's in the interesting bit? Glad you asked. Here we go. First we dig into the message to access the page URL and the receipt handle:

```
                                    chapter_06/fetch_page.php (excerpt)

    $messageDetail = $message['MessageDetail'];
    $receiptHandle = $message['ReceiptHandle'];
    $pageURL       = $messageDetail['Data'];
```

This is the message format that we created in our **load_crawl_urls.php** utility command script.

Now that we have a URL, we can go fetch the HTML using the PHP file_get_contents function:

```
                                    chapter_06/fetch_page.php (excerpt)

    print("Processing URL '${pageURL}':\n");
    $html = file_get_contents($pageURL);
    print("  Retrieved " . strlen($html) . " bytes of HTML\n");
```

With the HTML in hand we can store it in S3 using the uploadObject function that we developed in Chapter 4:

```
chapter_06/fetch_page.php (excerpt)
$key = 'page_' . md5($pageURL) . '.html';
if (uploadObject($s3, BOOK_BUCKET, $key, $html, S3_ACL_PUBLIC))
{
  $s3URL = $s3->get_object_url(BOOK_BUCKET, $key);
  print(" Uploaded page to S3 as '${key}'\n");
```

This code uses PHP's md5 function to turn the page URL into a 32-character hexa-decimal string. This string will make a convenient unique key for the page.[2]

We then upload the HTML to S3, and store the new object's S3 URL in $s3URL.

With the page successfully stored in S3, it's time to create a message that contains the information needed by the next stage in the pipeline. Here's the code:

```
chapter_06/fetch_page.php (excerpt)
$origin    = $messageDetail['Origin'];
$history   = $messageDetail['History'];
$history[] = 'Fetched by ' . $argv[0] . ' at ' . date('c');

$message = json_encode(array('Action'  => 'ParsePage',
     'Origin'  => $origin,
     'Data'    => $s3URL,
     'PageURL' => $pageURL,
     'History' => $history));
```

The Data element of the message contains the S3 URL of the HTML that will be parsed in the next step. The PageURL is the URL of the original page, and the History element is a timestamped array of all the processing steps that have been performed on the data as it passes through the pipeline. The Action elements indicate the next action to be performed on the data. Strictly speaking, the S3 URL is the only element that must be passed from stage to stage. I included the other values in order to show you how to create more complex messages.

The message is then inserted into the next queue, the parser queue, effectively handing responsibility for the page to the parser stage:

---

[2] There's a very small chance that multiple URLs could have the same MD5 value. If this is a valid concern, you can simply append another unique value, such as the current time in microseconds.

chapter_06/fetch_page.php *(excerpt)*

```
$res = $sqs->send_message(PARSE_QUEUE, $message);
print("  Sent page to parser\n");
```

If all went well, the message is deleted from the input queue:

chapter_06/fetch_page.php *(excerpt)*

```
if ($res->isOK())
{
  $sqs->delete_message(URL_QUEUE, $receiptHandle);
  print("  Deleted message from URL queue\n");
}
print("\n");
```

We also add an `else` clause to the `if` statement we began previously, with `if (up-loadObject($s3, BOOK_BUCKET, $key, $html))`. This prints a message if the upload fails:

chapter_06/fetch_page.php *(excerpt)*

```
}
else
{
  print("Error uploading HTML to S3\n");
}
```

And our loop is complete. As all the interesting bits are within the main loops in the rest of the code you'll find in this chapter, I'll focus on the code inside the `while` loops. You can find the complete code in the code archive for the book.

Stage 2: Parsing HTML and Extracting Image URLs

Let's work on the second stage of the pipeline. This stage pulls the raw HTML from S3, parses it using a third-party HTML parser, extracts some of the image links, and passes those links on to the next stage. To simplify this example, we'll only process images that have an absolute URL.

We'll use the PHP Simple HTML DOM Parser[3] to parse the HTML. Download the file from the site and put it in your **include** folder. The script setup and loop outline look like this:

chapter_06/parse_page.php (excerpt)

```php
#!/usr/bin/php
<?php

error_reporting(E_ALL);

require_once('cloudfusion.class.php');
require_once('include/simple_html_dom.php');
require_once('include/book.inc.php');

$sqs = new AmazonSQS();
$s3  = new AmazonS3();

while (true)
{
  $message = pullMessage($sqs, $queueParse);

  if ($message != null)
  {
    : process the message…
  }
}
?>
```

Let's examine what happens inside the loop for each message pulled from the parse queue. The first step is to access the page from S3. The parser allows us to combine fetching and parsing, so this is really simple:

chapter_06/parse_page.php (excerpt)

```php
    $messageDetail = $message['MessageDetail'];
    $receiptHandle = (string)$message['ReceiptHandle'];
    $pageURL       = $messageDetail['Data'];

    print("Processing URL '${pageURL}':\n");
    $dom = new simple_html_dom();
    $dom->load_file($pageURL);
```

---

[3] http://simplehtmldom.sourceforge.net/

Using the DOM, it's very easy to locate and process individual HTML tags or collections of tags. Here's how to extract the page title:

chapter_06/parse_page.php *(excerpt)*

```php
$pageTitle = $dom->find('title', 0)->innertext();
print("  Retrieved page '${pageTitle}'\n");
```

This is a handy value to have, so we'll save it in the $pageTitle variable so that we can pass it along the processing pipeline.

Now it's time to process the image links. We'll capture up to 16 of them:

chapter_06/parse_page.php *(excerpt)*

```php
$imageURLs = array();
foreach ($dom->find('img') as $image)
{
  $imageURL - $image->src;
  if (preg_match('!^http://!', $imageURL))
  {
    print("  Found absolute URL '${imageURL}'\n");
    $imageURLs[] = $imageURL;
    if (count($imageURLs) == 16)
    {
      break;
    }
  }
}
```

In the code above, the expression $dom->find('img') retrieves an array that contains all the HTML <img/> tags from the page. The expression $image->src retrieves the src attribute from the tag; this is the URL of the image.

If the URL begins with the string "http://" it's added to the $imageURLs array. When the array has 16 images, the loop is terminated.

At this point we have an array of up to 16 image URLs, ready to be sent along to the next stage, the image fetcher. It's time to construct the message, like this:

chapter_06/parse_page.php *(excerpt)*

```php
if (count($imageURLs) > O)
{
  $origin     = $messageDetail['Origin'];
  $history    = $messageDetail['History'];
  $history[] = 'Processed by ' . $argv[0] . ' at ' . date('c');

  $message = json_encode(array('Action'    => 'FetchImages',
       'Origin'    => $origin,
       'Data'      => $imageURLs,
       'History'   => $history,
       'PageTitle' => $pageTitle));

  $res = $sqs->send_message(IMAGE_QUEUE, $message);
  print("  Sent page to image fetcher\n");

  if ($res->isOK())
  {
    $sqs->delete_message(PARSE_QUEUE, $receiptHandle);
    print("  Deleted message from parse queue\n");
  }

  print("\n");
}
```

This code represents the final part of the inside of our loop. If the parser has found any images, we construct a message to the image-fetching queue, passing the array of image URLs as the message data, and also including the page title, since we'll be able to use that later.

At this point we've parsed the page. We extracted the image title and have also located URLs for up to 16 images. The image fetcher is handed everything it will need in order to do its job.

Stage 3: Fetching Image URLs

It's time to build the third stage. This one will use the now familiar processing loop. This stage takes the array of image URLs from the previous stage, and fetches each one. It then uses the thumbnailImage function that we wrote in Chapter 4 to scale the image to a smaller size, as defined by the THUMB_SIZE constant.

At this point you could probably write the code for this stage yourself, but let's take a quick look anyway. As in the previous stages, we obtain references to the queues we need and begin the loop:

chapter_06/fetch_images.php (excerpt)

```php
#!/usr/bin/php
<?php

error_reporting(E_ALL);

require_once('cloudfusion.class.php');
require_once('include/book.inc.php');

$sqs = new AmazonSQS();
$s3  = new AmazonS3();

while (true)
{
  $message = pullMessage($sqs, $queueFetch);

  if ($message != null)
  {
    : process the message…
  }
}
?>
```

Within the loop, the code reads the array of image URLs from the queue message, fetches all the images, and stores them in S3:

chapter_06/fetch_images.php (excerpt)

```php
    $messageDetail = $message['MessageDetail'];
    $receiptHandle = (string)$message['ReceiptHandle'];
    $imageURLs     = $messageDetail['Data'];

    print("Processing message with " .
    count($imageURLs)              .
    " images:\n");

    $s3ImageKeys = array();
    foreach ($imageURLs as $imageURL)
    {
```

```
      print("  Fetch image '${imageURL}'\n");
      $image = file_get_contents($imageURL);
      print("  Retrieved " . strlen($image) . " byte image\n");


      $imageThumb = thumbnailImage($image, 'image/png');


      $key = 'image_' . md5($imageURL) . '.png';


      if (uploadObject($s3, BOOK_BUCKET, $key, $imageThumb))
      {
        print("  Stored image in S3 using key '${key}'\n");
        $s3ImageKeys[] = $key;
      }
    }
}
```

The above code uses the `file_get_contents` function to download the images, our `thumbnailImage` function to create the thumbnails, and our `uploadObject` function to upload the new image thumbnails to the S3 bucket.

The message is then passed along the pipeline in the usual fashion:

chapter_06/fetch_images.php (excerpt)

```
if (count($imageURLs) == count($s3ImageKeys))
{
  $origin   = $messageDetail['Origin'];
  $history  = $messageDetail['History'];
  $pageTitle = $messageDetail['PageTitle'];

  $history[] = 'Processed by ' . $argv[0] . ' at ' . date('c');

  $message = json_encode(array('Action'   => 'RenderImages',
      'Origin'   => $origin,
      'Data'     => $s3ImageKeys,
      'History'   => $history,
      'PageTitle' => $pageTitle));

  $res = $sqs->send_message(RENDER_QUEUE, $message);
  print("  Sent page to image renderer\n");


  if ($res->isOK())
  {
    $sqs->delete_message(IMAGE_QUEUE, $receiptHandle);
    print("  Deleted message from fetch queue\n");
```

```
    }
    print("\n");
}
```

The $s3ImageKeys array stores all the keys to our thumbnails, so we test that the number of thumbnail keys matches the number of images we're processing. If they match it means we've successfully processed all the images, and the message for this site can be sent to the next queue. If the message is successfully sent to the next queue, the message in the image-fetching queue can be deleted.

Our crawler is now three-quarters complete; there's just one more stage left.

Stage 4: Rendering Images

The fourth and final stage takes the S3 object keys and fetches each object from S3 before generating a thumbnail mosaic image. This code uses a number of functions from PHP's GD library.

The setup and loop outline look almost identical to the other stages, except that we create a set of constants to govern the rendering process, and only a reference to one queue is needed. Since this is the last stage, there are no more queues to send messages to:

chapter_06/render_images.php (excerpt)

```php
#!/usr/bin/php
<?php

error_reporting(E_ALL);

require_once('cloudfusion.class.php');
require_once('include/book.inc.php');

define('BORDER_LEFT', 12);
define('BORDER_RIGHT', 12);
define('BORDER_TOP', 12);
define('BORDER_BOTTOM', 12);
define('IMAGES_ACROSS', 4);
define('IMAGES_DOWN', 4);
define('GAP_SIZE', 6);

$sqs = new AmazonSQS();
```

```
$s3  = new AmazonS3();

while (true)
{
  $message = pullMessage($sqs, RENDER_QUEUE);

  if ($message != null)
  {
    : process the message…
  }
}
?>
```

The constants that start with BORDER_ control the amount of space between each edge of the main image and thumbnails. IMAGE_ACROSS and IMAGES_DOWN control the number of images in the mosaic grid. GAP_SIZE is the amount of space between thumbnails.

The code inside the loop begins in the usual way—retrieving the message data from the queue—and then we create the base mosaic image. The constants are used to figure out how big the final image should be:

chapter_06/render_images.php *(excerpt)*

```
$messageDetail = $message['MessageDetail'];
$receiptHandle = (string)$message['ReceiptHandle'];
$imageKeys     = $messageDetail['Data'];
$pageTitle     = $messageDetail['PageTitle'];

print("Processing message with " .
count($imageKeys)             .
" images:\n");

$outX = BORDER_LEFT + BORDER_RIGHT   +
        (IMAGES_ACROSS * THUMB_SIZE) +
        ((IMAGES_ACROSS - 1) * GAP_SIZE);

$outY = BORDER_TOP + BORDER_BOTTOM +
        (IMAGES_DOWN * THUMB_SIZE) +
        ((IMAGES_DOWN - 1) * GAP_SIZE);

$imageOut = ImageCreateTrueColor($outX, $outY);
```

chapter_06/render_images.php *(excerpt)*

```php
ImageFill($imageOut, 0, 0,
    ImageColorAllocate($imageOut, 255, 255, 255));
ImageRectangle($imageOut, 0, 0,
    $outX - 1, $outY - 1,
    ImageColorAllocate($imageOut, 0, 0, 0));
```

We need to track the position where the next thumbnail will be drawn. We'll do this using $nextX and $nextY, and we'll set them to the top-left corner to start off:

chapter_06/render_images.php *(excerpt)*

```php
$nextX = BORDER_LEFT;
$nextY = BORDER_TOP;
```

Now we must process each thumbnail image in turn, so we'll loop over the set of S3 keys like this:

chapter_06/render_images.php *(excerpt)*

```php
foreach ($imageKeys as $imageKey)
{
```

With this superstructure in place, it's easy to retrieve each thumbnail image and draw it on the destination image:

chapter_06/render_images.php *(excerpt)*

```php
    print("  Fetch image '${imageKey}'\n");
    $image = $s3->get_object(BOOK_BUCKET, $imageKey);

    $imageBits = ImageCreateFromString($image->body);

    print("  Render image at ${nextX}, ${nextY}\n");
    ImageCopy($imageOut, $imageBits, $nextX, $nextY,
        0, 0, ImageSx($imageBits), ImageSy($imageBits));
```

To make the image look attractive, we'll also draw a border around each thumbnail:

chapter_06/render_images.php *(excerpt)*

```php
ImageRectangle($imageOut, $nextX, $nextY,
  $nextX + ImageSx($imageBits),
  $nextY + ImageSy($imageBits),
  ImageColorAllocate($imageOut, 0, 0, 0));
```

The last step when processing each thumbnail is to update the output position, and that closes our `foreach` loop:

chapter_06/render_images.php *(excerpt)*

```php
$nextX += THUMB_SIZE + GAP_SIZE;
if (($nextX + THUMB_SIZE) > $outX)
{
  $nextX = BORDER_LEFT;
  $nextY += THUMB_SIZE + GAP_SIZE;
}
}
```

Once all the thumbnail images have been rendered, we can upload the final image to S3:

chapter_06/render_images.php *(excerpt)*

```php
$imageFileOut = tempnam('/tmp', 'aws') . '.png';
ImagePNG($imageOut, $imageFileOut, 0);
$imageBitsOut = file_get_contents($imageFileOut);
unlink($imageFileOut);

$key = 'page_image_' . md5($pageTitle) . '.png';

if (uploadObject($s3, BOOK_BUCKET, $key, $imageBitsOut,
    S3_ACL_PUBLIC))
{
```

There's just a little bit of cleanup work left, and we're done. First of all, we need to report on the location of the final image. Then the message has to be deleted, and we can also display the processing history that we've maintained as the message has moved from stage to stage:

chapter_06/render_images.php *(excerpt)*

```
    print(" Stored final image in S3 using key '${key}'\n");
    print_r($messageDetail['History']);

    $sqs->delete_message($queueRender, $receiptHandle);
    print(" Deleted message from render queue\n");
  }

  print("\n");
```

Here's an example of what the message history looks like:

```
Array(
    [0] => Posted by load_crawl_urls.php at 2009-06-29T09:28:10-04:00
    [1] => Fetched by fetch_page.php at 2009-06-29T09:28:11-04:00
    [2] => Processed by parse_page.php at 2009-06-29T09:28:12-04:00
    [3] => Processed by fetch_images.php at 2009-06-29T09:28:15-04:00
)
```

You can see how long the message spent in each stage. This output was generated when I ran the URL http://www.sitepoint.com through our processing pipeline. Figure 6.7 shows the image it generated.

Figure 6.7. Image generated by our processing pipeline

The final image represents the cooperative work of four processing stages and the loader program. Each stage can run at its own speed, with work accumulating in the queues as necessary. The application can easily scale up to handle dozens or even hundreds of requests per minute without too much trouble.

Running the Code

You'll need to be good at window manipulation if you'd like to run the code in this chapter. First, create five terminal windows—each will represent a stage, with the final window for loading the URLs. Connect to your AMI and run one command in each. If possible, arrange the windows in order so that you can see the processing pipeline in action. Here's what you need to do:

1.   Window 1—fetch and store a page:

```
<dev>: php fetch_page.php
```

2.   Window 2—parse a page:

```
<dev>: php parse_page.php
```

3.   Window 3—fetch thumbnail images:

```
<dev>: php fetch_images.php
```

4.   Window 4—render the final image:

```
<dev>: php render_images.php
```

5.   Window 5—load URLs into the pipeline. You can do this connected to your AMI or locally:

```
$ php load_crawl_urls.php http://www.sitepoint.com
```

As soon as you start this command, you'll see each stage of the pipeline come to life in turn. You can run this command more than once, or you can simply list multiple URLs on the command line.

You can also run the **crawl_queue_status.php** command at any time to check on the queue status:

```
$ php rawl_queue_status.php
```

You may also like to experiment with running more than one copy of each pipeline stage at a time. Stage 3 is a good candidate for this, since it spends a few seconds downloading the images, generating the thumbnails, and uploading the thumbnails to S3.

When you're done with the pipeline, be sure to return to windows 1 through 4 to kill each processing stage using **ctrl+c**. This way, you'll avoid incurring SQS request charges for no good reason.

Wrapping Up

Amazon SQS is a simple yet powerful service. Once you have mastered the basics of queues and messages, you can use them to build programs in a new way, as we just saw.

In this chapter we took a process, broke it down into parts, and implemented each part as a standalone program, connecting the programs with Amazon SQS queues. When writing this book the program was actually built and tested in small parts. In fact, I wrote the code at each stage as I wrote the corresponding section of the chapter. I left messages sitting in queues until the code was ready.

The architectural models discussed in this chapter will allow you to build large, complex, and highly scalable applications. As is always the case, investing some time on up-front design will pay considerable dividends at implementation and runtime.

Chapter 7

EC2 Monitoring, Auto Scaling, and Elastic Load Balancing

In this chapter, you will learn how to use three powerful Amazon EC2 features: monitoring, auto scaling, and elastic load balancing. You'll see how these features can be used separately or together to build scalable and powerful web applications. Along the way you'll also learn how to leverage the CloudFusion library to make use of these features. We'll then take a short detour to learn how to use the Apache JMeter application to generate a predictable test load. Finally, we'll wrap up the chapter by learning how to load test an actual application to make sure that it scales as desired.

Introduction

The monitoring, auto scaling, and elastic load balancing features of the Amazon EC2 services give you easy on-demand access to capabilities that once required a complicated system architecture and a large hardware investment.

Any real-world web application must have the ability to scale. This can take the form of **vertical scaling**, where larger and higher capacity servers are rolled in to replace the existing ones, or **horizontal scaling**, where additional servers are placed side-by-side (architecturally speaking) with the existing resources. Vertical scaling is sometimes called a scale-up model, and horizontal scaling is sometimes called a scale-out model.

Vertical Scaling

At first, vertical scaling appears to be the easiest way to add capacity. You start out with a server of modest means and use it until it no longer meets your needs. You purchase a bigger one, move your code and data over to it, and abandon the old one. Performance is good until the newer, larger system reaches its capacity. You purchase again, repeating the process until your hardware supplier informs you that you're running on the largest hardware that they have, and that you've no more room to grow. At this point you've effectively painted yourself into a corner.

Vertical scaling can be expensive. Each time you upgrade to a bigger system you also make a correspondingly larger investment. If you're actually buying hardware, your first step-ups cost you thousands of dollars; your later ones cost you tens or even hundreds of thousands of dollars. At some point you may have to invest in a similarly expensive backup system, which will remain idle unless the unthinkable happens and you need to use it to continue operations.

Horizontal Scaling

Horizontal scaling is slightly more complex, but far more flexible and scalable in the long term. Instead of upgrading to a bigger server, you obtain another one (presumably of the same size, although there's no requirement for this to be the case) and arrange to share the storage and processing load across two servers. When two servers no longer meet your needs, you add a third, a fourth, and so on. This scale-out model allows you to add resources incrementally and economically. As your fleet of servers grow, you can actually increase the reliability of your system by eliminating dependencies on any particular server.

Of course, sharing the storage and processing load across a fleet of servers is sometimes easier said than done. Loosely coupled systems tied together with SQS message queues like those we saw and built in the previous chapter can usually scale easily. Systems with a reliance on a traditional relational database or another centralized storage can be more difficult.

Monitoring, Scaling, and Load Balancing

We'll need several services in order to build a horizontally scaled system that automatically scales to handle load.

First, we need to know how hard each server is working. We have to establish how much data is moving in and out across the network, how many disk reads and writes are taking place, and how much of the time the CPU (Central Processing Unit) is busy. This functionality is provided by Amazon CloudWatch. After CloudWatch has been enabled for an EC2 instance or an elastic load balancer, it captures and stores this information so that it can be used to control scaling decisions.

Second, we require a way to observe the system performance, using it to make decisions to add more EC2 instances (because the system is too busy) or to remove some running instances (because there's too little work for them to do). This functionality is provided by the EC2 auto scaling feature. The auto scaling feature uses a rule-driven system to encode the logic needed to add and remove EC2 instances.

Third, we need a method for routing traffic to each of the running instances. This is handled by the EC2 elastic load balancing feature. Working in conjunction with auto scaling, elastic load balancing distributes traffic to EC2 instances located in one or more Availability Zones within an EC2 region. It also uses configurable health checks to detect failing instances and to route traffic away from them.

Figure 7.1 depicts how these features relate to each other.

An incoming HTTP load is balanced across a collection of EC2 instances. CloudWatch captures and stores system performance data from the instances. This data is used by auto scale to regulate the number of EC2 instances in the collection.

As you'll soon see, you can use each of these features on their own or you can use them together. This modular model gives you a lot of flexibility and also allows you to learn about the features in an incremental fashion.

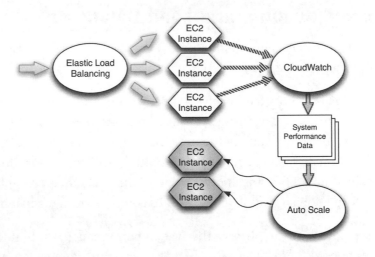

Figure 7.1. The relationship between elastic load balancing, CloudWatch, and auto scale

Installing the Command Line Tools

We'll be using the Amazon command line tools in this chapter, so let's take a moment to install them and have them working. Start by downloading the appropriate **.zip** file(s):

- Amazon EC2 API Tools[1]
- Amazon CloudWatch API Tools[2]
- Auto Scaling API Tools[3]
- Elastic Load Balancing API Tools[4]

Unzip the files into separate top-level directories without spaces in the names.

The command line tools are written in Java, so you'll need to have the Java Runtime Environment (JRE) installed; otherwise, download it from http://www.java.com and install. Again, a directory name without spaces is preferable.

The CloudWatch, elastic load balancer, and auto scaling tools will need your AWS account access key ID and secret key. Again, these values are accessible on your

---

[1] http://developer.amazonwebservices.com/connect/entry.jspa?externalID=351
[2] http://developer.amazonwebservices.com/connect/entry.jspa?externalID=2534
[3] http://developer.amazonwebservices.com/connect/entry.jspa?externalID=2535
[4] http://developer.amazonwebservices.com/connect/entry.jspa?externalID=2536

AWS account page at http://aws.amazon.com when you select **Security Credentials** from the **Your Account** menu, or else they're in your CloudFusion **config.inc.php** file.

Copy the file **credentials-file-template** in the directory where you installed CloudWatch to **credentials.txt** in the same directory. Open **credentials.txt** with your favorite text editor and insert your keys.

You'll also need the X.509 certificate associated with the private key. You can access this file by logging into http://aws.amazon.com, clicking onto **Account**, and selecting **Security Credentials**. Select the **X.509 Certificates** tab and click on the **Create a New Certificate** link. This will reveal a dialog from which you can download the certificate files to your local machine. Click the **Download Private Key File** and the **Download X.509 Certificate** buttons to download the two required files. Make sure you put them in a safe and private place.

We now should set a long list of environment variables. In the following examples you'll have to adjust the paths as appropriate to your environment. The Windows examples include my own environment settings.

Start by adding some commands to set up the HOME environment variables. On Windows you set them up as follows:

```
C:\> set EC2_HOME=C:\ec2-api-tools-1.3-36506
C:\> set AWS_ELB_HOME=C:\ElasticLoadBalancing-1.0.1.23
C:\> set AWS_CLOUDWATCH_HOME=C:\CloudWatch-1.0.0.24
C:\> set AWS_AUTO_SCALING_HOME=C:\AutoScaling-1.0.4.4
```

On Mac OS X and Linux the syntax is slightly different:

```
$ export EC2_HOME=path_to_tools
$ export AWS_ELB_HOME=path_to_tools
$ export AWS_CLOUDWATCH_HOME=path_to_tools
$ export AWS_AUTO_SCALING_HOME=path_to_tools
```

Next, we need to set the full paths to the key and the certificate. On Windows:

```
C:\> set EC2_PRIVATE_KEY=U:\jeff\pk-5NFGWY … DRPFFK3.pem
C:\> set EC2_CERT=U:\jeff\cert-5NFGWY … DRPFFK3.pem
```

On Mac OS X and Linux:

```
$ export EC2_PRIVATE_KEY=path_to_private_key.pem
$ export EC2_CERT=path_to_certificate.pem
```

We also have to tell the tools where to find your credentials. On Windows:

```
C:\> set AWS_CREDENTIAL_FILE=C:\CloudWatch-1.0.0.24\credentials.txt
```

And on Mac OS X and Linux:

```
$ export AWS_CREDENTIAL_FILE=path_to_credentials.txt
```

Now set up the PATH environment variable so that the shell can find the command line tools. On Windows:

```
C:\> set PATH=%PATH%;%EC2_HOME%\bin
C:\> set PATH=%PATH%;%AWS_ELB_HOME%\bin
C:\> set PATH=%PATH%;%AWS_CLOUDWATCH_HOME%\bin
C:\> set PATH=%PATH%;%AWS_AUTO_SCALING_HOME%\bin
```

On Mac OS X and Linux:

```
$ export PATH=$PATH:$EC2_HOME/bin
$ export PATH=$PATH:$AWS_ELB_HOME/bin
$ export PATH=$PATH:$AWS_CLOUDWATCH_HOME/bin
$ export PATH=$PATH:$AWS_AUTO_SCALING_HOME/bin
```

The tools also need the location of the Java runtime executable. On Windows:

```
C:\> set JAVA_HOME=C:\Java\jre1.5.0_09
```

On Mac OS X and Linux:

```
$ export JAVA_HOME=path_to_java
```

Mac OS X users should set the JAVA_HOME environment variable to /System/Library/Frameworks/JavaVM.framework/Home.

If your instances are in a region other than the default, you can set the region to be used by the command line tools by setting the EC2_URL environment variable. If you don't do this, you'll need to specify the `--region` parameter each time you use the command line tools. On Windows:

```
C:\> set EC2_URL=https://eu-west-1.ec2.amazonaws.com
```

On Mac OS X and Linux:

```
$ export EC2_URL=https://eu-west-1.ec2.amazonaws.com
```

And you've done it.

I find the best way to do this is to write a batch file and include all the above statements. For example, if you're using Windows, create a batch file named **ec2-tool-setup.bat** and run it to set up all the variables. On Mac OS X or Linux, put all the above statements in a file called **ec2-tool-setup** and run this command:

```
$ source ec2-tool-setup
```

Verify that you have everything right by running one or more of the following commands. On Windows:

```
C:\> mon-cmd --help
C:\> ec2-describe-images
C:\> elb-describe-lbs
```

On Mac OS X or Linux:

```
$ mon-cmd --help
$ ec2-describe-images
$ elb-describe-lbs
```

If you see connection errors or Java stack traces (my favorite), you'll need to retrace your steps and figure out what went wrong.

With any luck, you have succeeded in setting up the AWS command line tools. Otherwise, your next step is to visit the EC2 forum[5] and politely ask for help.

---

[5] http://developer.amazonwebservices.com/connect/forum.jspa?forumID=30

Monitoring EC2 Data with Amazon CloudWatch

It's time to learn about Amazon CloudWatch concepts and its pricing model, add support for CloudWatch to the CloudFusion library, and then write some code to retrieve and display the collected data.

Amazon CloudWatch Concepts

Amazon CloudWatch collects, aggregates, stores, and dispenses data from a number of AWS resources. The current release of Amazon CloudWatch collects data from EC2 instances and elastic load balancers; support for additional services may be added in the future.

There are a number of terms and concepts associated with Amazon CloudWatch. These terms build on each other and are essential to understanding the CloudWatch model.

A **namespace** represents a source of data. The "AWS/EC2" namespace is associated with data collected from the Amazon EC2 infrastructure and the "AWS/ELB" namespace is associated with data collected from the Elastic Load Balancer.

A **measure** is a raw, observed data value. Measures are accumulated and rolled up to represent one minute's worth of observation. A measure is always part of a namespace and has a unit such as bit, byte, or percent. Each measure has a name and a timestamp. Measures can be aggregated across one or more dimensions. The combination of the namespace, measure name, and zero or more dimensions is the complete measure name. Measures, once observed, are retained for two weeks (14 days).

A **unit** is an attribute of a measure. CloudWatch supports the following units: none, seconds, percent, bytes, bits, count, bytes/second, bits/second, and count/second. The unit is optional and the default is none. Some numbers, like ratios, have no units.

A **dimension** is a refined view of a certain type of data. CloudWatch supports the following dimensions: `AvailabilityZone`, `ImageType` (an AMI Id), `InstanceId`, `InstanceType`, and `AutoScaleGroup`.

A **metric** is a stored, processed measure. The CloudWatch API provides a function to retrieve metrics based on namespace, measure, unit, period, statistic, and dimension parameters.

Metrics without dimensions represent highly aggregated data; for instance, this could be disk activity or average CPU utilization across all EC2 instances of a particular instance type (or even for all instances in the account).

A **period** is used to specify a time granularity, in seconds, when requesting metrics from CloudWatch.

A **statistic** is a computed attribute of a metric and reflects the attributes of the measures that compose the metric. CloudWatch supports the following metrics: minimum, maximum, average, and sum. A fifth statistic, samples, denotes the number of measurements used to compute the value for the statistics.

Amazon CloudWatch Operation

You must enable CloudWatch for each of your EC2 instances in order to start the data collection process. Once enabled, the process starts within a minute and metrics become available within a few minutes. You can enable CloudWatch when you launch the instances. You can also enable or disable CloudWatch for any EC2 instances that are already running. The enable and disable operations are part of the EC2 API. There is a per-instance hourly charge for the use of CloudWatch; this covers the overhead of collecting and storing the data.

Each elastic load balancer automatically forwards certain measurements to CloudWatch. There's no need to enable monitoring for these load balancers and there's no charge for storing or using the collected metrics.

CloudWatch stores accumulated data for two weeks; older data is automatically discarded.

After CloudWatch has been enabled, you can retrieve the list of measures and the actual metrics using the command line tools or the CloudWatch API. Viewed in this way, CloudWatch appears a lot simpler than it actually is. In fact, the real power of CloudWatch manifests itself in the parameters used to access the data.

Amazon CloudWatch Pricing

There's a charge of $0.015 (1.5 cents) per hour per monitored EC2 instance for the use of CloudWatch. This charge covers monitoring, data storage, and access to the stored data using the command line tools and the CloudWatch API.

There's no charge for the storage or use of elastic load balancer data in CloudWatch.

Amazon CloudWatch from the Command Line

The easiest way to put CloudWatch through its paces is to use the command line. There's one interesting twist that you need to be aware of, though. The EC2 tools are used to enable or disable CloudWatch for an EC2 instance. The CloudWatch tools are used to access the collected data.

Here is how to enable CloudWatch for a single EC2 instance. The first step is to determine the instance's ID using the `ec2-describe-instances` command:

```
$ ec2-describe-instances
INSTANCE i-aaba69c3 ami-2b5fba42 ec2-75-101-154-199.compute-1.amazon
➥aws.com domU-12-31-38-00-A0-01.compute-1.internal running gsg-keyp
➥air 0 m1.small 2008-07-13T03:44:43+0000 us-east-1a  aki-a71cf9ce
➥ari-a51cf9cc monitoring-disabled
```

In this case the instance ID is `i-aaba69c3`. With this value in hand, the `ec2-monitor-instances` command is used to enable CloudWatch (substituting the ID of your own instance, of course):

```
$ ec2-monitor-instances i-aaba69c3
i-aaba69c3 monitoring-pending
```

This command can be run again (after a short delay) to confirm that CloudWatch has been enabled for the specified instance:

```
$ ec2-monitor-instances i-aaba69c3
i-aaba69c3 monitoring-enabled
```

The `mon-list-metrics` command (from the CloudWatch tools) displays the list of available metrics:

```
$ mon-list-metrics
CPUUtilization   AWS/EC2   {ImageId=ami-3c47a355}
CPUUtilization   AWS/EC2   {InstanceType=m1.small}
CPUUtilization   AWS/EC2
CPUUtilization   AWS/EC2   {InstanceId=i-aaba69c3}
: a big long list…
```

The results are broken down by metric (`DiskReadBytes`, `DiskReadOps`, `NetworkIn`, `NetworkOut`, `DiskWriteBytes`, `DiskWriteOps`, and so on) and denote the dimensions (`ImageId`, `InstanceId`, `InstanceType`, and so on) that may be requested from CloudWatch. Metrics are retained and can be retrieved for instances that you've recently terminated. Witness the following dimensions for CPU utilization below.

Here is the dimension for the CPU utilization of all your running or recently terminated EC2 instances:

```
CPUUtilization   AWS/EC2
```

And this denotes the CPU utilization of running/recently terminated EC2 instances of type m1.small:

```
CPUUtilization   AWS/EC2   {InstanceType=m1.small}
```

This is the same again, only it's for those launched using the indicated AMI:

```
CPUUtilization   AWS/EC2   {ImageId=ami-3c47a355}
```

And here it's for the specific running or recently terminated EC2 instance:

```
CPUUtilization   AWS/EC2   {InstanceId=i-aaba69c3}
```

Once you have chosen a dimension, you can use the `mon-get-stats` command to retrieve any metrics that you'd like. For example, all CPU utilization, by hour, for the last 24 hours:

```
$ mon-get-stats CPUUtilization --statistics Average
➡ --start-time 2010-07-27 --end-time 2009-07-28 --period 3600
➡ --namespace AWS/EC2
2009-07-18 00:00:00  60.0  5.9479999999999995  Percent
```

```
2009-07-18 01:00:00   60.0   6.910833333333331   Percent
2009-07-18 02:00:00   60.0   6.614666666666667   Percent
: a big long list…
```

The first two columns represent the date and time of the aggregated data. The third column is the number of samples that CloudWatch aggregated to produce the metric. In this case we asked for results by the hour (**--period 3600**), so CloudWatch used 60 samples (taken one per minute) for each result. The next column is the requested metric, average CPU utilization over the hour. The final column is the units (percent CPU utilization).

You should experiment with a variety of parameters to `mon-get-stats` to obtain a better feel for the metrics and the associated units.

Programming Amazon CloudWatch

Now that we've seen how to access CloudWatch from the command line, let's have a look at the functions CloudFusion has to offer, and use its `AmazonCloudWatch` class to draw some cool charts.

Listing Available Metrics

Here's a program to list all the available metrics:

chapter_07/list_metrics.php *(excerpt)*

```php
#!/usr/bin/php
<?php

error_reporting(E_ALL);

require_once('cloudfusion.class.php');
require_once('cloudwatch.class.php');

$cW = new AmazonCloudWatch();
$res = $cW->list_metrics();

if ($res->isOK())
{
  $metrics     = $res->body->ListMetricsResult->Metrics->member;
  $metricsRows = array();
```

```php
  foreach ($metrics as $metric)
  {
    $metricsRows[] =
      array('MeasureName' => (string) $metric->MeasureName,
      'Namespace'   => (string) $metric->Namespace,
      'Name'        => (string) $metric->Dimensions->member->Name,
      'Value'       => (string) $metric->Dimensions->member->Value);
  }

  usort($metricsRows, 'CmpMetrics');

  printf("%-16s  %-16s  %-16s  %-16s\n",
    "Namespace", "Measure Name", "Name", "Value");

  printf("%-16s  %-16s  %-16s  %-16s\n",
    "=========", "============", "====", "=====");

  foreach ($metricsRows as $metricsRow)
  {
    printf("%-16s  %-16s  %-16s  %-16s\n",
      $metricsRow['Namespace'],
      $metricsRow['MeasureName'],
      $metricsRow['Name'],
      $metricsRow['Value']);
  }
}
else
{
  $error = $res->body->Error->Message;
  exit("Could not list metrics: ${error}\n");
}

function CmpMetrics($m1, $m2)
{
  $k1 = $m1['Namespace'] . $m1['MeasureName'] . $m1['Name'];
  $k2 = $m2['Namespace'] . $m2['MeasureName'] . $m2['Name'];

  return strcmp($k1, $k2);
}

?>
```

This program calls the list_metrics method and then copies the results into a PHP array. PHP's usort function is used to sort the array so that the elements are grouped by `Namespace`, then `Measure`, then `Name`, as indicated by the `CmpMetrics` function in the code above.

The program produces the following output:

```
Namespace            Measure Name      Name          Value
=========            ============      ====          =====
AWS/EC2              CPUUtilization
AWS/EC2              CPUUtilization    ImageId       ami-3c47a355
AWS/EC2              CPUUtilization    InstanceId    i-aaba69c3
AWS/EC2              CPUUtilization    InstanceType  m1.small
: a long list…
```

This is, of course, very similar to the output produced by the `mon-list-metrics` command.

Charting Multiple Metrics

Let's build a web page with charts of some CloudWatch metrics. The code to do this will be fairly involved, so we'll build it in sections. The program in this section will generate a web page, so you'll want to run it on your web server.

This program will use the Google Chart API,[6] and will draw seven charts on the same page, like the example in Figure 7.2.

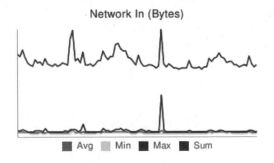

Figure 7.2. The **Network In** chart

---

[6] http://code.google.com/apis/chart/

Our script begins in the usual way:

chapter_07/statistics_chart_page.php *(excerpt)*

```php
<?php

error_reporting(E_ALL);

require_once('cloudfusion.class.php');
```

We will need to do some data processing. By default, the program will report on the metrics collected in the preceding 24 hours. The $startDate_DT variable will represent the starting date and time, while the $endDate_DT variable will represent the ending date and time. Let's declare them and set them up:

chapter_07/statistics_chart_page.php *(excerpt)*

```php
$startDate_DT = new DateTime('now');
$endDate_DT   = new DateTime('now');
$startDate_DT->modify('-1 day');
```

CloudWatch expresses all dates in terms of GMT (Greenwich Mean Time). You'll have to adjust your queries if you want to express your dates and date ranges in local time.

The next step is to convert the date values into the format needed to use them in CloudWatch queries. This is done using the format method of PHP's DateTime class, like this:

chapter_07/statistics_chart_page.php *(excerpt)*

```php
$startDate = $startDate_DT->format('Y-m-d');
$endDate   = $endDate_DT->format('Y-m-d');
```

If parameters were supplied as part of the request, go ahead and fetch them. Otherwise, we'll use reasonable default values:

```
                        chapter_07/statistics_chart_page.php (excerpt)
$period = IsSet($_GET['period']) ? $_GET['period'] : 15;
$start  = IsSet($_GET['start'])  ? $_GET['start']  : $startDate;
$end    = IsSet($_GET['end'])    ? $_GET['end']    : $endDate;
$period *= 60;
```

Note how handy and concise the ternary (? :) operator turns out to be in this situation? With proper formatting, it becomes easy to recognize this construct and to mentally process it as a very compact if-then-else.

The period parameter is specified in minutes for convenience, but CloudWatch needs it in seconds so we adjust it.

The program will produce a series of seven charts, driven by the information in the $charts array. It looks like this:

```
                        chapter_07/statistics_chart_page.php (excerpt)
$charts = array(
    array('M' => 'NetworkIn',
          'U' => 'Bytes',
          'L' => 'Network In (Bytes)'),

    array('M' => 'NetworkOut',
          'U' => 'Bytes',
          'L' => 'Network Out (Bytes)'),

    array('M' => 'CPUUtilization',
          'U' => 'Percent',
          'L' => 'CPU Utilization (Percent)'),

    array('M' => 'DiskReadBytes',
          'U' => 'Bytes',
          'L' => 'Disk Read Bytes'),

    array('M' => 'DiskReadOps',
          'U' => 'Count',
          'L' => 'Disk Read Operations/Second'),

    array('M' => 'DiskWriteBytes',
          'U' => 'Bytes',
          'L' => 'Disk Write Bytes'),
```

```
    array('M' => 'DiskWriteOps',
          'U' => 'Count',
          'L' => 'Disk Write Operations/Second'),

    );
```

Each element of the array contains three strings. The M element specifies the CloudWatch measure for the chart, the U element specifies the CloudWatch units, and the L element specifies the chart title.

With all that completed, it's time to create an instance of the `AmazonCloudWatch` class:

chapter_07/statistics_chart_page.php *(excerpt)*

```
$cW = new AmazonCloudWatch();

$opt = array('Namespace' => 'AWS/EC2', 'Period' => $period);
$statistics = array('Average','Minimum','Maximum','Sum');
```

We'll also need an array of optional parameters. These will stay the same from call to call, so we can set them up now in the $opt array above. The same holds true for the desired statistics, which we put in a $statistics array.

Now let's return to the $charts array that we just set up. In the code below we start a simple loop through the elements to provide us with the information needed to generate our charts. We've also created the $chartImages array to hold the source URLs for our charts that we'll use in the HTML template to follow:

chapter_07/statistics_chart_page.php *(excerpt)*

```
$chartImages = array();
foreach ($charts as &$chart)
{
  $measure = $chart['M'];
  $unit    = $chart['U'];
  $label   = $chart['L'];
```

This code sets up the loop and fetches the measure, unit, and label for each chart.

With this information in hand it's time to fetch the desired metrics from CloudWatch, like this:

```
chapter_07/statistics_chart_page.php (excerpt)

$res = $cW->get_metric_statistics($measure,
        $statistics,
        $unit,
        $start,
        $end,
        $opt);


if ($res->isOK())
{
```

There is no dimension specified in this request; instead, it retrieves information about all running and recently terminated EC2 instances. As always, we need to ensure that this request succeeded before processing the results.

The metrics are returned in an unpredictable order. Since we're planning to use them to draw a chart, we'll need to capture them all and then sort them. Let's dig into the returned value and find the Datapoints item:

```
chapter_07/statistics_chart_page.php (excerpt)

$datapoints =
  $res->body->GetMetricStatisticsResult->Datapoints->member;
```

Now we create an empty array and then extract the metrics from Datapoints, storing them in $dataRows, indexed by the returned timestamp:

```
chapter_07/statistics_chart_page.php (excerpt)

$dataRows = array();
foreach ($datapoints as $datapoint)
{
  $timestamp = (string) $datapoint->Timestamp;

  $dataRows[$timestamp] =
    array('Timestamp' => (string) $datapoint->Timestamp,
        'Units'    => (string) $datapoint->Unit,
        'Samples'  => (string) $datapoint->Samples,
        'Average'  => (float)  $datapoint->Average,
```

```
        'Minimum'   => (float) $datapoint->Minimum,
        'Maximum'   => (float) $datapoint->Maximum,
        'Sum'       => (float) $datapoint->Sum);
}
ksort ($dataRows);
```

At the end of the code above we sort the metrics by the array key (the timestamp for each metric).

The metrics are now sorted. Since we'll be producing a chart, we actually need to have four separate arrays, one for each statistic to be graphed. The following code takes the $dataRows array and produces these separate arrays:

chapter_07/statistics_chart_page.php *(excerpt)*

```
$averages = array();
$minimums = array();
$maximums = array();
$sums     = array();

foreach ($dataRows as $dataRow)
{
  $averages[] = $dataRow['Average'];
  $minimums[] = $dataRow['Minimum'];
  $maximums[] = $dataRow['Maximum'];
  $sums[]     = $dataRow['Sum'];
}
```

There are several different ways to specify the data values for the Google Chart API. The simplest one restricts the values to the range 0 to 100, inclusive. So, the next step is to compute the scale factor needed to map all the statistics to this range, and with it in hand, scale each of the arrays:

chapter_07/statistics_chart_page.php *(excerpt)*

```
$chartMax = max(max($averages), max($minimums),
    max($maximums), max($sums));
$scale    = 100.0 / $chartMax;

for ($i = 0; $i < count($averages); $i++)
{
  $averages[$i] = (int) ($averages[$i] * $scale);
```

```
    $minimums[$i] = (int) ($minimums[$i] * $scale);
    $maximums[$i] = (int) ($maximums[$i] * $scale);
    $sums[$i]     = (int) ($sums[$i]     * $scale);
}
```

The chart API accepts the data values for each line in the chart as a comma-separated string. The values for the lines are separated by the pipe or vertical bar character. Here's the code to set this up:

chapter_07/statistics_chart_page.php (excerpt)

```
$average = implode(',', $averages);
$minimum = implode(',', $minimums);
$maximum = implode(',', $maximums);
$sum     = implode(',', $sums);

// Combine arrays for use in chart
$series  = $average . '|' .
           $minimum . '|' .
           $maximum . '|' .
           $sum;
```

Hang in there, we're almost ready to generate the charts! The next step is to replace embedded spaces in the chart title with plus (+) signs and to set up the colors:

chapter_07/statistics_chart_page.php (excerpt)

```
$label = str_replace(' ', '+', $label);
$colors = 'ff0000,00ff00,0000ff,800080';
```

With all the information at our disposal, we can now compose the URL for the chart. Here's the code:

chapter_07/statistics_chart_page.php (excerpt)

```
$chartURL = "http://chart.apis.google.com/chart";
$chartURL .= '?chs=300x180';                // Chart size
$chartURL .= '&cht=lc';                     // Line chart
$chartURL .= '&chtt=' . $label;             // Label
$chartURL .= '&chdlp=b';                    // Legend at bottom
$chartURL .= '&chdl=Avg|Min|Max|Sum';       // Legend
$chartURL .= '&chco=' . $colors;            // Colors
$chartURL .= '&chd=t:' . $series;           // Data series
```

The Google Chart API includes many advanced formatting and labeling options, but I kept this example fairly minimal so as to leave room for you to improve it.

The final step is to store the URL in the $chartImages array:

chapter_07/statistics_chart_page.php *(excerpt)*

```
$chartImages[] = $chartURL;
```

The final step, after the URLs of all the charts have been saved, is to include our HTML template and then exit:

chapter_07/statistics_chart_page.php *(excerpt)*

```
$output_title = 'Chapter 7 Sample - Charts of CloudWatch ' .
    'Statistics';
$output_message = "Charts of CloudWatch Statistics from ${start}" .
    " to ${end}";

include 'include/statistics.html.php';
```

Finally, here's the simple HTML template for our page:

chapter_07/statistics_chart_page.php *(excerpt)*

```
<!DOCTYPE html PUBLIC "-//W3C//DTD XHTML 1.0 Strict//EN"
  "http://www.w3.org/TR/xhtml1/DTD/xhtml1-strict.dtd">
<html xmlns="http://www.w3.org/1999/xhtml" xml:lang="en" lang="en">
<head>
  <title><?php echo $output_title ?></title>
</head>
<body>
  <h1><?php echo $output_title ?></h1>
  <p><?php echo $output_message ?></p>
  <?php foreach($chartImages as $image): ?>
    <img src="<?php echo $image ?>"/>
  <?php endforeach ?>
</body>
</html>
```

The important point to realize is that this program never does any actual drawing. Instead, it creates an HTML page that asks Google to do the work. When the browser renders the page it will make a call to the Google Chart API for each chart on the page. A server at Google will process the URL, draw the chart, and return it to the browser; then the browser will draw the chart as part of the page.

Figure 7.3 shows what the finished page looks like.

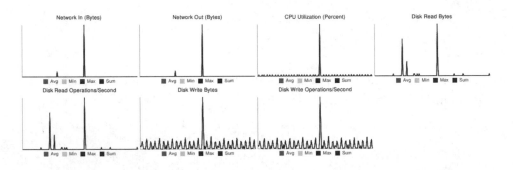

Figure 7.3. Seven CloudWatch metrics in chart form

Remember that this page accepts some parameters. You can experiment with the period parameter to aggregate metrics over different periods of time. You can set the `start` and `end` parameters to dates (use values like `2009-07-07`) or dates with times (values like `2009-07-07T12:00:00`). Simply append the parameters to the page URL. Here's a sample:

```
statistics_chart_page.php?period=60&start=2009-07-20T12:00:00&end=
➡2009-07-20T18:00:00
```

If your page fails to show any data, you might have to experiment with the date values. For example, if you only enabled monitoring an hour ago, restrict the time range to the last hour while you test. If you do reduce the time span to, say, an hour, reduce the `period` value so that your graphs will have some detail. Finally, make sure dates are expressed in Greenwich Mean Time, or else you may see wildly inaccurate results depending on your local time zone.

The Google Chart API imposes a limit on the overall length of the chart URL. Small values or broad time ranges will generate more metrics (and an overly long URL), and the chart will fail to draw. You can maneuver around this by adjusting the parameters or by modifying the code to draw fewer statistics per chart. You could also use a more powerful charting package, such as JpGraph.[7]

---

[7] http://www.aditus.nu/jpgraph/

You can extend this program in various ways, such as combining it with the previous one and creating a user interface to allow the user to choose the dimension to be displayed. You might let the user choose the date range using two copies of the jQuery Datepicker.[8] Also, you could embed this program into a larger monitoring or system control program. It can be as useful as you make it.

We've learned a lot in this section. We covered the fundamental concepts of CloudWatch, and saw how to enable Amazon CloudWatch for an EC2 instance and how to access the collected metrics. We also used the CloudFusion library to list the available CloudWatch metrics and to generate charts.

Learning and Using Apache JMeter

Let's take a short detour to learn more about a very useful program, the Apache JMeter.

Why JMeter?

If you're running the charting program from the previous section and monitoring a nearly idle EC2 instance, you'll see little in the way of highs and lows. You can generate a system load manually by doing tasks such as:

- copying large files from place to place (generates disk read and write operations)
- downloading large files from the Internet (generates a load that's reflected in the Network In metric)
- placing large files on the server and downloading them externally (generates a load that's reflected in the Network Out metric)
- sorting very large files (increases CPU utilization, and disk read and disk write operations)

Unless you write some sophisticated test scripts, you'll quickly tire of doing this. Also, since generating a load is often the first step in a system optimization effort, you'll need to be able to reproduce the load with some degree of precision.

The Apache JMeter application simplifies the process of stress-testing a web-based application. Once a test plan has been created, it can be run at any time with a single click. The results are measured and stored for analysis.

---

[8] http://docs.jquery.com/UI/Datepicker

In order to keep this section to a reasonable length, I'm going to provide a straightforward set of steps for the use of JMeter. Space definitely precludes a complete description of the entire JMeter feature set.

Installing and Running JMeter

JMeter[9] is a free, open source program. Download the binary file and choose a directory so that the resulting path will exclude any spaces.[10]

Now go into the **bin** subdirectory of the installation directory and run `jmeter` if you're on Mac OS X or Linux; **jmeter.bat** if you're on Windows. On Windows it's best to run the batch file from a command because some of JMeter's reports (also known as listeners) will produce their output there.

The main window is shown in Figure 7.4.

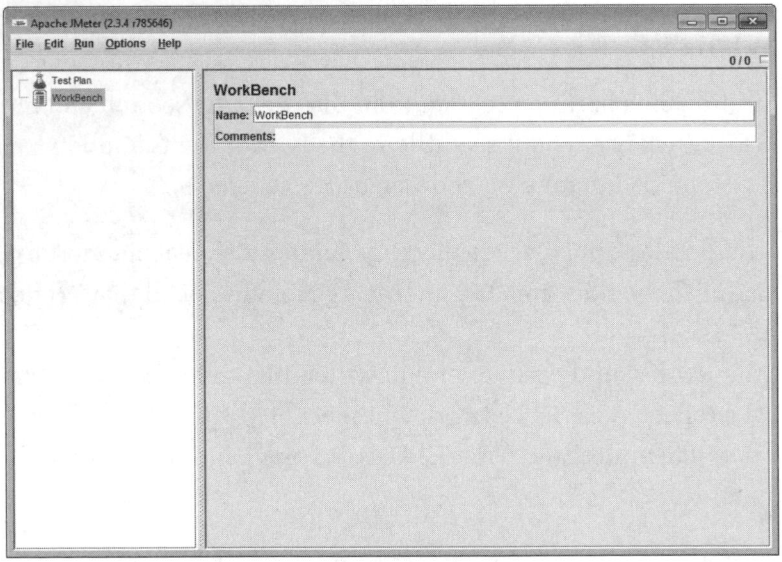

Figure 7.4. JMeter's main window

---

[9] http://jakarta.apache.org/site/downloads/downloads_jmeter.cgi
[10] It's hard to believe that this particular Java shortcoming is still present. I was bitten by it for the first time in 1996.

Creating a Test Plan

The next step is to create a JMeter test plan. The test plan specifies the number of parallel threads to run, the HTTP requests to make in each thread, and a disposition for the results.

Here's how to create a simple test plan:

1. Right-click on the **Test Plan** node and choose **Add > Threads (Users) > Thread Group**.

2. Configure the thread group with four threads, a ramp-up period of ten seconds, and a loop count of 16.

3. Right-click on the new Thread Group node and choose **Add > Sampler > HTTP Request**.

4. Enter your server host name or IP address (mine is www.captaincloud.com— omit the `http://` protocol prefix) and port (80 should be fine).

5. Enter "/" for the path to retrieve the home page from the site.

6. Repeat the previous step for other pages on the same server. And enter a different name for each one.

7. Right-click on the **Test Plan** node once again. Add the following listener nodes: **Generate Summary Results**, **Aggregate Report**, and **Graph Results**

The completed test plan should look similar to Figure 7.5.

Figure 7.5. The completed test plan

Once you're happy with the plan, choose **File** > **Save**.

Running the Test

Make sure that your server is ready to go. Log in to your server via SSH, and go to the Apache log file directory—if you're running the LAMP Web Starter AMI, this will be **/home/webuser/helloworld/logs**—and run `tail`:

```
$ cd /home/webuser/helloworld/logs
$ tail -f access_log
```

Return to JMeter and choose **Run** > **Start**. Watch your server log to verify that the requests are arriving as expected.

While the test is running, click on the **Aggregate Report** or **Graph Results** nodes to see the request statistics measured by JMeter.

Continue to watch your server log file. You may also want to use the w command to check your server's load average:

```
<dev>: w
19:17:15 up 373 days, 1:24, 4 users, load average: 0.01, 0.02, 0.09
USER     TTY        FROM            LOGIN@   IDLE   JCPU   PCPU   WHAT
root     pts/0      71.112.36.28    Mon17    2:47m  6.90s  6.88s  emacs
➥ -u jeff
root     pts/2      71.112.36.28    Mon19    0.00s  0.00s  0.00s  w
root     pts/4      71.112.36.28    14:46    3:02m  0.03s  0.03s  -bash
root     pts/3      71.112.36.28    Mon19    4:30m  0.00s  0.00s  —bash
```

The higher the load average—the last three numbers on the first line (representing system load for the past minute, five minutes, and 15 minutes, respectively)—the busier the system.[11]

Viewing the Results

The summary results are displayed in the command window where JMeter was launched. One line is written at the conclusion of each test run. Here's what mine looked like after I did some experimentation with various parameter values:

---

[11] This is the actual output from one of my EC2 instances. As you can see, it has been running for 373 days (more than a year).

```
Generate Summary Results +   68 in   4.9s =   13.8/s Avg:    432 Min:
➡   215 Max:    793 Err:     0 (0.00%)
Generate Summary Results =  192 in  11.9s =   16.1/s Avg:    419 Min:
➡   214 Max:    821 Err:     0 (0.00%)
Generate Summary Results =  576 in  25.1s =   23.0/s Avg:    455 Min:
➡   216 Max:   3294 Err:     0 (0.00%)
Generate Summary Results =  864 in  30.8s =   28.0/s Avg:    535 Min:
➡   216 Max:   3424 Err:     0 (0.00%)
Generate Summary Results +  454 in  12.7s =   35.8/s Avg:    596 Min:
➡   226 Max:   3332 Err:     0 (0.00%)
Generate Summary Results +  620 in  42.6s =   14.6/s Avg:    782 Min:
➡   217 Max:  40502 Err:     3 (0.48%)
Generate Summary Results = 1074 in  53.1s =   20.2/s Avg:    704 Min:
➡   217 Max:  40502 Err:     3 (0.28%)
```

The field ending in "/s" indicates the average number of requests per second issued during the test.

The **Aggregate Report**, shown in Figure 7.6, includes one detail line for each distinct HTTP request node in the test plan, followed by a line of totals.

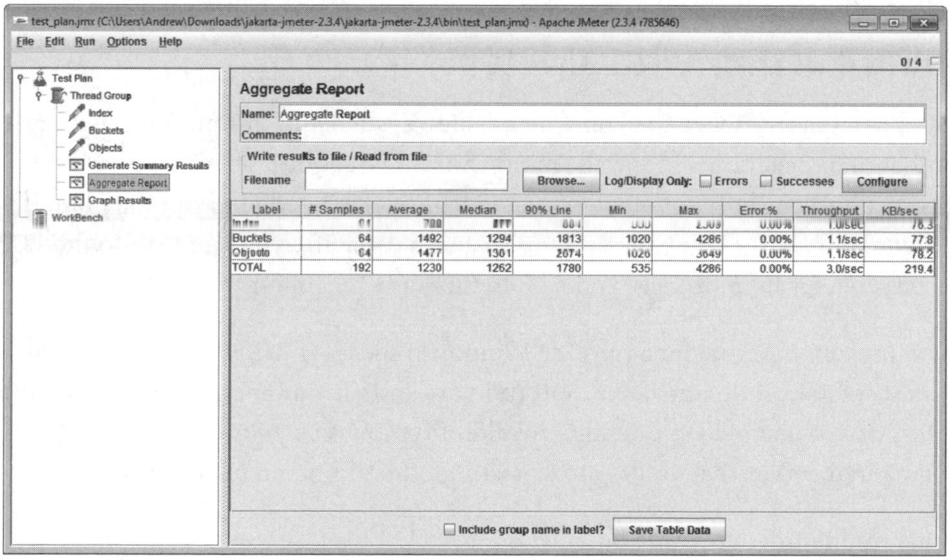

Figure 7.6. JMeter's Aggregate Report

The **Graph Results** report, shown in Figure 7.7, charts various statistics over time.

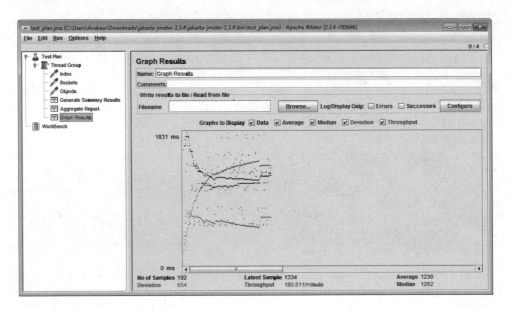

Figure 7.7. JMeter's **Graph Results**

You can use the checkboxes and the **Configure** window to control the content and appearance of the graph results.

Going Further with JMeter

JMeter can place a heavy load on your desktop system and internet connection. The number of request threads and the number of HTTP request objects in your test plan directly affect the amount of memory and bandwidth needed to run the plan. If you find yourself limited by your desktop system's capacity, you can turn to the EC2 web service for help. In fact, you can do this in two different ways:

■ Launch an EC2 instance running Windows, access it using Remote Desktop, install JMeter on this instance, and run your tests from there. If you launch the test driver instance in the same Availability Zones as your test subject (the EC2-powered server that you're stress-testing), there'll be no bandwidth charges.

■ Install the JMeter engine on an EC2 server (a Linux server will do just fine and will cost you less) and then control it from the JMeter instance running on your desktop. There's more information about this in the Remote Testing section of the JMeter manual.[12]

---

[12] http://jakarta.apache.org/jmeter/usermanual/remote-test.html

I hope that this brief introduction has given you a hint of what you can do with JMeter. If so, you may want to spend some time reading the user's manual[13] to learn more about this powerful tool.

Scaling EC2 Instances with Elastic Load Balancing

In this section, you'll learn about the elastic load balancing feature. We'll review the process model and the pricing, and then we'll put the service to use, creating a load balancer for a couple of EC2 instances. We'll do a quick review of the programming model (without writing any code) and then you'll be ready to use this feature in your own applications.

Elastic Load Balancing Concepts

By using EC2's elastic load balancing feature, you can create software load balancers in any AWS region. Each **load balancer** listens on one or more network ports and routes traffic to one or more EC2 instances, possibly spread across more than one Availability Zone. The load balancers check the health of each instance and route traffic only to healthy instances, while also seeking to equalize the amount of traffic sent to each instance.

A load balancer is an entity specific to a particular AWS region. When you create the load balancer you will supply a reference name, such as `LoadBal`. Each load balancer is represented externally by a fully qualified host name; for example, LoadBal-79377590.us-east-1.elb.amazonaws.com. This name is assigned when the load balancer is created. A list of EC2 instances is attached to each load balancer. Each instance has an associated health (healthy or unhealthy). Each load balancer also has a list of Availability Zones and will route traffic only to healthy EC2 instances in those zones.

Each load balancer must have one or more listeners. Each listener accepts requests on a specific network port and forwards them to a specific port on an EC2 instance. Listeners can listen on ports 80, 443, and 1024 through 65,535, and can forward requests to any port.

---

[13] http://jakarta.apache.org/jmeter/usermanual/index.html

A health check is attached to each load balancer. The health check provides the load balancer with a target (a port, a protocol, and (for HTTP checks) a URL fragment) to be checked, along with thresholds representing the number of checks to be made before changing the state of the instance.

Elastic Load Balancing Processing Model

The processing model is very straightforward. Here's what you need to do:

1. Create an elastic load balancer by providing a reference name, an initial list of Availability Zones, the parameters for the health check, and the list of listeners. You will receive an externally visible host name in return; for example: LoadBal-79377590.us-east-1.elb.amazonaws.com. With this name in hand you can use a CNAME entry in your application's DNS record to make the load-balanced cluster a part of your application's web namespace.[14]

2. Add one or more EC2 instances to the load balancer using their instance IDs after ensuring that they're prepared to respond to health checks and actual requests. The load balancer will begin to track the state (InService or OutOfService) of each instance.

3. Start to route traffic to the load balancer using the externally visible host name.

4. Add additional EC2 instances (and possibly Availability Zones) to the load balancer as traffic increases.

5. Delete the load balancer when you no longer need it.

As usual, all these operations can be performed using the command line tools or through the elastic load balancing API. You can also use CloudWatch to monitor the overall state of the load balancer.

The load balancer will perform health checks (or probes) on each instance under its care using the parameters that you supplied when you created it. Let's say that a load balancer is configured with the following health check parameters (which happen to be the default values):

---

[14] For reasons that are far too complex to explain in this footnote, you can't use a CNAME record to define the root of your domain. You can map www.example.com to your load balancer using a CNAME, but you can't map example.com.

Parameter	Value	Units
HealthyThreshold	3	probes
UnhealthyThreshold	3	probes
Interval	30	seconds
Timeout	5	seconds

Here's what happens:

1. A probe is started every 30 seconds. If the instance responds as expected within five seconds then the probe succeeded, otherwise it failed.

2. If the instance's state is InService and three successive probes fail, the state is changed to OutOfService and no further traffic is routed to the instance.

3. If the state of the instance is OutOfService and is found to be healthy for three successive probes, the state is changed to InService and traffic is once again routed to the instance.

Health probes can be set to be TCP-style or HTTP-style:

- A **TCP-style probe** attempts to open a connection to a specified port on the target instance. If the connection is made, it's immediately closed and the instance is considered healthy.

- **HTTP-style probes** are more involved. The connection is opened and then a GET request is made for the URL fragment. If the target is HTTP:80/check.html, the HTTP GET request will be made on port 80 for page /check.html. If the server replies with a 200 OK response, it's deemed healthy. Any other response (or no response altogether) is considered unhealthy. These requests will show up in your web server's log files; you may want to arrange to filter them out if you're collecting statistics on visits to your site.

You can use the HTTP-style probe in some creative ways. The simplest and most obvious task to perform is to refer to a static page. If the server is up and the web server is running, the page will be available and the instance will receive traffic.

However, what if it's a dynamic page? Then your application could, for example, take itself offline for periodic database backups by returning a response like 503

`Service Unavailable`. If you do this, you'd want to make sure that there are other instances available to handle the load rather than all the instances going offline at the same time.

Elastic Load Balancing Pricing

Pricing for this feature is fairly simple. You pay for your load balancers by the hour. You also pay for all data transfer through your load balancers. You'll be charged $0.025 (2.5 cents) per hour per load balancer and $0.008 (slightly less than a cent) for each gigabyte of data transferred through any of your load balancers. This is in addition to the normal EC2 bandwidth charges.

This is definitely more economical than purchasing a hardware load balancer or running a software load balancer on an EC2 instance. You could run an elastic load balancer for several years before the hourly costs approached the purchase price of a similarly featured hardware load balancer.

Elastic Load Balancing in Operation

Setting up a traditional hardware load balancer is an expensive, complicated, and time-consuming task. You need to acquire and install the hardware, attach it to your network, and then learn how to set it up. Once you have it up and running, the last thing you want to do is experiment with the settings in a way that could destabilize your production system.

EC2's elastic load balancing is inexpensive to use and can be set up in a matter of minutes. It's easy to create test configurations, so that experimentation becomes risk-free and affordable.

In this section we'll set up an elastic load balancer and then use it to direct traffic to a pair of EC2 instances. We'll alter some of the health check parameters along the way and retrieve some statistics using CloudWatch.

You'll need to have the API Tools installed in order to do this yourself.

In the rest of this section, commands with the $ prompt were run from my local desktop. Commands with the <lb1>: prompt were run on an EC2 instance.

Use the AWS Management Console to launch an instance of the LAMP Web Starter AMI in Availability Zone us-east-1a. Wait for the instance to launch, and then open up an SSH session to it. Write down the instance ID; you'll need it soon.

Edit the file **/home/webuser/helloworld/htdocs/index.php**. Find the following statement:

```
<h2>PHP Information</h2>
```

Change it to read as follows:

```
<h2>PHP Information For First Instance!</h2>
```

Leave the SSH window open as you'll need it later.

Visit the instance's public IP address in a browser and confirm that you see the new message and the output from the phpinfo function.

Now create a load balancer named LoadBal using this command:

```
$ elb-create-lb LoadBal --availability-zones us-east-1a
➥ --listener "protocol=HTTP,lb-port=80,instance-port=80"
```

This load balancer will direct HTTP traffic on port 80 to EC2 instances running in Availability Zone us-east-1a.

The command will create the load balancer, and then it will display a key piece of information—the host name of the load balancer:

```
DNS-NAME LoadBal-79377590.us-east-1.elb.amazonaws.com
```

At this point the load balancer is running. The next step is to have it manage the EC2 instance. Here's all you need to do (replace the instance ID with your own):

```
$ elb-register-instances-with-lb LoadBal --instances i-0f414766
INSTANCE-ID  i-0f414766
```

Now take the host name of the load balancer and visit it in your browser. You should see the same output you saw when you used the name of the EC2 instance. In fact, visit that name once again to see that the load balancer avoids interfering with direct access to the instance.[15]

We've just set up the minimal load balancer configuration: one load balancer and one EC2 instance. If a single EC2 instance can handle your off-peak traffic, you can actually use the load balancer in this fashion. That way, you can easily place additional EC2 instances to deal with more traffic. Let's go ahead and see how to do that.

Create a second EC2 instance using the same AMI you used to create the first one, but create this one in Availability Zone us-east-1b. While you're waiting for it to start, go ahead and add the zone to the load balancer like this:

```
$ elb-enable-zones-for-lb LoadBal --availability-zones us-east-1b
AVAILABILITY_ZONES us-east-1b, us-east-1a
```

After the instance has started, edit its **/home/webuser/helloworld/htdocs/index.php** file to emit the message "PHP Information For Second Instance!" (or another exciting and distinctive phrase of your choice). Leave the SSH window to this instance running; you're going to need it again soon.

Add the instance to the load balancer, and Bob's your uncle:

```
$ elb-register-instances-with-lb LoadBal --instances i-c95650a0
INSTANCE-ID i-0f414766
INSTANCE-ID i-c95650a0
```

Refresh your browser once or twice and (if you're lucky) you should see the message from the second instance.

If you're out of luck and the message fails to change, there's no need to worry. The current version of the elastic load balancer provides no guarantee that successive requests from the same IP address or browser will be routed to the same EC2 instance, but this seems to happen more often than not. You could try to access the page from another computer or from your cell phone, or perhaps email the URL to a close friend and ask them what they see.

---

[15] On a production system you can remove entries from the appropriate security group to block direct external access to the instance on port 80.

So far, so good. One load balancer and a pair of instances. If one of the instances (or an instance's entire Availability Zone) were to fail, the load balancer would notice this and route all the traffic to the other instance. Let's make that happen!

Return to the SSH window connected to your first EC2 instance and shut down Apache:

```
<lb1>: /home/webuser/helloworld/bin/stop_apache
```

Refresh your browser a couple of times, pausing for a sip of a tasty beverage perhaps,[16] to allow time for the load balancer to detect that the instance is no longer passing its health check. Once this happens you'll see the web page from the other instance.

You can confirm that the load balancer is aware that the first instance is unhealthy with the elb-describe-instance-health command:

```
$ elb-describe-instance-health LoadBal --headers
INSTANCE-ID   INSTANCE-ID   STATE
INSTANCE-ID   i-c95650a0    InService
INSTANCE-ID   i-0f414766    OutOfService
```

Now start up Apache on the first instance:

```
<lb1>: /home/webuser/helloworld/bin/run_apache
```

Have another sip of your beverage and then check the instance health again:

```
$ elb-describe-instance-health LoadBal --headers
INSTANCE-ID   INSTANCE-ID   STATE
INSTANCE-ID   i-c95650a0    InService
INSTANCE-ID   i-0f414766    InService
```

Recall that the elastic load balancer uses a health check to ascertain the state of each instance. The default health check has some fairly long delays and also checks three times before deciding that an instance is unhealthy. Let's be more aggressive:

---

[16] The weather in Seattle is uncharacteristically warm as I write these words in the middle of the evening. I've consumed well over two liters of water today!

```
$ elb-configure-healthcheck LoadBal --target HTTP:80/ --interval 5
➡ --timeout 2 --healthy-threshold 2 --unhealthy-threshold 2
HEALTH-CHECK  HTTP:80/  5  2  2  2
```

This command changes the interval from the default (30 seconds) to the minimum (five seconds). It also reduces the HealthyThreshold from three to two and does the same for the UnhealthyThreshold. We'll increase the number of health checks sixfold, but the load balancer will be able to detect and respond to changes that much quicker as a result of the changes to the interval and the thresholds.

After making this change, spend some time starting and stopping Apache; you'll observe that the load balancer is now more responsive to changes in the health of the instances.

As I mentioned before, the load balancers automatically report their statistics to CloudWatch. You can use the mon-list-metrics command to view the available metrics—they'll have the AWS/ELB namespace. You'll find the following metrics: HealthyHostCount, Latency, RequestCount, and UnHealthyHostCount.

Here's an example of how to obtain the average and maximum latency for requests handled by the load balancer:

```
$ mon-get-stats Latency --namespace "AWS/ELB" --period 3600
➡ --start-time 2009-07-22 --statistics Average,Maximum
```

Once you're done testing and experimenting shut down all your test instances, either from the AWS Management Console or by means of the halt command.

You can verify that the load balancer has noticed the missing instances by checking the instance health one last time:

```
$ elb-describe-instance-health LoadBal --headers
INSTANCE-ID  INSTANCE-ID  STATE
INSTANCE-ID  i-c95650a0   OutOfService
INSTANCE-ID  i-0f414766   OutOfService
```

Wrap up by deleting the load balancer:

```
$ elb-delete-lb LoadBal
```

You'll be asked to confirm your intention to delete the load balancer.

Programming Elastic Load Balancing

As is the case with all the Amazon Web Services, you can access the elastic load balancing functionality through the programming interface.

Unfortunately, however, CloudFusion does not currently (as of version 2.5) include support for elastic load balancing.

That said, it's possible to add support by creating a new class patterned after the EC2 class. The details on how this would be done are beyond the scope of this book, but should you be interested in trying your hand at this task, you'll need some basic information: the DEFAULT_URL is elasticloadbalancing.amazonaws.com and the API version is 2009-05-15.

There are nine elastic load balancing API calls:

CreateLoadBalancer creates new load balancers and DeleteLoadBalancer deletes old ones. ConfigureHealthCheck sets up a non-default health check that will be used for all the instances.

RegisterInstancesWithLoadBalancer attaches a list of EC2 instances to a load balancer and DeregisterInstancesFromLoadBalancer does the opposite.

DescribeLoadBalancers returns detailed information about each extant load balancer and DescribeInstanceHealth returns the health of all or selected EC2 instances.

EnableAvailabilityZonesForLoadBalancer allows the load balancer to access instances in additional Availability Zones, while the opposite is achieved with DisableAvailabilityZonesForLoadBalancer.

Now that you know how to create, monitor, and destroy elastic load balancers with some simple commands, you're one big step closer to creating highly scalable and available applications.

Auto Scaling

In this section you'll learn about Amazon EC2's Auto Scaling feature. We'll review key terminology and concepts, address pricing, and then we'll put the service through its paces using the command line tools. We'll review the programming model, once again leaving the actual code up to you.

Auto Scaling Concepts

You can create auto scaling groups in any EC2 region using EC2's auto scaling feature. Each auto scaling group has a reference name and can span one or more Availability Zones. An auto scaling group relies on a launch configuration to provide the information needed to launch EC2 instances. A trigger attached to the group supplies the information needed to initiate a scaling activity. A **scaling activity** is generated each time an auto scaling group launches or terminates EC2 instances. Instances are added as part of a **scale-out event** and terminated as part of a **scale-in event**. Each group also has a minimum size and a maximum size.

An **Auto Scaling launch configuration** includes an AMI ID, the name of an EC2 key pair, a list of EC2 security groups, an EC2 instance type, and other information needed to launch EC2 instances as needed.

An auto scaling trigger references a CloudWatch metric such as EC2 `CPUUtilization` or elastic load balancing `HealthyHostCount`. The trigger also includes upper and lower threshold values and scaling increments. The scaling increments can be absolute ("add 1 more instance") or relative ("add 50% more instances"). The trigger's breach duration specifies the time period over which the trigger's thresholds are evaluated against the metrics.

Auto Scaling Processing Model

Although auto scaling is independent of elastic load balancing, the two features were designed to work hand-in-glove to allow you to easily load balance large numbers of requests across an automatically scaled cluster of EC2 instances. Once everything is set up, you can simply route all your traffic to the load balancer and AWS will take care of the rest.

The auto scaling processing model is clean and easy to understand. To make a start, create the following:

1. an elastic load balancer for one or more Availability Zones

2. a launch configuration, specifying the ID of the AMI to be launched, the instance type, and other sought parameters

3. an auto scaling group for the desired set of Availability Zones, supplying the names of the load balancer and the launch configuration, the desired minimum and maximum size of each group, and a reference name for the group

4. a trigger for the group

Then sit back and relax as the auto scaling process ensures that you have sufficient EC2 instances in place to meet your application's requirements, as expressed in the group size and in the trigger.

Once an auto scaling group is up and running, it operates as follows:

1. The CloudWatch metrics specified in the group's trigger are retrieved using the parameters (`Namespace`, `Dimension`, `Measure`, `Statistic`, and `Unit`) for a time range that extends back in time by the trigger's `BreachDuration` value.

2. The metrics are checked against the trigger's thresholds. If the metrics are larger than the `UpperThreshold`, and the number of EC2 instances in the group is less than the `MaxSize`, a scale-out event is initiated. One or more EC2 instances is launched using the group's launch configuration parameters. The number of instances launched depends on the trigger's `UpperBreachScaleIncrement`. If the value of this parameter ends with a percent sign ("%") then sufficient instances are launched to raise the total number in the group by that percentage. Otherwise, the value is used as the actual number of instances to launch. New instances are automatically added to the load balancer (if any) associated with the group.

In similar fashion, if the metric is smaller than the `LowerThreshold`, and the number of instances in the group is more than `MinSize`, a scale-in event is initiated. One or more EC2 instances are terminated, again using the parameters from the group's launch configuration. The number of instances terminated depends on the trigger's `LowerBreachScaleIncrement`, which can be a percentage value or a number. In either case the numeric value should be negative. The excess instances are removed from the load balancer (if any) before they're terminated.

After a scale-in or scale-out event, no further automatic scaling actions will be triggered until after the group's cool-down period has passed. All the scale-in and scale-out events are logged and can be retrieved for later analysis.

In most cases you'll configure the trigger to use minimum or maximum values as the basis for scaling decisions. Here are some examples:

Namespace	Metric	Statistic
AWS/EC2	CPUUtilization	Average

Scale up or scale down when the average CPU utilization (across all the instances in the group) exceeds `UpperThreshold`. Scale down when it is less than `Lower-Threshold`.

Namespace	Metric	Statistic
AWS/EC2	NetworkIn	Maximum

Scale up when the incoming network traffic exceeds `UpperThreshold`. Scale down when it is less than `LowerThreshold`.

Namespace	Metric	Statistic
AWS/ELB	HealthyHostCount	Minimum

Scale down when the number of healthy hosts exceeds `UpperThreshold`. Scale up when the number of healthy hosts is less than `LowerThreshold`.[17]

You can also create an auto scale group without a trigger. In this case the group will start out by creating enough EC2 instances to reach the minimum number specified for the group. You can increase the instance count programmatically at any time using the `SetDesiredCapacity` function or the `as-set-desired-capacity` command.

There are a couple of important aspects to this model that you need to take into account as you consider ways to put elastic load balancing to use in your application:

- The EC2 instances are run as needed and are immediately put into service. Therefore, the specified AMI is responsible for all startup chores, including the ones that you sometimes do manually in more traditional environments. Put a different way, there's no opportunity for you to log in to the newly launched instances and tweak them between the time they're launched and put into service.

---

[17] In order to implement this behavior, the `UpperBreachScaleIncrement` must be a negative value and the `LowerBreachScaleIncrement` must be a negative value.

■ The EC2 instances are shut down when they are no longer needed and any information stored on them is lost, including log files. If you need to retain log files, you should use an elastic block storage volume.

Auto Scaling Pricing

There is no charge for the use of this feature. EC2 usage is charged at the standard rates. Because the auto scaling groups are launching instances per your rules, you should pay close attention to your "burn rate" for the first hours and days to make sure that the overall cost is in line with your expectations.

Auto Scaling in Operation

In this section we'll set up a load balancer, named `LoadBal`, and an auto scaling group. The first step is to create a load balancer:

```
$ elb-create-lb LoadBal --listener "lb-port=80,instance-port=80,
➡protocol=HTTP" --availability-zones us-east-1b
DNS-NAME   LoadBal-1395306781.us-east-1.elb.amazonaws.com
```

As we saw earlier in this chapter, this command returns the host name of the load balancer—in this case LoadBal-1395306781.us-east-1.elb.amazonaws.com.

The next step is to create an auto scaling group launch configuration:

```
$ as-create-launch-config Config --image-id ami-60da3d09
➡ --instance-type m1.small
OK-Created launch config
```

This configuration, named `Config`, specifies the use of the LAMP Web Starter AMI on a small EC2 instance. This AMI is ideal for testing purposes because it's preconfigured to launch Apache and return a default page.

Now we're ready to create the auto scaling group. Here's all it takes:

```
$ as-create-auto-scaling-group AutoScale --launch-configuration
➡ Config --availability-zones us-east-1b --min-size 1 --max-size 5
➡ --load-balancers LoadBal
OK-Created AutoScalingGroup
```

The group, called `AutoScale`, references the load balancer (`LoadBal`) and the launch configuration (`Config`). It'll run up to five instances in Availability Zone `us-east-1b`. Now we need a trigger. Here's the command to create a trigger named `Trigger1`:

```
$ as-create-or-update-trigger Trigger1 --auto-scaling-group
➥ AutoScale --namespace "AWS/EC2" --measure CPUUtilization
➥ --statistic Average --dimensions "AutoScalingGroupName=AutoScale"
➥ --units "Percent" --period 60 --lower-threshold 30
➥ --upper-threshold 70 --lower-breach-increment"=-1"
➥ --upper-breach-increment "1" --breach-duration 120
OK-Created/Updated trigger
```

That's a fairly long command, so let's break it down. It's driven by the EC2 metric `CPUUtilization`. It will initiate a scale-out action when average CPU utilization for the set of EC2 instances in the group exceeds 70% over a two-minute interval. It will initiate a scale-in operation when the average CPU utilization falls below 30%, also over a two-minute interval. It will add one new instance on scale-out and remove one instance on scale-in.

Once the trigger has been set, the group becomes active. Here's how to see what's happening:

```
$ as-describe-scaling-activities AutoScale
ACTIVITY    a479869e-14d8-4b02-98f5-33e9a8b7afda    2009-07-25T04:53:33Z
➥ Successful   "At 2009-07-25 04:50:57Z a user request created an
➥ AutoScalingGroup changing the desired capacity from 0 to 1.
➥ At 2009-07-25 04:52:05Z an instance was started in response to a
➥ difference between desired and actual capacity, increasing the
➥ capacity from 0 to 1."
```

The `as-describe-scaling-activities` command displays the most recent scaling activities in reverse chronological order.

You should shut the group down cleanly once you're done with it. Here's how to do that. Start by deleting the trigger (you'll be asked to confirm):

```
$ as-delete-trigger Trigger1 --auto-scaling-group AutoScale
```

Next, set the minimum and maximum size of the group to zero to force all its instances to terminate:

```
$ as-update-auto-scaling-group AutoScale --min-size 0 --max-size 0
```

Now, watch for a scaling activity that actually terminates the instances. Run this command:

```
$ as-describe-scaling-activities AutoScale
```

Run it a couple of times over the course of a minute or two, until you see an entry like this:

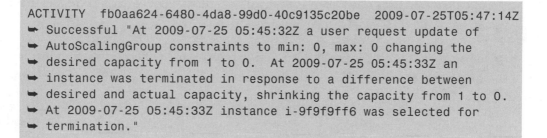

```
ACTIVITY   fb0aa624-6480-4da8-99d0-40c9135c20be   2009-07-25T05:47:14Z
➥ Successful "At 2009-07-25 05:45:32Z a user request update of
➥ AutoScalingGroup constraints to min: 0, max: 0 changing the
➥ desired capacity from 1 to 0.  At 2009-07-25 05:45:33Z an
➥ instance was terminated in response to a difference between
➥ desired and actual capacity, shrinking the capacity from 1 to 0.
➥ At 2009-07-25 05:45:33Z instance i-9f9f9ff6 was selected for
➥ termination."
```

Now you can go ahead and delete the group (as usual, you'll be asked to confirm):

```
$ as-delete-auto-scaling-group AutoScale
```

Finally, delete the load balancer:

```
$ elb-delete-lb LoadBal
```

And we're done!

Programming Auto Scaling

As is always the case with AWS, all the auto scaling functionality is available through a set of APIs. Unfortunately, as with ELB, CloudFusion currently does not provide support for auto scaling.

Again, if you want to add support for this feature to CloudFusion, you'll need some basic information: the DEFAULT_URL is autoscaling.amazonaws.com and the API version is 2009-05-15.

The Auto Scaling API consists of five groups of functions:

- The `CreateAutoScalingGroup`, `DeleteAutoScalingGroup`, `DescribeAutoScalingGroups`, `SetDesiredCapacity`, and `UpdateAutoScalingGroup` functions operate on auto scaling groups; the operations should be self-evident from the names. The update function allows you to change the group's parameters while it's operational.

- The `CreateLaunchConfiguration`, `DeleteLaunchConfiguration`, and `DescribeLaunchConfigurations` functions operate on launch configurations.

- The `CreateOrUpdateScalingTrigger` is used to create a new scaling trigger or to update an existing one. `DescribeTriggers` returns a list of triggers for an auto scale group, and `DeleteTrigger` deletes a trigger.

- The `DescribeScalingActivities` function returns a list of scaling activities for an auto scale group.

- The `TerminateInstanceInAutoScaleGroup` explicitly terminates an instance.

Off the Scale

And with that, we are done with our description of Amazon EC2's Auto Scaling. You have all the information to start utilizing this feature in your own applications.

Wrapping It Up

We've covered a lot of ground in this chapter! We started out by taking a look at Amazon CloudWatch, and saw how to interact with it using CloudFusion. We then took a short (but worthwhile) detour to learn how to create an artificial load on your system using JMeter. From there we examined the Elastic Load Balancing and Auto Scaling features.

Now that you have a good understanding of these features, you should be able to create applications that are both scalable and fault-tolerant.

Chapter

Amazon SimpleDB: A Cloud Database

In this chapter you'll discover how to use Amazon SimpleDB to store data for your application. Amazon SimpleDB is a refreshingly simple alternative to the traditional (and very complex) relational database. We'll review the conceptual basis behind Amazon SimpleDB, then learn how to use it with a number of self-contained code samples and a more complex real-world example. We'll finish with a quick look at a browser-based tool for SimpleDB.

Introduction

Many web applications would use a general purpose relational database such as Oracle or MySQL to store user data: account names, passwords, file lists, preferences, links, and so forth. Because they're general purpose, these products have become very complex over time, with thousands of pages of documentations, layers of libraries and tools, and an entire industry devoted to training and support.

Amazon SimpleDB is a cloud-based database. There's no need to buy, install, or maintain any hardware or configure any software. You only spend half the time designing the database schema ahead of schedule because changes are easy to make and there's no requirement to take the database offline to do so.

Building a highly scalable system and then actually scaling it becomes much simpler. SimpleDB itself makes sure that sufficient disk space and CPU power are available, automatically taking advantage of parallelism by spreading the load across multiple disks and servers as needed. This intrinsic, under-the-covers scaling and redundancy provides for fault tolerance and high availability without the need for monitoring or manual intervention.

The data storage model is clean, simple, and easy to learn, as is the programming model. SimpleDB excels at storing semi-structured data where the items (rows) are similar but not necessarily identical to each other.

All data stored in Amazon SimpleDB is automatically indexed, so you're free from having to make any indexing decisions. Your existing knowledge of SQL (Structured Query Language) will still be relevant; you can retrieve data using SQL select queries. There are no software upgrade issues, because you're always running the current version of the code.

The Amazon SimpleDB model lacks support for joins across domains (roughly equivalent to relational tables); instead, you can store data in non-normalized form for more efficient access.

As you'll soon see, Amazon SimpleDB's model supports the data storage needs of many types of applications. You can spend your time focusing on your application and on meeting the needs of your users, instead of worrying about low-level database issues.

Amazon SimpleDB

The Amazon SimpleDB model encompasses a small number of concepts and a compact programming interface. You can learn the basics of SimpleDB and have some code up and running in an hour or two. In this section, we'll review the concepts that comprise SimpleDB, take a peek at the programming model, and then examine the SimpleDB pricing model.

Amazon SimpleDB Concepts

An Amazon SimpleDB **domain** is roughly analogous to a table in a relational database. Each domain exists within the scope of a particular AWS account and has a readable name, such as `employees` or `feeds`. Each domain can store up to 10GB of data. Applications with a need to store more than ten gigabytes can easily spread the data across multiple domains. Each AWS account is allotted 100 domains.[1]

Each item in a SimpleDB domain has a name (unique to the domain) and up to 256 **attributes** (name-value pairs). Item names, attribute names, and attribute values can each be up to 1,024 bytes long. Each domain can store up to one billion attributes.

Item attributes can be multivalued. In fact, each attribute can have up to 256 values. For example, the attribute `Size` could be three distinct values `"8"`, `"10"`, and `"12"`. Each value in an attribute counts toward the limit of 256 attributes per item. All attribute values are treated as strings. This has some important and less obvious implications when storing and querying numerical values. All values are automatically indexed.

Inserts, deletes, and updates to SimpleDB items are done using the API. Queries are done using SQL select queries through the API.

Let's take a look at some of the ways that SimpleDB's data model can be used to store complex data sets in a single domain.

Imagine that we need to store data about some people (I'll refer to this as the `People` domain in the SQL examples below). We start off with a simple model like this:

Item Name	FirstName	LastName	Age	Sex
Rec1	Tom	Basic	12	M
Rec2	Nancy	Hacker	15	F

Later, we decide to store middle names if known. We start storing this attribute for newly added records:

Item Name	FirstName	LastName	Age	Sex	Middle
Rec1	Tom	Basic	12	M	
Rec2	Nancy	Hacker	15	F	
Rec3	Joan	Hughes	44	F	K

---

[1] You can request additional domains if you require more than 100 for your application.

There's no need to update records Rec1 and Rec2 (but this can be done, of course). The attribute Middle simply doesn't exist for those records. Next, we decide to store the states where each person has lived. Again, we just start storing this new attribute:

Item Name	FirstName	LastName	Age	Sex	Middle	State
Rec1	Tom	Basic	12	M		
Rec2	Nancy	Hacker	15	F		MD
Rec3	Joan	Hughes	44	F	Kraft	NY, NJ, DC, IL, MD, PA

As you can see, this could easily be extended to store other one-to-many relationships such as children, parents, job titles, and so forth.

Amazon SimpleDB Programming Model

We'll dive into some real code shortly. The Amazon SimpleDB programming model consists of just nine calls:

■ At the domain level, CreateDomain creates a new domain, ListDomains returns a list of existing domains, and DeleteDomain deletes a domain. DomainMetadata returns usage information about the domain.

■ At the item level, PutAttributes creates new items and adds or replaces (your choice) additional attributes to existing items. BatchPutAttributes is an extended version of this call that handles multiple items at once. DeleteAttributes removes attributes from an item and GetAttributes retrieve specified attributes. Select issues a SQL query.

And that's it! A complete data storage system.

Amazon SimpleDB's SQL language takes the form of a standard select statement with extensions to handle multi-valued attributes. Here are some samples:

```
select * from People where FirstName="Tom"
```

The above query would retrieve Rec1 in the previous table.

```
select FirstName,Middle,LastName from People where LastName >= "H"
```

The above query retrieves `Rec2` and `Rec3`.

```
select * from People where every(State)="MD"
```

While this query retrieves `Rec2`.

```
select * from People where State="PA"
```

And here, `Rec3` is retrieved.

Amazon SimpleDB Pricing

Your Amazon SimpleDB usage is charged based on three usage dimensions: data transfer, data storage, and machine utilization.

Your data transfer charges are based on the amount of data transferred in and out of SimpleDB. Data transferred into SimpleDB is charged at a rate of $0.10 per gigabyte. Once again, this amount is prorated. Data transferred out of SimpleDB is charged on a sliding scale starting at $0.17 per gigabyte and reduces based on volume, reaching $0.10 per gigabyte for all outgoing data transfer in excess of 150 terabytes per month. There's no charge for data transferred within a Region; you pay nothing to transfer data between an EC2 instance and a SimpleDB domain in the same Region.

You pay $0.25 (a quarter) per gigabyte per month to store data in SimpleDB, prorated on time and on the actual amount stored. There's an overhead of 45 bytes per item, 45 bytes per attribute name, and 45 bytes per name-value pair.

Finally, you pay $0.14 per hour for the machine time used to process each SimpleDB request. Complex requests (for instance, more items, more attributes, or sophisticated select queries) will take more time than simple ones. SimpleDB returns the time used by each request in the `BoxUsage` field.

As of this writing (but subject to change), there's a free tier of usage for SimpleDB. The first 25 hours of machine time, the first gigabyte of data storage, and the first gigabyte of data transfer are all free.

Programming Amazon SimpleDB

In this section you'll see how you can use CloudFusion to access all of SimpleDB's functionality. Because CloudFusion already includes support for Amazon SimpleDB, we'll be able to jump right into the code.

We'll create domains and list them, then populate them with items. Then we'll see how to deal with numeric data and run some queries. We'll update existing items with additional data, and then delete some items and item attributes. We'll see how to monitor domain statistics and then wrap up with a real-world example: fetching, parsing, and storing RSS feeds in SimpleDB.

I will be using three SimpleDB domains in this chapter. Here are the definitions we'll add to **book.inc.php**:

chapter_08/include/book.inc.php (excerpt)

```
define('BOOK_FILE_DOMAIN', 'files');
define('BOOK_FEED_DOMAIN', 'feeds');
define('BOOK_FEED_ITEM_DOMAIN', 'feed_items');
```

BOOK_FILE_DOMAIN will be used to store information about files.

BOOK_FEED_DOMAIN will be used to store information about RSS feeds, and

BOOK_FEED_ITEM_DOMAIN will be used to store information about the items found in the RSS feeds.

You'll need to sign up for SimpleDB[2] before you begin to use it. Simply visit the site and click on the **Sign Up for Amazon SimpleDB** button.

---

[2] http://aws.amazon.com/simpledb/

Creating a Domain

Here's a script that creates all the SimpleDB domains needed for the examples in this chapter:

```
                                          chapter_08/create_domain.php (excerpt)

#!/usr/bin/php
<?php

error_reporting(E_ALL);

require_once('cloudfusion.class.php');
require_once('include/book.inc.php');

$sdb = new AmazonSDB();

foreach (array(BOOK_FILE_DOMAIN,
    BOOK_FEED_DOMAIN,
    BOOK_FEED_ITEM_DOMAIN) as $domain)
{
  $res = $sdb->create_domain($domain);
  if (!$res->isOK())
  {
    exit("Create domain operation failed for domain ${domain}\n");
  }

  print("Domain ${domain} created.\n");
}
exit(0);
?>
```

The program simply creates a new AmazonSDB object, iterates through an array of domain names, and calls the create_domain method for each one. create_domain will do nothing (and return a successful result) if the domain already exists.

If you'd like a challenge, you should easily be able to modify the above script to accept new domain names on the command line.

Listing Domains

The next step is to list the domains. Here's how to do that:

chapter_08/list_domains.php *(excerpt)*

```php
#!/usr/bin/php
<?php

error_reporting(E_ALL);

require_once('cloudfusion.class.php');

$sdb = new AmazonSDB();
$res = $sdb->list_domains();

if (!$res->isOK())
{
  exit("List domain operation failed\n");
}

foreach ($res->body->ListDomainsResult->DomainName as $domainName)
{
  print($domainName . "\n");
}
exit(0);
?>
```

The `list_domains` method returns an array of domain names. The code iterates through the list and prints each one.

Here's the output from the command:

```
$ php list_domains.php
feed_items
feeds
files
```

Storing Data

The next step is to store some data in a domain. This is done using the `put_attributes` method. This method can be used to create new items or to add additional attributes to existing items.

The following program creates an item for each file in the current directory with a name that matches the regular expression /^[a-zA-ZO-9_-]*\.php$/—all the PHP files with reasonable names. It uses the file's name as the item name and creates three attributes:

- Name (the file's name)
- Hash (the MD5 hash of the file's contents)
- Size (the size of the file in bytes)

Here's the code:

```
                                        chapter_08/insert_items.php (excerpt)
#!/usr/bin/php
<?php

error_reporting(E_ALL);

require_once('cloudfusion.class.php');
require_once('include/book.inc.php');

$sdb = new AmazonSDB();

$dir = opendir(".");
while (($file = readdir($dir)) !== false) ❶
{
  if (preg_match("/^[a-zA-ZO-9_-]*\.php$/", $file)) ❷
  {
    $data = file_get_contents($file); ❸
    $hash = md5($data);
    $size = filesize($file);

    $attrs = array('Name' => $file,
        'Hash' => $hash,
        'Size' => $size);

    $res = $sdb->put_attributes(BOOK_FILE_DOMAIN, $file,
        $attrs, true); ❹

    if ($res->isOK())
    {
      print("Inserted item $file\n");
    }
    else
```

```
    {
      $error = $res->body->Errors->Error->Message;
      print("Could not insert item: ${error}\n");
    }
  }
}
closedir($dir); 5
exit(0);
?>
```

1 PHP's opendir and readdir are used to access the list of files in the current
directory (".").

2 Each file's name is read and checked against the regular expression.

3 If the file's name matches the regular expression, the file's contents are read
using file_get_contents, and then the MD5 hash of the contents is computed
using the md5 function. With this information in hand, the $attrs array is set
up with the name-value pairs of attributes.

4 The put_attributes method is called to store the information in the SimpleDB
domain denoted by BOOK_FILE_DOMAIN. The final parameter (*true*) in the call
to put_attributes indicates that any existing values for an attribute will be
removed and then replaced with the new ones. If this parameter is set to *false*
the new values will augment the existing ones, resulting in an attribute that's
multivalued.

5 Finally, we close the directory and exit the script.

Storing Multiple Items Efficiently

Another SimpleDB function, BatchPutAttributes, can be used to perform multiple
PutAttributes calls with a single request. This can be faster and more efficient
than making a long series of individual requests. Here's a modified version of the
previous example that uses the batch requests:

chapter_08/batch_insert_items.php *(excerpt)*

```php
#!/usr/bin/php
<?php

error_reporting(E_ALL);

require_once('cloudfusion.class.php');
require_once('include/book.inc.php');

$sdb = new AmazonSDB();

$items = array();

$dir = opendir(".");
while (($file = readdir($dir)) !== false)
{
  if (preg_match("/^[a-zA-Z0-9_-]*\.php$/", $file))
  {
    $data = file_get_contents($file);
    $hash = md5($data);
    $size = filesize($file);

    $items[$file] = array('Name' => $file, ❶
                          'Hash' => $hash,
                          'Size' => $size);
  }

  if (count($items) == 25) ❷
  {
    WriteBatch($sdb, $items);
    $items = array();
  }
}
closedir($dir);

if (count($items) > 0) ❸
{
  WriteBatch($sdb, $items);
}
```

❶   The main difference between this and the previous version of the insert script
     is that each array of attribute name-value pairs is added to an $items array,
     instead of immediately being inserted into SimpleDB.

When the `$items` array reaches 25 elements, we call a custom function called WriteBatch.

 Finally, we call the WriteBatch function if there are any remaining items.

Here's the custom WriteBatch function:

```
                                    chapter_08/batch_insert_items.php (excerpt)

function WriteBatch($sdb, &$items)
{
  $res = $sdb->batch_put_attributes(BOOK_FILE_DOMAIN, $items, true);

  if ($res->isOK())
  {
    print("Inserted " . count($items) . " items\n");
    return true;
  }
  else
  {
    $error = $res->body->Errors->Error->Message;
    print("Could not insert items: ${error}\n");
    return false;
  }
}
?>
```

The WriteBatch function uses the `batch_put_attributes` method to insert all the items in the `$items` array in one operation.

When doing performance testing, I found that the first insert script inserts 99 files in 8.6 seconds, while the batch script inserts the same files in just 0.88 seconds, or ten times faster. Structuring your program to take advantage of SimpleDB is clearly worthwhile.

Handling Numeric Data

SimpleDB stores all data as strings. When the data is the subject of a select query, a lexicographic comparison is used. This can lead to some surprising results when numerical values are stored. For example, the string `"10"` is less than the string `"2"`. Leading minus signs are also problematic.

Numeric values should be left-padded with zeros to create fixed-length strings. This can be done using PHP's `sprintf` function and an appropriate format string. In our previous scripts, we should update the item value for the `Size` attribute to use left-padding:

```
array('Name' => $file,
      'Hash' => $hash,
      'Size' => sprintf("%08s", $size));
```

If your numeric values can be negative, you should offset them by a large positive number when you store them, and then compensate for this offset when you retrieve them. Choose an offset value that ensures the smallest expected negative value will end up as a positive value. For example, if your values will range from -32,768 to 32,767, add 50,000 to adjust the range to 17,232 to 82,767 (stored as `"17232"` through `"82767"`).

Running a Query

With the data stored, running queries is simple:

chapter_08/query_domain.php *(excerpt)*

```php
#!/usr/bin/php
<?php

error_reporting(E_ALL);

require_once('cloudfusion.class.php');
require_once('include/book.inc.php');

$query = "select * from " .
         BOOK_FILE_DOMAIN .
         " where Name like '%items%'";

$sdb = new AmazonSDB();
```

```
$res = $sdb->select($query);

if (!$res->isOK())
{
  exit("Select operation failed\n");
}

foreach ($res->body->SelectResult->Item as $item)
{
  foreach ($item->Attribute as $attribute)
  {
    print($attribute->Name . ": " . $attribute->Value . ", ");
  }
  print("\n");
}
exit(0);
?>
```

The above script uses the `select` method to run a query that will return all items with a `Name` attribute containing the string `"items"`. It'll then loop through all the returned items and output their attributes and values. Here's an example of the output if the database contained file information about all the files in the **chapter_08** folder from the code archive:

```
$ php query_domain.php
Hash: a446a0c1d252042cf065e7bc4d743336, Name:
➥ augment_items.php, Size: 00001191,
Hash: 280434b0478b68aecacef61e329d337e, Name:
➥ batch_insert_items.php, Size: 00001337,
Hash: 49cb20ea103caeb654ce4aad307ecdcd, Name:
➥ delete_items.php, Size: 00001003,
Hash: e77f57f95676ac156318123c4e428c40, Name:
➥ insert_items.php, Size: 00000937,
```

By default, the `select` call returns 100 items (or 1MB worth, whichever is smaller) at a time. The `limit` clause can be used to request the return of up to 2,500 items, although this is still limited to 1MB.

If a `select` call has failed to return all the items due to these limits, a `NextToken` value will be included in the response. This can be passed to subsequent, repeated calls to `select` to receive additional results. Here's a hypothetical representation of a loop that takes advantage of the `NextToken` value to make repeated `select` calls until there are no more results returned:

```
$next = null;
do
{
  $attrs = ($next == null) ? null : array('NextToken' => $next);
  $res   = $sdb->select($query, $attrs);
  $next  = (string) $res->body->SelectResult->NextToken;

  : Process results here…
}
while ($next != null);
```

We'll see more of this kind of loop in the remaining chapters.

Advanced Queries

Let's alter the previous script so that the query comes from the command line by adding the following code:

chapter_08/query_domain_cmd.php *(excerpt)*

```
#!/usr/bin/php
<?php

error_reporting(E_ALL);

require_once('cloudfusion.class.php');
require_once('include/book.inc.php');

$query = "select * from " . BOOK_FILE_DOMAIN;

if ($argc > 1)
{
  $query .= " where ";

  for ($i = 1; $i < $argc; $i++)
  {
    $query .= ' ' . $argv[$i] . ' ';
  }
}

print("Final query: ${query}\n");
```

```
$sdb = new AmazonSDB();
$res = $sdb->select($query);

: process the results...


?>
```

Now we can run arbitrary queries, like so:

```
$ php query_domain_cmd.php
```

The above command will retrieve all the records—the default action for this script.

We specify a query like so:

```
$ php query_domain_cmd.php "Size < '00000900'"
```

This command will find all files smaller than 900 bytes.

The special field `itemName()` can be used to refer to the item's name in a select query:

```
$ php query_domain_cmd.php "itemName() like '%items%'"
```

The above command will retrieve items with names containing `"items"`.

And finally, this command is used to retrieve items with the specified names:

```
$ php query_domain_cmd.php "itemName() in
➥('disable_mon.php', 'list_metrics.php')"
```

SimpleDB queries have the following general form:

```
select output_list
from domain_name
[where expression]
[order by clause]
[limit clause]
```

Let's take a look at these. The *output_list* can be * for all attributes, itemName() for the name of the item, or a list of attribute names, or count(*) to retrieve an item count instead of items. The *domain_name* refers to the SimpleDB domain, of course.

The optional where expressions are a combination of attribute names, constant values, itemName(), and operators. The following table shows the operators that can be used in the where expression.

Table 8.1. Available Operators

Operator	Description
=	Equal to
!=	Not equal to
>	Greater than
>=	Greater than or equal to
<	Less than
<=	Less than or equal to
and	Both conditions must be true
or	Either condition can be true
intersection	Returns results that appear in a pair of independent queries
like	Contains the specified constant, with "%" as a wildcard
not like	Does not contain the specified constant
between/and	In a specified range
in	Matches an item from a list
is null	Attribute does not exist
is not null	Attribute exists
every()	Every value of a multi-valued attribute satisfies the expression

The optional order by clause can be used to order the results by a single attribute or item name. All sorts are performed in lexicographical order and the sort attribute must be mentioned by name in the associated expression. It's impossible to sort against null values.

The optional limit clause can be used to limit the number of results to a given value.

Augmenting Items with Additional Data

Once an item has been created, additional calls to the `put_attributes` method can be used to create additional attributes or additional values for an existing attribute. Let's augment each item in the `BOOK_FILE_DOMAIN` with the file's modification time using this script:

chapter_08/augment_items.php (excerpt)

```php
#!/usr/bin/php
<?php

error_reporting(E_ALL);

require_once('cloudfusion.class.php');
require_once('include/book.inc.php');

$sdb = new AmazonSDB();
$res1 = $sdb->select("select Name from " . BOOK_FILE_DOMAIN);

if ($res1->isOK())
{
  foreach ($res1->body->SelectResult->Item as $item)
  {
    $itemName = $item->Name;
    $file     = $item->Attribute[0]->Value;

    $modTime = filemtime($file);
    if ($modTime !== false)
    {
      $attrs = array('ModTime' => sprintf("%010s", $modTime));

      $res2 = $sdb->put_attributes(BOOK_FILE_DOMAIN, $itemName,
          $attrs, false);

      if ($res2->isOK())
      {
        print("Updated item $itemName\n");
      }
    else
    {
      $error = $res2->body->Errors->Error->Message;
      print("Could not update item: ${error}\n");
    }
```

```
    }
  }
}
else
 {
  $error = $res1->body->Errors->Error->Message;
  exit("Could not run query: ${error}\n");
}
exit(0);
?>
```

It's as simple as calling the `put_attributes` method again for each item supplying the new attribute and value data.

This program illustrates another useful programming model. A SimpleDB query is used to obtain the list of items to be processed. Each item is processed in turn: the file name is extracted from the query results, the file's modification time is fetched, and the item is updated.

The code I just showed you took one slightly choosy shortcut:

```
$file = $item->Attribute[0]->Value;
```

The above line accesses the first returned attribute using a positional index. Code like this is fragile and hard to maintain. There's a better way to do this, and I'll show you what it is in just a minute.

Storing Multiple Values for an Attribute

Storing multiple values for a single attribute is very easy; there are two ways to do this.

If you're storing the values one at a time and want them to accumulate over time, you can simply pass the value `false` for the *replace* parameter. You can store multiple modification times using the code from the last section, with repeated calls like so:

```
$attrs = array('ModTime' => sprintf("%010s", $modTime));
$res2 = $sdb->put_attributes(BOOK_FILE_DOMAIN, $itemName,
    $attrs, false);
```

You can store several values at the same time like this:

```
$attrs2 = array('Flavors' => array('Vanilla', 'Chocolate'));
$res2 = $sdb->put_attributes(BOOK_FILE_DOMAIN, $itemName,
    $attrs2, false);
```

Accessing Attribute Values

Let's improve on the cheesy attribute access code above. Here's a function to turn the array of SimpleXML nodes in the returned response into a PHP associative array:

chapter_08/include/book.inc.php *(excerpt)*

```
function getItemAttributes($item)
{
  $attrs = array();

  foreach ($item->Attribute as $attribute)
  {
    $name  = (string) $attribute->Name;
    $value = (string) $attribute->Value;

    if (IsSet($attrs[$name]))
    {
      if (is_array($attrs[$name]))
      {
        $attrs[$name][] = $value;
      }
      else
      {
        $attrs[$name] = array($attrs[$name], $value);
      }
    }
    else
    {
      $attrs[$name] = $value;
    }
  }
  return $attrs;
}
```

Here's what the returned data looks like:

```
Array
(
  [Hash] => c7158ad4d0961016fb3f531ccc90da5e
  [Size] => 00001535
  [Name] => query_domain_cmd.php
  [ModTime] => 1249514406
  [Flavors] => Array
  (
    [0] => Chocolate
    [1] => Vanilla
  )
)
```

Deleting Attributes

If you've no more need for an attribute, you can use the `delete_attributes` method
to delete it like this:

chapter_08/delete_attrs.php *(excerpt)*

```php
#!/usr/bin/php
<?php

error_reporting(E_ALL);

require_once('cloudfusion.class.php');
require_once('include/book.inc.php');

$sdb = new AmazonSDB();

$attrs = array('ModTime', 'Flavor');

$res1 = $sdb->select("select Name from " . BOOK_FILE_DOMAIN);
if ($res1->isOK())
{
  foreach ($res1->body->SelectResult->Item as $item)
  {
    $itemName = (string)$item->Name;

    $res2 = $sdb->delete_attributes(BOOK_FILE_DOMAIN,
        $itemName, $attrs);
```

```
    if ($res2->isOK())
    {
      print("Updated item $itemName\n");
    }
    else
    {
      $error = $res2->body->Errors->Error->Message;
      print("Could not update item: ${error}\n");
    }
  }
}
else
{
  $error = $res1->body->Errors->Error->Message;
  exit("Could not run query: ${error}\n");
}
exit(0);
?>
```

In the above code we delete the `ModTime`and `Flavor` attributes with one call to the `delete_attributes` method per item.

Deleting Items

You can also use the `delete_attributes` method to delete an entire item, by deleting all the attributes. Here's how to do it:

chapter_08/delete_items.php (excerpt)

```
#!/usr/bin/php
<?

error_reporting(E_ALL);

require_once('cloudfusion.class.php');
require_once('include/book.inc.php');

$sdb = new AmazonSDB();

$res1 = $sdb->select("select * from " . BOOK_FILE_DOMAIN);
if ($res1->isOK())
{
  foreach ($res1->body->SelectResult->Item as $item)
  {
```

```
    $itemName = (string)$item->Name;

    $attrs = array_keys(getItemAttributes($item));

    $res2 = $sdb->delete_attributes(BOOK_FILE_DOMAIN,
        $itemName, $attrs);

    if ($res2->isOK())
    {
      print("Deleted item $itemName\n");
    }
    else
    {
      $error = $res2->body->Errors->Error->Message;
      print("Could not delete item: ${error}\n");
    }
  }
}
else
{
  $error = $res1->body->Errors->Error->Message;
  exit("Could not run query: ${error}\n");
}
exit(0);
?>
```

The code constructs an array of each item's attributes using our `getItemAttributes` function, like this:

```
$attrs = array_keys(getItemAttributes($item));
```

The attributes are then deleted, causing the item itself to be deleted.

Monitoring Domain Statistics

The `domain_metadata` method returns information about a domain. Here's a script that calls the method and displays what it returns:

chapter_08/metadata.php (excerpt)

```
#!/usr/bin/php
<?php
```

```php
error_reporting(E_ALL);

require_once('cloudfusion.class.php');
require_once('include/book.inc.php');

$sdb = new AmazonSDB();

foreach (array(BOOK_FILE_DOMAIN,
          BOOK_FEED_DOMAIN,
          BOOK_FEED_ITEM_DOMAIN) as $domain)
{
  $res = $sdb->domain_metadata($domain);
  if ($res->isOK())
  {
    $metadata = $res->body->DomainMetadataResult;

    $itemCount           = (int) $metadata->ItemCount;
    $attributeNameCount  = (int) $metadata->AttributeNameCount;
    $attributeValueCount = (int) $metadata->AttributeValueCount;
    $itemNamesSize       = (int) $metadata->ItemNamesSizeBytes;
    $attributeNamesSize  = (int) $metadata->AttributeNamesSizeBytes;
    $attributeValuesSize =
        (int) $metadata->AttributeValuesSizeBytes;

    printf($domain . ":\n" .
      "\tItem Count:      " .
      number_format($itemCount)            . "\n" .
      "\tAttrs:           " .
      number_format($attributeNameCount)   . "\n" .
      "\tValues:          " .
      number_format($attributeValueCount)  . "\n" .
      "\tName Size:       " .
      number_format($itemNamesSize)        . "\n" .
      "\tAttr Name Size:  " .
      number_format($attributeNamesSize)   . "\n" .
      "\tAttr Value Size: " .
      number_format($attributeValuesSize)  . "\n" .
      "\n");
  }
}
exit(0);
?>
```

The script above fetches and then prints information about each domain used in this chapter's examples. The columns have the following meanings:

- Domain is the name of the domain, of course.
- Items is the number of items in the domain.
- Attrs is the number of unique attribute names in the domain.
- Values is the number of attribute name-value pairs in the domain.
- Name Size is the total size of all the item names in the domain, in bytes.
- Attr Name Size is the total size of all the unique attribute names in the domain, in bytes.
- Attr Value Size is the total size of all the attribute values in the domain, in bytes.

The sum of the last three values is the amount of storage used by the domain. Here's an example of the output:

```
$ php metadata.php
files:
   Item Count:       12
   Attrs:            3
   Values:           36
   Name Size:        201
   Attr Name Size:   12
   Attr Value Size:  681
```

Processing and Storing RSS Feeds with Amazon SimpleDB

Let's wrap up this chapter with a real-world example. SimpleDB is great for storing semi-structured data, where the items are similar to each other, but some variation exists at the detailed level.

In this section, the program will process a list of RSS feeds, typically representing blogs or another type of news or information source. Each feed is represented by a URL, such as http://www.jeff-barr.com/?feed=rss2. A feed starts out with some header data fields such as a title, a link, a publication date, and a description. Most of these fields are optional. The remainder of the feed is occupied by the individual news or blog items. Each one can have (among other things) a title, a link, a description, and a **GUID** (a globally unique identifier).

The program uses the Magpie RSS parser[3] open source library.

[3] http://magpierss.sourceforge.net/

To make the program more flexible, it will be able to obtain its list of feeds from one of two sources. The first source will be a file named **feeds.txt**. The file should have one feed URL per line. The second source will be an SQS queue identified by FEED_QUEUE. The code is going to store status information about each fetched feed, so we'll set up a couple of handy constants for status values. Let's add all these constants to our **book.inc.php** file:

```
chapter_08/include/book.inc.php (excerpt)

define('FEEDS', 'feeds.txt');
define('FEED_QUEUE', 'c_feed');

define('FEED_NO_FETCH', 'NoFetch');
define('FEED_YES_FETCH', 'Fetched');
```

Here's how the program starts out:

```
chapter_08/rss_process.php (excerpt)

#!/usr/bin/php
<?php

error_reporting(E_ALL);

require_once('cloudfusion.class.php');
require_once('include/book.inc.php');
require_once('include/rss_fetch.inc');

define('MAGPIE_CACHE_ON', 0);
```

The define statement turns off Magpie's cache of recently fetched feeds.

The first task is to determine whether the program will process the feed file (signified by the −f command line argument) or the queue (signified by the −q argument). Here's the code:

```
chapter_08/rss_process.php (excerpt)

$doFile  = false;
$doQueue = false;

if (($argc != 2) ||
    (($argv[1] != '-f') && ($argv[1] != '-q')))
```

```
{
  exit("Usage:\n".
      $argv[0] . " -f\n" .
      $argv[0] . " -q\n");
}

switch ($argv[1])
{
  case '-f':
    $doFile = true;
    break;

  case '-q':
    $doQueue = true;
    break;
}
```

The program will access SimpleDB and SQS, so we'll need to create access objects for both services:

chapter_08/rss_process.php (excerpt)

```
$sdb = new AmazonSDB();
$sqs = new AmazonSQS();
```

After each feed has been parsed, we'll store the most interesting fields. Here they are at the item and feed levels:

chapter_08/rss_process.php (excerpt)

```
$feedFields = array('link',
    'title',
    'pubdate',
    'tagline',
    'language',
    'generator',
    'description');

$itemFields = array('guid',
    'link',
    'title',
    'description');
```

Because none of the item fields are guaranteed to exist, we'll have to go to some effort to figure out which field can be used to form the item's unique key. We can set that up with a simple array:

chapter_08/rss_process.php *(excerpt)*

```php
$itemKeyFields = array('guid',
    'link',
    'title');
```

Now the code diverges into two parallel branches. The first branch deals with a file-based feed list:

chapter_08/rss_process.php *(excerpt)*

```php
if ($doFile)
{
  $urls = file(FEEDS);
  print("Begin processing " . count($urls) . " feeds\n");

  foreach ($urls as $url)
  {
    $url = trim($url);

    if (updateFeed($sdb, $url))
    {
      print($url . " - updated.\n");
    }
    else
    {
      print($url . " - not updated.\n");
    }
  }
}
```

The code simply extracts the list of feeds from the file and calls `updateFeed`, a custom function we'll write where most of the interesting work happens.

Here's the code to handle the queue-based feed list:

```
                                        chapter_08/rss_process.php (excerpt)

if ($doQueue)
{
  while (true)
  {
    $message = pullMessage($sqs, FEED_QUEUE);

    if ($message != null)
    {
      $messageDetail = $message['MessageDetail'];
      $receiptHandle = (string)$message['ReceiptHandle'];

      $url = $messageDetail['FeedURL'];

      if (updateFeed($sdb, $url))
      {
        print($url . " - updated.\n");
      }
      else
      {
        print($url . " - not updated.\n");
      }

      $sqs->delete_message(FEED_QUEUE, $receiptHandle);
    }
  }
}
```

This code uses the pullMessage function that we developed for our image crawler application in Chapter 6. Again, most of the interesting work happens in updateFeed. Let's take a look at it now. It's fairly long, so we'll examine it piece by piece.

The function starts by attempting to fetch the feed URL using the Magpie RSS parser:

```
                                        chapter_08/rss_process.php (excerpt)

function updateFeed($sdb, $url)
{
  global $stats;
  global $feedFields;
  global $itemFields;
```

```
global $itemKeyFields;

$rss = fetch_rss($url);
```

If the fetch succeeds, then BOOK_FEED_DOMAIN and BOOK_FEED_ITEM_DOMAIN will be updated. Before doing this, it's important to see if the fetch did succeed:

chapter_08/rss_process.php (excerpt)

```
if ($rss !== false)
{
```

The success case comes first. updateFeed builds up an attribute array for eventual storage into the domain using this code:

chapter_08/rss_process.php (excerpt)

```
$key = $url;
$attrs = array('feed_url' => $url,
    'fetch_date' => date('c'),
    'status' => FEED_YES_FETCH);

foreach ($feedFields as $field)
{
  if (IsSet($rss->channel[$field])
      && ($rss->channel[$field] != ''))
  {
    $attrs[$field] = $rss->channel[$field];
  }
}
```

The attribute array always has the feed's URL, the date of the fetch, and the status value. It also has any of the feed's fields that were listed in the $feedFields array and actually present in the parsed feed. Once this array has been built, it's a simple matter to store the item in SimpleDB:

chapter_08/rss_process.php (excerpt)

```
$res = $sdb->put_attributes(BOOK_FEED_DOMAIN, $key,
    $attrs, true);

if (!$res->isOK())
```

```
  {
    return false;
  }
```

The next task is to step through and process each of the individual items in the feed:

chapter_08/rss_process.php (excerpt)

```
foreach ($rss->items as $item)
{
```

Once again, the code extracts fields and constructs an attributes array, like this:

chapter_08/rss_process.php (excerpt)

```
$attrs = array();
foreach ($itemFields as $field)
{
  if (IsSet($item[$field]) && ($item[$field] != ''))
  {
    $attrs[$field] = $item[$field];
  }
}
```

The next step is to figure out a good unique key. Ideally, one of the fields in the $itemKeyFields array will exist, so we can use it:

chapter_08/rss_process.php (excerpt)

```
$itemKey = null;
foreach ($itemKeyFields as $field)
{
  if (IsSet($item[$field]) && ($item[$field] != ''))
  {
    $itemKey = $item[$field];
    break;
  }
}
```

If that fails to work, the MD5 hash of all the item's fields will have to do:

```
                                           chapter_08/rss_process.php (excerpt)
    if ($itemKey == null)
    {
      $all = '';
      foreach ($attrs as $key => $value)
      {
        $all .= $key . '_' . $value . '__';
      }
      $key = md5($all);
    }
```

Finally, the item is stored in SimpleDB:

```
                                           chapter_08/rss_process.php (excerpt)
    $res = $sdb->put_attributes(BOOK_FEED_ITEM_DOMAIN, $itemKey,
        $attrs, true);

    if (!$res->isOK())
    {
      return false;
    }
  }
  return true;
```

If the feed failed to be fetched or parsed, the following code will update its status:

```
                                           chapter_08/rss_process.php (excerpt)
  }
  else
  {
    $key   = $url;
    $attrs = array('feed_url'   => $url,
        'fetch_date' => date('c'),
        'status'     => FEED_NO_FETCH);

    $res = $sdb->put_attributes(BOOK_FEED_DOMAIN, $key,
        $attrs, true);

    if (!$res->isOK())
    {
      return false;        // We failed at failing!
```

```
    }

    return false;
  }
}
```

And that's all it takes to store variable RSS feed data in Amazon SimpleDB.

To make this program more useful, we need a script to stuff the queue with feeds. Here we go:

chapter_08/load_feed_urls.php *(excerpt)*

```php
#!/usr/bin/php
<?php

error_reporting(E_ALL);

require_once('cloudfusion.class.php');
require_once('include/book.inc.php');

if ($argc < 2)
{
  exit('Usage: ' . $argv[0] . " [URL] [-f FILE] ...\n");
}

$sqs = new AmazonSQS();

for ($i = 1; $i < $argc; $i++)
{
  if ($argv[$i] == '-f')
  {
    $urls = file($argv[++$i]);

    foreach ($urls as $url)
    {
      LoadURL($sqs, FEED_QUEUE, trim($url));
    }
  }
  else
  {
    LoadURL($sqs, $queue, $argv[i]);
  }
}
```

```php
function LoadURL($sqs, $queue, $url)
{

  $message  = json_encode(array('FeedURL' => $url));
  $res = $sqs->send_message($queue, $message);

  if ($res->isOK())
  {
    print("Posted '${message}' to queue '${queue}'\n");
  }
  else
  {
    $error = $res->body->Error->Message;
    print("Could not post message to queue: ${error}\n");
  }
}

?>
```

This program will stuff the FEED_QUEUE with URLs specified on the command line or in a file specified by −f and the file name. Here's how to process a file:

```
$ php load_feed_urls.php -f feeds.txt
```

And here's how to specify the feed URLs directly:

```
$ php load_feed_urls.php http://arden.blogs.com/swn/index.rdf
```

The best way to see this program in action is to host it on an EC2 instance. Launch several terminal windows simultaneously. First, load up the queue with some feeds:

```
<dev>: php load_feed_urls.php -f feeds.txt
Posted '{"FeedURL":"http:\/\/angrybethshortbread.blogspot.com\/
➥atom.xml"}' to queue 'https://queue.amazonaws.com/c_feed'
Posted '{"FeedURL":"http:\/\/secondlife.blogs.com\/change\/index.rdf
➥"}' to QueueURL 'https://queue.amazonaws.com/c_feed'
⋮
```

Start up the feed processor in another window:

```
<dev>: php rss_process.php  -q
http://blogs.electricsheepcompany.com/chris/?feed=rss2 - updated.
http://www.catherineomega.com/feed/ - updated.
⋮
```

Now, let's make it more interesting. The feed processor pulls feeds from SQS and writes data to SimpleDB. It has no persistent state of its own. Therefore, we can start up as many additional copies as we would like in order to perform the work more quickly. I actually ran 40 (yes, *forty*) copies of **rss_process.php** in parallel and processed over 50 feeds per second on my m1.small EC2 instance.

Here's the script that I used to start up 40 copies of the RSS processor:

chapter_08/start_rss_procs.bash *(excerpt)*

```
# start_rss_procs.bash
Count=40
Pids=''
for ((i = 1; i <= Count; i++));
do
  Log=parse_out_$i.txt
  echo $Log
  ./rss_process.php -q > $Log 2>&1 &
  Pids="$Pids $!"
done
echo $Pids
```

The script starts the processes and then displays their **PID**s (Process IDs) so that they can be easily killed when you no longer need them.

I did all this to illustrate an important point—that parallelism is often the key to high performance when dealing with cloud-based web services such as RSS feeds and SimpleDB. I can easily add more processes (and more EC2 instances) to speed up the job or to deal with an increased load. I can trade off time and processing power any way that I like.

All Stored

Okay, that about wraps up the chapter!

We took a look at the issues that make relational databases difficult to create, maintain, and scale, and then we took a look at SimpleDB. We reviewed the most important SimpleDB concepts and then we learned how to create, list, populate, and query domains using PHP and CloudFusion. We wrapped up with a highly parallelizable example and learned a bit about RSS feeds in the process.

Chapter

9

Amazon Relational Database Service

In Chapter 8, I told you why your application might have no need for the full power of a relational database. That's all well and good, but what if you want to move an existing MySQL-powered application to the cloud? Or, what if you need to perform complex queries or join data stored in two or more tables?

In this chapter, we'll take a look at the Amazon Relational Database Service (RDS). We'll see how it lets you take advantage of MySQL's power, while keeping you shielded from many of the more complex and time-consuming operational issues.

Introduction

The Relational Database Service makes it easy for you to set up, operate, and scale a relational database in the cloud. You can use MySQL without spending time provisioning a server, installing an operating system, installing MySQL, watching for and installing operating system or database patches, upgrading the server and storage as your needs change, configuring failover, or scheduling backups and managing backup files. Amazon RDS handles many of these chores automatically, and packages the rest of them as simple web service calls. For example, you can create an RDS DB Instance with a single web service call. The instance will be up and running and ready for use within a few minutes.

After you finish reading this chapter, I think you'll agree that Amazon RDS can actually change the way you think about a relational database. You can create, use, terminate, and restore your DB Instances on an as-needed basis.

Perhaps you're moving an application to the cloud and each installation of the application requires a private MySQL database. You can automate the entire installation and provisioning process. Each time a new customer signs up for your service, your code can call the RDS `CreateDBInstance` API operation to create a new DB Instance.

Maybe you have a multi-tier application and you want to set up a fully automated test environment. Again, using the Amazon RDS APIs (or the command line tools), you can create, use, and terminate DB Instances as part of your testing process.

Or, consider this: say your application accumulates data slowly but consistently throughout the month, and provides access to the data through some simple, low-overhead queries. At the end of each month, however, your application initiates a day-long billing run, during which the queries become complex and time-consuming. Using Amazon RDS, you can host the database on a system of moderate power for 95% of the month, scale up once per month to support the billing run, and then scale back down afterwards. You could do this on a daily, weekly, or even seasonal basis as your needs change. You can also add extra storage space to your database as your needs grow.

Sound interesting? Let's learn more!

MySQL Code Ahead

This chapter assumes that you have some basic familiarity with MySQL. If you know how to use the `mysql` command from the command line, you're in good shape. Of course, you'll need to have MySQL installed on your system; chances are you're already good to go, as you've likely installed it along with PHP. If that's not the case, Chapter 1 of Kevin Yank's *Build Your Own Database Driven Web Site Using PHP and MySQL* is freely available on sitepoint.com,[1] and contains detailed installation instructions for every platform.

---

[1] http://articles.sitepoint.com/article/php-amp-mysql-1-installation

Amazon Relational Database Service

As we've seen time and time again throughout this book, AWS takes care of many of the underlying details so that you can focus on your application. Amazon RDS handles much of the operational complexity associated with the creation and maintenance of a relational database. Despite this, everything that you already know about MySQL still applies. You can use your existing tools, code, data, and queries. In this section we'll examine some key Amazon RDS and MySQL concepts, take a peek at the Amazon RDS programming model, and wrap up with a look at the Amazon RDS pricing model.

Amazon RDS Concepts

Most of the operations involving Amazon RDS are centered around a **DB Instance**. You can create the DB Instance as a **Single-AZ** or as a **Multi-AZ Deployment** (recall that, as we saw in the section called "Availability Zone" in Chapter 2, AZ is short for Availability Zone, and that AWS is designed so that failures affecting one AZ will not affect the others). The Multi-AZ Deployment offers increased availability and durability by synchronously replicating database updates between multiple Availability Zones, with automatic failover to a standby in the event of a failure.[2]

You must specify the DB Instance Class when you create a DB Instance. There are currently five DB Instance Classes, as shown in Table 9.1.[3]Unlike EC2, which offers a choice of 32-bit and 64-bit instance classes, all of the RDS DB Instance Classes are 64 bit.

---

[2] This is a great example of the ability of AWS to turn a very complex system-building task (setting up a MySQL database with a hot spare, automated failover, and automated recovery) into a very simple and straightforward menu option.

[3] As was the case with Amazon EC2, the set of available DB Instance Classes is expected to grow and change over time. You can always find the latest list of DB Instance types at http://aws.amazon.com/rds.

Table 9.1. Amazon RDS DB Instance Classes[a]

Name	CPU Virtual Cores	CPU Core Speed (EC2 Compute Units)	RAM	Cost/Hour
Small	1	1	1.7GB	$0.11
Large	2	2	7.5GB	$0.44
Extra Large	4	2	15GB	$0.88
Double Extra Large	4	3.25	34GB	$1.55
Quadruple Extra Large	8	3.25	68GB	$3.10

[a] As is the case with all prices mentioned in this book, these are subject to change over time.

You can change the class of a DB Instance in a matter of minutes, so avoid spending too much time trying to decide which one you'll need up-front. The costs in Table 9.1 reflect the cost of the Single-AZ deployment for a DB Instance. For Multi-AZ deployments, the cost for the DB Instance is double that for a Single-AZ deployment.

The DB Instances have no fixed amount of storage. Instead, you specify an initial storage allocation of 5GB to 1,024GB when you create the DB Instance. You can add more space (up to the limit of 1,024GB) as your needs (and data) expand. The amount of space that you specify is known as the **allocated storage** for the DB Instance. Additional storage allocation can be added to your DB Instance on the fly without incurring downtime.

You must specify a **DB Instance identifier** when you create a DB Instance. This is a string that must start with a lower-case letter and can contain up to 63 lower-case letters, digits, and hyphens. The identifier cannot end with a hyphen, nor contain consecutive hyphens. The identifier must be unique within your account.

Each DB Instance hosts a single copy of a particular **database engine**. The only supported engine at press time is version 5.1 of MySQL; the corresponding database engine identifier is MySQL5.1.

Storage Engines

MySQL uses the word "engine" to refer to storage engines such as InnoDB and MyISAM. Each table in a MySQL instance uses a particular storage engine. The automated backup feature of Amazon RDS (which we'll get to in a minute) is currently supported only for InnoDB tables, since InnoDB supports reliable crash recovery. If you must use MyISAM tables with RDS, it's vital that you stop all activity on each table, lock it, and then flush it before backing it up.[4]

A DB Instance is always in a particular state. The principal states are **creating**, **backing-up**, **available**, **modifying**, and **deleting**. The DB Instance will spend most of its life in the available state; the other states are transient.

Your application program and database tools must be able to establish a network connection with your DB Instances. In order to make this possible, you must associate a DB Security Group with the DB Instance, and you must authorize ingress (inbound access) to the DB Instance from a network address range or EC2 Security Group. Once you've done this, you can configure your program and tools to use the DB Instance's Endpoint to establish a connection.

Amazon RDS gives you the ability to control the parameters that affect low-level aspects of the database engine's performance and behavior using DB Parameter Groups. Each group contains a list of configuration variables specific to the database engine. For the MySQL database, the DB Parameter Group will include values such as innodb_additional mem pool size and innodb_buffer_pool_size. Some of the values are absolute, and others are specified using a formula; for example, innodb_buffer_pool_size is specified by the formula {DBInstanceClassMemory*3/4}. This allows the Parameter Group to apply to all of the DB Instance Classes—as the value will be adjusted based on the features of the Instance Class. If a particular Parameter Group has no value for a parameter, then a default value that's specific to RDS or the database engine is used. Your AWS account contains a default DB Parameter Group that you can use until you need to change a parameter. When you modify a parameter group you can choose to apply the update immediately, or on the next reboot of the DB Instance or Instances associated with the group. Some

---

[4] The Amazon Relational Database Service Developer Guide contains more information about this topic; you can find it at http://docs.amazonwebservices.com/AmazonRDS/latest/DeveloperGuide/.

parameters are dynamic and can be applied straight away. Others are static and re-quire a reboot of the DB Instance.

When you create a new DB Instance you must supply a master user name and a master user password. Amazon RDS will create an account on the database engine using the supplied values, which must then be used to create a connection to the database. This user is given the following MySQL permissions: SELECT, INSERT, UPDATE, DELETE, CREATE, DROP, RELOAD, PROCESS, REFERENCES, INDEX, ALTER, SHOW DATABASES, CREATE TEMPORARY TABLES, LOCK TABLES, EXECUTE, CREATE VIEW, SHOW VIEW, CREATE ROUTINE, ALTER ROUTINE, CREATE USER, EVENT, and TRIGGER.

The Master User also has the GRANT option, so that they can grant permissions to user accounts that are created after the DB Instance is up and running.

You can optionally supply a database name when you create a new DB Instance. If you supply a name, Amazon RDS will create an empty database with that name on the DB Instance.

Each DB Instance has an associated maintenance window. The maintenance window gives you the flexibility to control when DB Instance modifications (such as scaling to a different DB Instance Class) and software patching occur. If a maintenance event is scheduled for a given week, it will be initiated and completed at some point during the four-hour maintenance window that you specify. Amazon RDS will apply any pending patches and parameter updates during the weekly four-hour period. By default, the window is set to a "quiet" time specific to each AWS Region. You can set the window to any desired part of the week if you have more insight into the best time (when the least number of users will be affected) for your particular application. The only maintenance events that require Amazon RDS to take your DB Instance offline are scale compute operations (which generally take a few minutes from start to finish) and required software patching. Required patching is automat-ically scheduled only for patches that affect security or durability. Such patching occurs infrequently (typically every few months) and should seldom require more than a fraction of the time in the maintenance window.

The Amazon RDS APIs make the process of backing up a DB Instance simple and painless. RDS will initiate an automatic backup each day during the DB Instance's backup window. The backup files will be retained for the number of days specified by the instance's backup retention period. You can also create a DB Snapshot at any time, which will be retained until you decide to delete it. You must assign a unique name to each DB Snapshot. Amazon RDS also stores the change logs for each database. The logs give you the ability to restore the database to the way it was at any point in time that's within the backup retention period, yet older than the DB Instance's latest restorable time. This time is typically within five minutes of the current time.

In any of the cases described above, restoring the database actually means creating a new DB Instance from the associated backup files. If you think creatively, you should be able to come up with some really interesting ways to use this feature. What if your production application starts to misbehave and you want to dig into the database to see what's going on? Take a snapshot, restore it to a new DB Instance, and analyze it in depth without impacting the production system. Deploying a new version of your code? Take a snapshot of the database first, and you can easily roll it back if you make a big mistake.

Amazon RDS keeps track of events related to the following sources: DB Instances, DB Snapshots, DB Security Groups, and DB Parameter Groups. Each event includes a date and time, a source type, a source name, and a message. You can retrieve events by source type, source name, and date range.

Each DB Instance reports the following metrics to CloudWatch:

- CPU utilization
- free storage
- number of DB connections
- number of read operations per second
- number of write operations per second
- read latency
- write latency
- read throughput
- write throughput

You can use these metrics to track the overall status and performance of each of your DB Instances. You can monitor the CPU utilization to drive your decision to scale to a larger or smaller DB Instance type, and you can watch the Free Storage to let you know when it's time to allocate more storage to one of your DB Instances.

Amazon RDS Programming Model

As is always the case with AWS, each aspect of the Amazon Relational Database Service is available through web service APIs. You can also use command line tools and the AWS Management Console to access and manipulate your RDS resources. The current version (2.5) of CloudFusion does not support RDS, so the examples in this chapter will make use of the command line tools and the console. It's worth examining RDS at the API level, so let's do that now.

The `CreateDBInstance` function is used to create a new DB Instance. Other functions that operate on DB Instances include `DescribeDBInstances`, `ModifyDBInstance`, `RebootDBInstance`, and `DeleteDBInstance`.

Another set of functions are used to create and manipulate DB Snapshots. These include `CreateDBSnapshot`, `DescribeDBSnapshots`, `DeleteDBSnapshot`, `RestoreDBInstanceFromDBSnapshot`, and `RestoreDBInstanceToPointInTime`.

Functions for manipulating DB Parameter Groups include `CreateDBParameterGroup`, `DeleteDBParameterGroup`, `DescribeEngineDefaultParameters`, and `ModifyDBParameterGroup`.

Similarly, the functions for manipulating DB Security Groups include `CreateDBSecurityGroup`, `DescribeDBSecurityGroups`, `DeleteDBSecurityGroup`, `AuthorzeDBSecurityGroupIngress`, and `RevokeDBSecurityGroupIngress`.

The `DescribeDBEvents` function is used to gain access to the events produced by each of your RDS resources.

Amazon RDS Pricing

Your use of the Amazon Relational Database Service is charged based on five usage dimensions: DB Instance hours, provisioned storage, storage I/O, backup storage, and data transfer.

DB Instance Hours

Hourly pricing for the use of single-AZ RDS DB Instances ranges from $0.11 to $3.10 per hour, as we saw in Table 9.1. Pricing for Multi-AZ DB Instances is double what's shown in the table, but this price covers both your primary DB Instance and the associated standby.

Billing begins when you create the DB Instance and continues, hour by hour, until you terminate the DB Instance. Note that this is a different model than that used by SimpleDB, so avoid confusing the two. As mentioned previously, you can change the class of a DB Instance in a matter of minutes, so don't be afraid to scale up and down as your needs dictate.

Provisioned Storage

The provisioned storage associated with a DB Instance is billed at $0.10 per GB per month for a Single-AZ instance, and twice that for a Multi-AZ instance. You'll pay for the amount that you provision, even if you fail to use it. It's easy (and quick) to provision additional storage, so there's no need to over-provision in advance. You can watch the free storage metric for each of your DB Instances to know when it's time to add additional storage.

Storage I/O

You're charged $0.10 for each million I/O requests you make to the storage provisioned for a DB Instance. Like all other AWS charges, this amount will be prorated based on actual usage. A Multi-AZ instance will accumulate write requests twice as fast as a Single-AZ instance, since the data is synchronously replicated as it's written.

Backup Storage

Backup storage is used for automated daily backups and for any snapshot backups that you initiate.

There's no charge for backup storage up to 100% of the amount of storage that you've provisioned for an active DB Instance. If you exceed this level, or if you terminate the instance, additional backup storage is priced at $0.15 per GB per month.

Data Transfer

This one is a little bit more complicated. Here are the rules:

- The first gigabyte of data transfer in and out of Amazon RDS is free.

- If you transfer data back and forth between an EC2 Instance and a DB Instance in different Availability Zones of the same Region, you pay only for the EC2 side of the data transfer ($0.01 per GB).

- There's no charge for the zone-to-zone data transfer that occurs as part of a Multi-AZ deployment.

- There's no charge for data transfer between an EC2 Instance and a DB Instance in the same Availability Zone.

- Data transferred into Amazon RDS that *isn't* coming from an EC2 Instance is charged at $0.10 per GB.

- Data transferred *out* of Amazon RDS that isn't going to an EC2 Instance is charged on a sliding scale that starts at $0.15 per GB.

Using Amazon RDS

With the preliminaries out of the way, let's now start playing with Amazon RDS. In this section you'll sign up to use the Amazon Relational Database Service, take a tour of the AWS Management Console's RDS support, and launch a Single-AZ DB Instance. We'll configure the DB Instance's DB Security Group, connect to the DB Instance from a remote client, and import some data. Once the DB Instance is up and running, we'll monitor its performance, initiate a backup, and then learn how to scale up both processing and storage. We'll create a DB Instance from a snapshot, and then terminate both of the DB Instances. You'll be all set to use RDS in your own application.

I'll be using some test data for the exercises in this section, and I will size my DB Instance accordingly. If you already know how you'll put Amazon RDS to use, feel free to adjust the parameters to suit.

Signing Up

If you've yet to do so, you'll need to go to the Amazon RDS page[6] and click on the button labeled **Sign Up For Amazon RDS**.

Tour the Console

Once you're signed up for Amazon RDS, open up the AWS Management Console at http://aws.amazon.com/, logging in to your AWS account again if necessary. To

---

[6] http://aws.amazon.com/rds

avoid having to log in to the console so frequently, click on the **Settings** item and uncheck the **Sign out on inactivity** option, as shown in Figure 9.1.

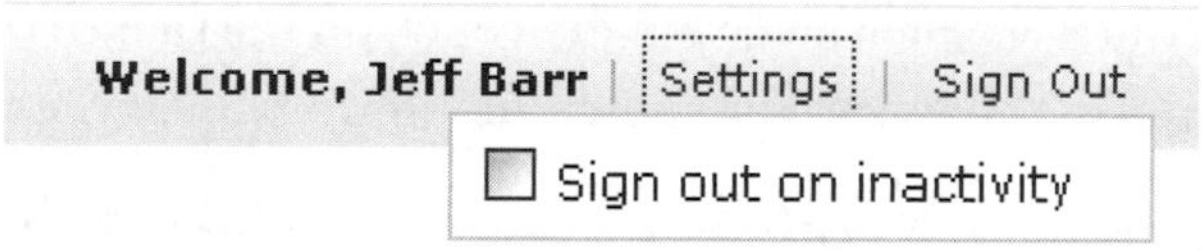

Figure 9.1. Disabling automatic sign-out

Click on the **Amazon RDS** tab. Select the nearest AWS Region from the drop-down menu, and your screen will look like Figure 9.2.

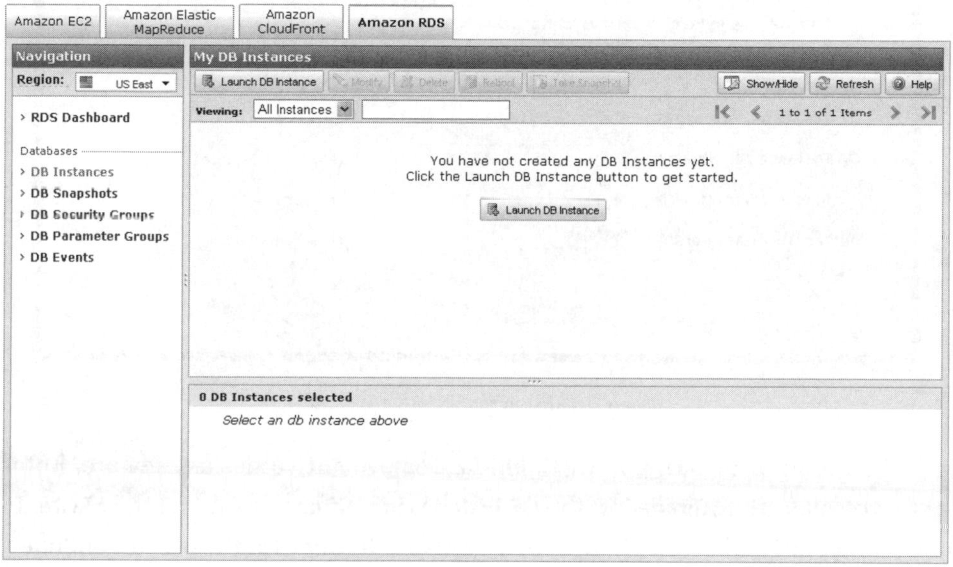

Figure 9.2. The Amazon RDS Console

Launching a DB Instance

Let's create a Single-AZ DB Instance using the Launch DB Instance Wizard. Click on **DB Instances** in the **Navigation** area, and then click on the **Launch DB Instance** button. Fill in the first page of the wizard as shown in Figure 9.3.

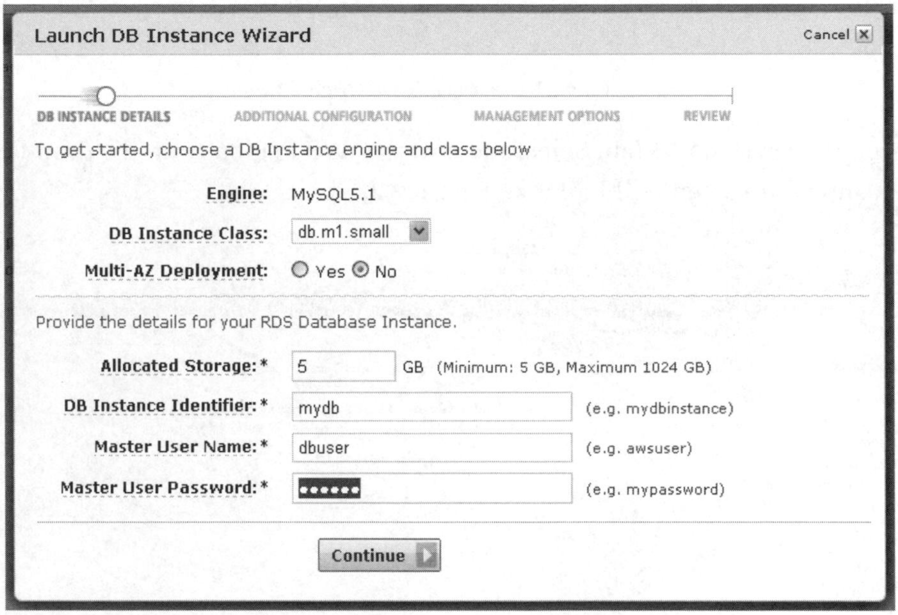

Figure 9.3. The Launch DB Instance Wizard

Leave the **DB Instance Class** and the **Multi-AZ Deployment** values as they are. Enter 5GB for the **Allocated Storage**, set the **DB Instance Identifier** to **mydb**, set the **Master User Name** to **dbuser**, and set the **Master User Password** to **dbpass**. Press the **Continue** button, and fill in the second page of the wizard as in Figure 9.4.

Figure 9.4. Page two of the launch wizard

Set the **Database Name** to **mydata** and leave the other fields as they are. Press the **Continue** button and move onto completing page three of the wizard as shown in Figure 9.5.

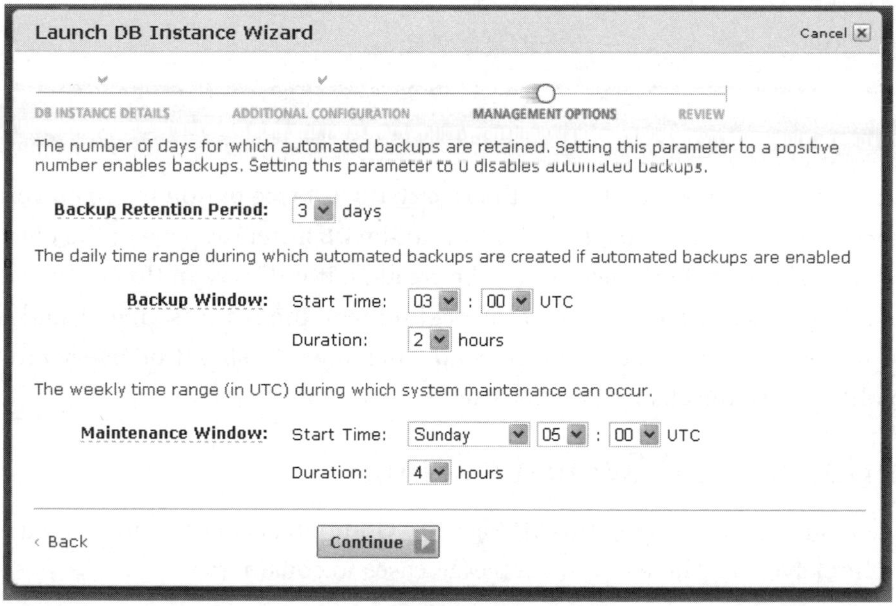

Figure 9.5. And to page three of the wizard

Set the **Backup Retention Period** to 3 days. Leave the other fields as they come. Click on the **Continue** button and verify that you've entered the values as desired, as shown in Figure 9.6.

Figure 9.6. Reviewing your settings

When everything looks good, press the **Launch DB Instance** button to create your DB Instance. Close the status page, and return to the **DB Instances** page of the console. The status of your DB Instance should be **creating**. It will stay in this status for a couple of minutes. If the spinner at the beginning of the row disappears and the status of your new instance is still **creating**, click the refresh button every minute or so until the status changes to **available**.

Configure a DB Security Group

The next step is to configure the DB Security Group to accept connections from your client system. There are two separate cases to consider:

- Connection from an EC2 Instance running on the same AWS account—if you already have an EC2 Instance up and running, you can use it as your client machine. You'll need to know the name of one of the Security Groups associated with the EC2 Instance. You'll also need your twelve-digit AWS Account ID.[6]

- Connection from a desktop PC or a server—if your MySQL client application runs on your desktop or on an existing server, you can also use it as your client machine. You'll need to know the machine's IP address. If your desktop machine is part of a network that uses network address translation (NAT), use an online service such as http://www.whatsmyip.org/ to determine the IP address your network presents to the outside world. Use the `ifconfig` command to determine the IP address of your Linux server, or the `ipconfig` command to determine your Windows server's IP address.

With the necessary information in hand, return to the AWS Management Console and click on **DB Security Groups**. Click on the DB Security Group named **default** and focus your attention on the bottom half of the page.

If you're planning to connect to your DB Instance from your EC2 Instance, select **EC2 Security Group** and fill in the form appropriately; then press the **Add** button, as seen in Figure 9.7.

Connection Type	Details		Status	Actions
No Authorizations				
EC2 Security Group ⌄	Security Group:			Add
	AWS Account ID.			

Figure 9.7. Adding an EC2 Security Group authorization

Otherwise, select **CIDR/IP** and enter an IP address or IP address range in CIDR notation. If you're connecting from a single address, simply enter that address followed by `/32` (this will ensure that only your machine will have access). If you're going to be connecting from a range of addresses, you'll need to ask for the CIDR address from your network administrator. Once you've entered the address, press the **Add** button, as shown in Figure 9.8.

---

[6] Log in to the AWS Management Console at http://aws.amazon.com. Your AWS Account ID is labeled Account Number and can be found on any of the pages linked from the Account section of the console (**Security Credentials**, **Account Activities**, or **Usage Reports**).

Connection Type	Details	Status	Actions
No Authorizations			
CIDR/IP ▾	**CIDR:** [ ] To authorize only the address of your current machine use 72.21.198.68/32		Add

Figure 9.8. Adding a CIDR/IP authorization

Access the DB Instance

Okay, where were we? Ah, right. You've launched a DB Instance, and it's up and running. You've added a rule to the DB Security Group and you should be able to access the database from an application. The next step is to retrieve the information needed to connect to the database. Return to the console and click on DB Instances. Click on your instance and focus your attention on the bottom half of the page. Locate the field labeled **Endpoint**. Select the name and copy it to your clipboard. Mine is shown in Figure 9.9.

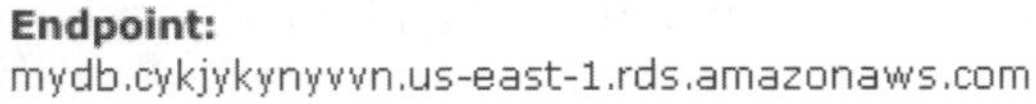

Endpoint:
mydb.cykjykynyvvn.us-east-1.rds.amazonaws.com

Figure 9.9. My DB Instance Endpoint

mydb is the DB Instance identifier that I specified when I created the DB Instance. us-east-1.rds.amazonaws.com indicates that I'm accessing a DB Instance located in the us-east-1 (Northern Virginia) Region. cykjykynyvvn is a unique identifier (and not, as you might otherwise assume, the Welsh word for "chicken").

Now head over to your client, and start up the mysql command like this:

```
$mysql -u dbuser -p -h mydb.cykjykynyvvn.us-east-1.rds.amazonaws.com
```

Replace dbuser with the master user name that you specified when you created the DB instance. Replace the string after –h with the value that you just copied from the console.

When the mysql command prompts you for a password, enter the master user password that you specified, and log in:

```
Enter password:
Welcome to the MySQL monitor.  Commands end with ; or \g.
Your MySQL connection id is 27
```

```
Server version: 5.1.45-log MySQL Community Server (GPL)

Type 'help;' or '\h' for help. Type '\c' to clear the buffer.

mysql>
```

Congratulations, you did it! You've launched a DB Instance and connected to it. Now you can verify that RDS created an empty database for you:

```
mysql>show databases;
+--------------------+
| Database           |
+--------------------+
| information_schema |
| innodb             |
| mydata             |
| mysql              |
+--------------------+
4 rows in set (0.00 sec)

mysql>use mydata;
Database changed
mysql>show tables;
Empty set (0.00 sec)
```

Import Some Data

The next step is to populate the database with some data. I happened to have a file with the URLs of about 200,000 RSS feeds handy, so I used that. First, I created a table for the data:

```
mysql>create table feeds (feedid int(11), url varchar(255));
Query OK, 0 rows affected (0.08 sec)
```

Then I imported the data into the DB Instance:

```
mysql>load data local infile "feeds.txt" into table feeds fields
➥terminated by "," enclosed by '"';
Query OK, 215825 rows affected (4.53 sec)
Records: 215825  Deleted: 0  Skipped: 0  Warnings: 0
```

And verified that it was present:

```
mysql>select * from feeds order by rand() limit 10;
+---------+----------------------------------------------------------+
| feedid  | url                                                      |
+---------+----------------------------------------------------------+
| 333143  | http://www.livejournal.com/users/so_delicate/data/atom/  |
| 166339  | http://www.vivat.be/rss_nl.asp?section=7                 |
| 422894  | http://sociable.blogspot.com/atom.xml                    |
| 276630  | http://www.livejournal.com/users/faizmagic/data/atom/    |
| 530872  | http://blogs.guardian.co.uk/games/index.xml              |
| 423608  | http://rss-lebanon.com/blogs/xmlsrv/rss2.php?blog=2       |
| 547146  | http://faboffer.com/articles/dwi-law/rss.xml             |
| 213177  | http://randomnumbers.us/wp-rss2.php                      |
| 500848  | http://feeds.healthywomen.org/nwhrc_newshcp              |
| 347547  | http://www.livejournal.com/users/_clearblur_/data/atom/  |
+---------+----------------------------------------------------------+
10 rows in set (1.08 sec)
```

You probably have some interesting data of your own, so feel free to use it for this step.

Administering RDS

Now that you know how to interact with your DB Instance, let's have a quick look at the various ways in which you can administer your instances.

Monitor Instance Performance

Head back over to the console and click on the instance. Then head towards the bottom of the page and click on the **Monitoring** tab. Figure 9.10 shows what my screen looked like.

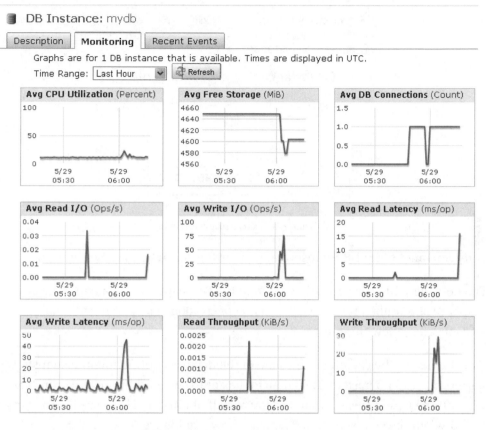

Figure 9.10. Monitoring the DB Instance

You can see that I loaded enough data to move the line on the graph labeled **Avg Free Storage**. The other graphs show momentary blips which correspond to the increased system load or network traffic related to the data that I loaded and then queried.

Initiate a Snapshot Backup

Let's make a snapshot backup before moving forward. Right-click on the DB Instance and choose **Take Snapshot**, as Figure 9.11 shows.

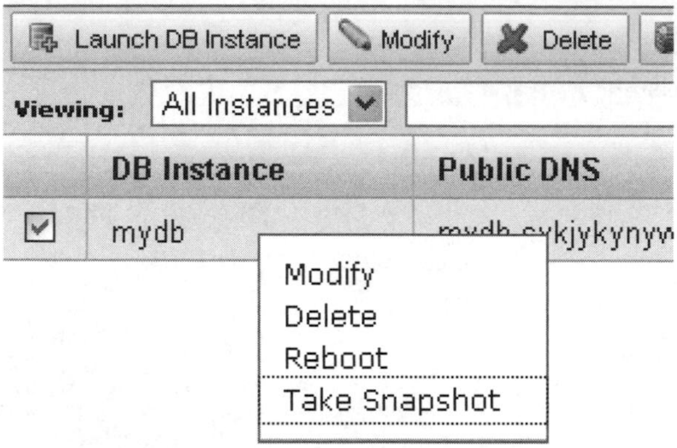

Figure 9.11. Taking a snapshot backup

Enter a name for the DB Snapshot and press the **Yes, Take Snapshot** button.

The console will automatically switch to the **DB Snapshots** page and your new snapshot should be present, with a status of **creating**. The status will change to **available** after a few minutes.

The snapshots always reflect the state of the database at the time the snapshot was started. There's no need to flush data to disk or to suspend the application. You can click on the **Recent Events** tab in the lower half of the console to see the events generated when the snapshot was taken, as shown in Figure 9.12.

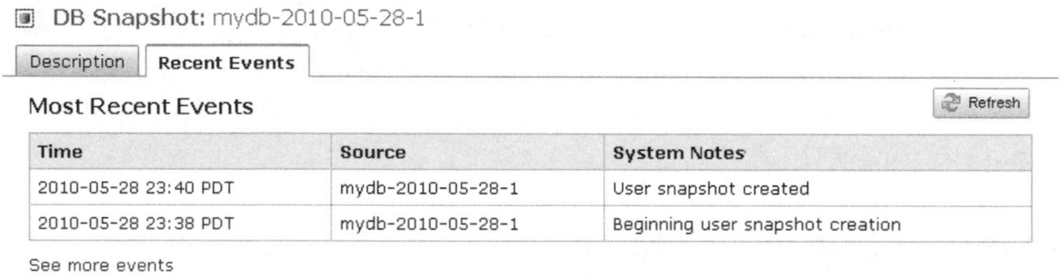

Figure 9.12. Recent events pertaining to our snapshot

Scale-up Processing

Let's pretend that you've used this DB Instance for testing, and you're now ready to move it into production. You're really happy with the system and expect to see a veritable flood of users on the first day. Because you'll be drinking champagne and eating cake while this is happening, you decide to scale up the processing power in advance of the flood. Right-click the DB Instance and select the **Modify** option; you'll be led to the screen shown in Figure 9.13.

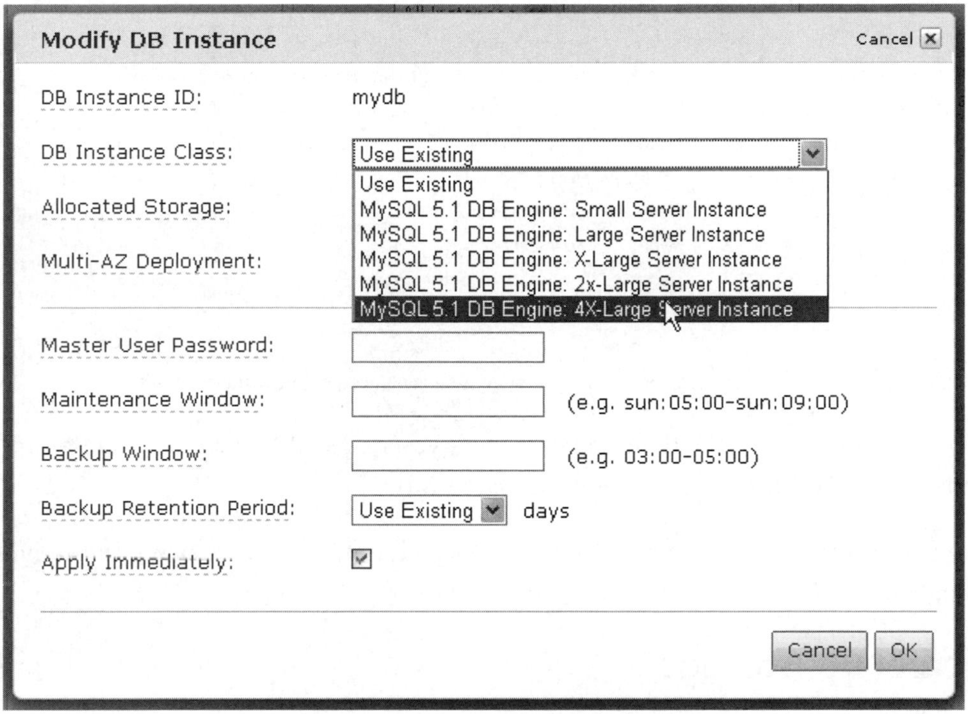

Figure 9.13. Scaling up a DB Instance

Select the new DB Instance Class and check **Apply Immediately,** then press the **OK** button. The state of the DB Instance will change to **modifying,** and a new entry will appear in the **Recent Events** tab to indicate that the Instance Class is being modified. Once the modification is complete, the state will be **available** and a corresponding event will appear. As you can see from my event log—shown in Figure 9.14—the entire scaling operation took just six minutes.

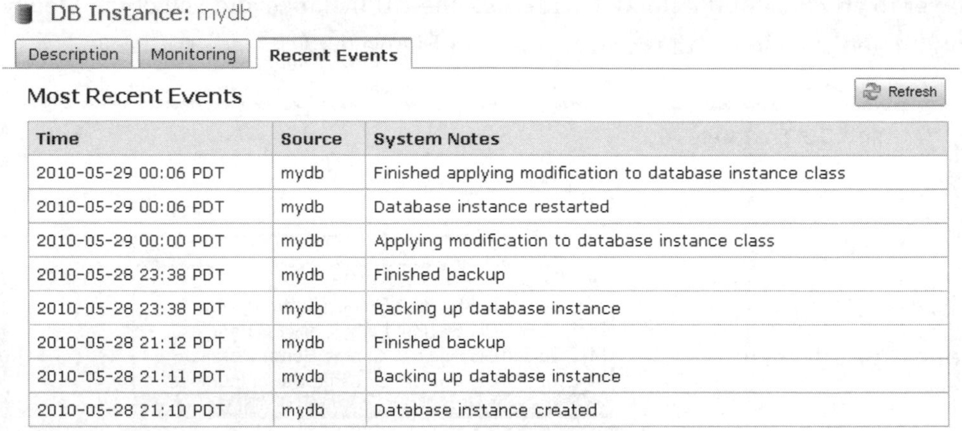

Time	Source	System Notes
2010-05-29 00:06 PDT	mydb	Finished applying modification to database instance class
2010-05-29 00:06 PDT	mydb	Database instance restarted
2010-05-29 00:00 PDT	mydb	Applying modification to database instance class
2010-05-28 23:38 PDT	mydb	Finished backup
2010-05-28 23:38 PDT	mydb	Backing up database instance
2010-05-28 21:12 PDT	mydb	Finished backup
2010-05-28 21:11 PDT	mydb	Backing up database instance
2010-05-28 21:10 PDT	mydb	Database instance created

Figure 9.14. The event log resulting from modifying the DB Instance

If you receive less traffic than you expected, you can scale down to a smaller and less expensive DB Instance type in the same way.

You can increase the amount of storage allocated to the instance using the same **Modify** operation, but you can never decrease it.

Scale-up Storage

After you return from your champagne and cake, you check your RDS monitoring and see that your free storage is now down to less than 1GB. Time to add more! Right-click the DB Instance and choose **Modify**. This time, change the **Allocated Storage** to a larger value, as shown in Figure 9.15. Remember to check **Apply Immediately**.

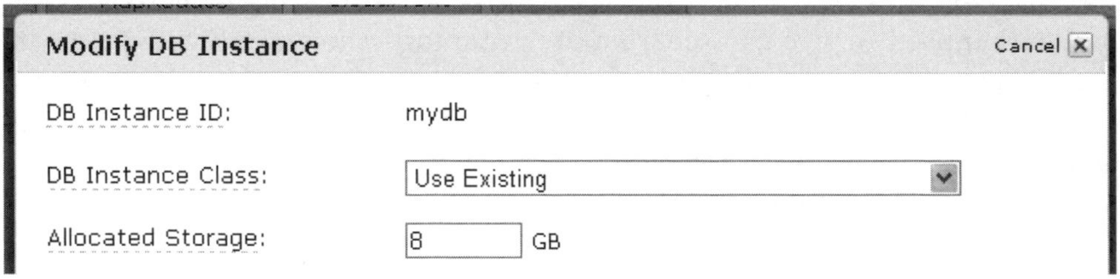

Figure 9.15. Scaling up the DB Instance's allocated storage

Your instance will remain operational and accessible while Amazon RDS adds more storage, so you can do this at any time. Again, use the **Recent Events** tab to check on the progress of the modification. My event log showed that increasing allocated storage from 5GB to 8GB took less than five minutes. The increased storage allocation is visible in the Monitoring tab, as you can see in Figure 9.16.

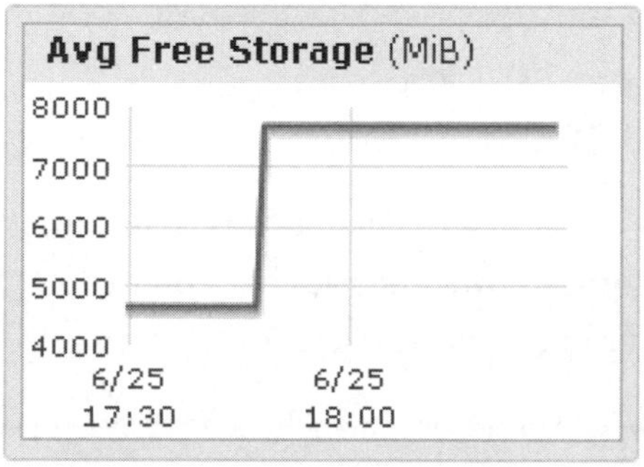

Figure 9.16. The Monitoring tab shows the increase in allocated storage

Create a DB Instance from a DB Snapshot or to a Point in Time

The AWS Management Console also allows you to create a DB Instance from any of your DB Snapshots or to the exact state in which it was at any point in time within the backup retention period. You can initiate these operations from the **DB Snapshots** and **DB Instances** pages, respectively.

Convert to Multi–AZ

You can convert your Single-AZ DB Instance to a Multi-AZ DB Instance (and vice versa) at any time. You can initiate this process from the console by invoking the **Modify** operation and changing the value of the **Multi-AZ Deployment** setting, as shown in Figure 9.17.

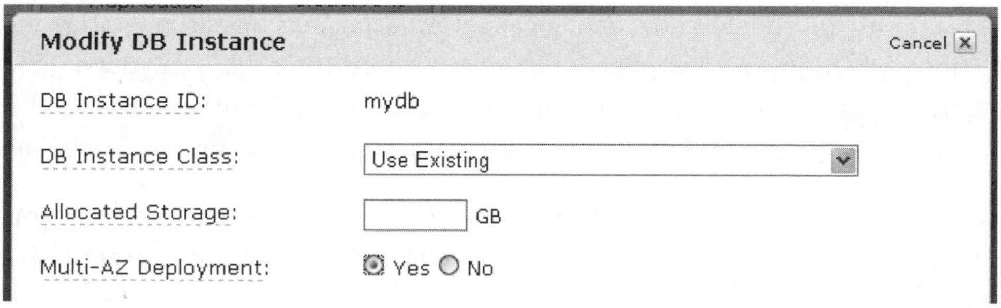

Figure 9.17. Changing a DB Instance to Multi-AZ Deployment

The conversion from Single-AZ to Multi-AZ took just seven minutes for my sample instance with 8GB of allocated storage. The state of the DB Instance will transition from **available** to **modifying** (and back) during the modification process, but the DB Instance remains online.

Delete DB Instances

The final step in the life cycle of a DB Instance is deletion. Amazon RDS allows you to take a final snapshot of your instance so that you can capture its state just before you terminate it, as Figure 9.18 shows.

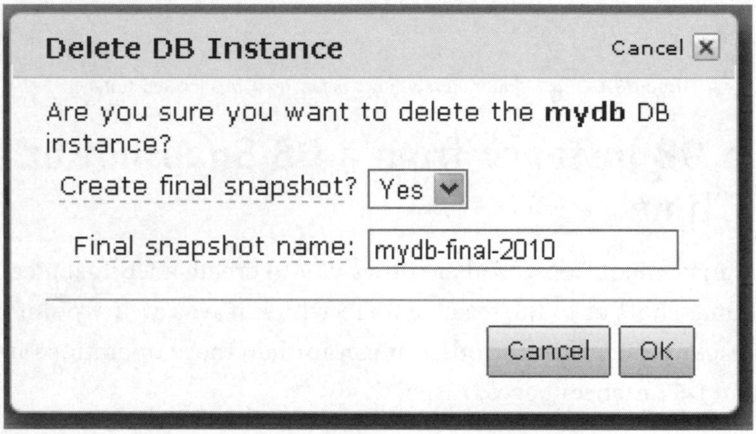

Figure 9.18. Creating a snapshot before deleting an instance

The state of the DB Instance will transition from **available** to **deleting** before the instance disappears entirely.

And That's a Wrap

At this point you should know enough about Amazon RDS to start migrating your existing MySQL-powered application. You can export the data from your existing database and then import it into a new DB Instance using the information in the section called "Access the DB Instance" and the section called "Import Some Data".

You'll need to alter your existing code to use the new connection string, and you'll have to set up your DB Security Group to allow network access from your application layer.

You can remove your existing backup regimen, and set up automated backups using the console.

Once everything is working as desired, you can start to take advantage of additional Amazon RDS features such as the ability to change DB Instance types on demand or Multi-AZ deployment. From there you can think about how to incorporate Amazon RDS into your development and testing process in new and unique ways.

Chapter 10

Advanced AWS

In this chapter we'll build on what we've already learned. We'll take a look at some advanced topics including accounting and tracking of your AWS usage, use of elastic block storage volumes, access to EC2's instance metadata, and dynamic diagramming of your AWS-powered system.

Accounting and Tracking

The dynamic nature of AWS—the ease with which you can store more data in Amazon S3, create and populate domains in SimpleDB, and launch EC2 instances—means that you should stay aware of your usage (and the associated costs).

Account Activity

You can track your account activity manually by visiting http://aws.amazon.com and selecting **Account Activity** from the **Your Account** menu. After logging in you'll be able to see detailed usage and cost information for each of the services that you use. You can expand each section using the + icon next to the name of the service. Figure 10.1 shows my account activity for August of 2009:

Account Activity

View Previous Statement

Summary of This Month's Activity as of August 19, 2009

Billing Cycle for this Report: August 1 - August 31, 2009
AWS service usage charges on this page currently show activity through approximately 08/19/2009 12:59 GMT

Expand All | Collapse All

Rate	Usage	Totals
⊞ **Amazon CloudFront**		
View/Edit Service		
United States		
$0.170 per GB - first 10 TB / month data transfer out	0.213 GB	0.04
$0.010 per 10,000 GET Requests	5,340 Requests	0.01
	View Usage Report	**0.05**
⊟ **Amazon Elastic Compute Cloud**		
View/Edit Service		
Amazon EC2 running Linux/UNIX Reserved Instances		
$0.03 per Small Instance (m1.small) instance-hour (or partial hour)	431 Hrs	12.93
Amazon EC2 running Linux/UNIX		
$0.10 per Small Instance (m1.small) instance-hour (or partial hour)	8 Hrs	0.80
Amazon EC2 Bandwidth		
$0.100 per GB Internet Data Transfer - all data transfer into Amazon EC2	2.940 GB	0.29
$0.170 per GB Internet Data Transfer - first 10 TB / month data transfer out of Amazon EC2	5.374 GB	0.91
$0.010 per GB Regional Data Transfer - in/out /between AZs or when using public or Elastic IPs or Elastic Load Balancing	0.105 GB	0.01
Amazon CloudWatch		
$0.015 per monitored instance-hour (or partial hour)	439 Hrs	6.59
	View Usage Report	**21.53**
Amazon Elastic MapReduce		
View/Edit Service		
	View Usage Report	**0.00**
⊟ **Amazon Simple Queue Service**		
View/Edit Service		
$0.01 per 10,000 requests ($0.000001 per request)	34,011 Requests	0.03
	View Usage Report	**0.03**
⊟ **Amazon Simple Storage Service**		
View/Edit Service		
$0.150 per GB - first 50 TB / month of storage used	121.963 GB-Mo	18.29
$0.100 per GB - all data transfer in	0.088 GB	0.01
$0.170 per GB - first 10 TB / month data transfer out	3.126 GB	0.53
$0.01 per 1,000 PUT, COPY, POST, or LIST requests	6,609 Requests	0.07
$0.01 per 10,000 GET and all other requests	26,670 Requests	0.03
	View Usage Report	**18.93**
⊟ **Amazon SimpleDB**		
View/Edit Service		
$0.00 per Machine-Hour consumed	46.867 Hrs	0.00
$0.00 per GB-Month of storage used	0.103 GB-Mo	0.00
$0.000 per GB - all data transfer in	0.002 GB	0.00
$0.000 per GB - first 10 TB / month data transfer out	0.000786 GB	0.00
	View Usage Report	**0.00**

Taxes
Estimated Taxes
(Due September 1, 2009)

Charges due on September 1, 2009†   40.54

† All charges for this billing cycle will be charged to your credit card on your next billing date, September 1, 2009. These charges include 1) next billing cycle's subscription charges due on the next billing date and 2) usage charges from the current billing cycle. Not included in the charges displayed here are any additional usage charges you will accrue this billing cycle. Visit the Amazon Web Services FAQs to learn more about web services pricing models and billing.

†‼ ‼   ‼ ‼ ‼ ‼ ‼ by Amazon Web Services LLC

Figure 10.1. A month's worth of account activity for the author

If your AWS usage varies from day to day you should make a point of checking your account activity. This is doubly true if you're serving up large amounts of content or using the auto scale feature to launch additional EC2 instances in response to increased system load or traffic.

Access to Usage Data

The raw data used to generate account activity can be downloaded from the AWS portal by selecting the **Usage Reports** option from the menu. You can download reports for any service—with control of the time period, usage types, and data format (XML or CSV)—as depicted in Figure 10.2.

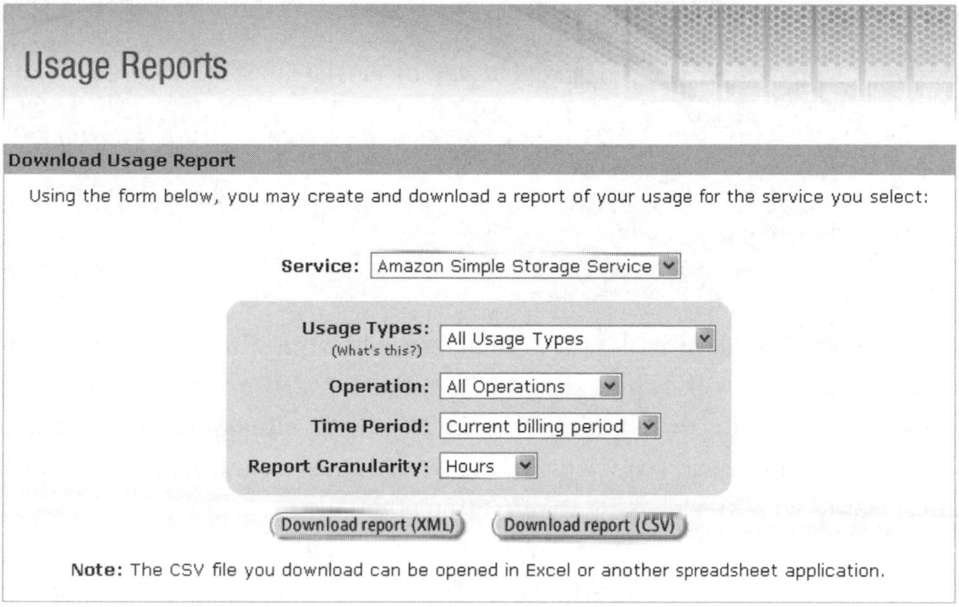

Figure 10.2. Downloading AWS usage reports

Since we've already learned how to process XML, let's work with a CSV (Comma-Separated Value) file this time so that we have the opportunity to learn a new skill. We'll access the data, store it in SimpleDB, and then retrieve and visualize it.

Start by downloading data for any (or all) of the services that you've used. Set the **Report Granularity** to **Days**, choose a **Time Period** that will represent your recent AWS usage (I started from January 1, 2009 and downloaded almost eight full months of data), and then click **Download report (CSV)**.

Depending on how your browser is configured, you may end up with a screen full of data or a new file in your download history. Either way, do what you need to do to transfer the data to your running EC2 instance. I opened the file in a local copy of Notepad, selected and copied the text, and then pasted it into an emacs buffer running on my EC2 instance. I named my EC2 usage file **ec2_usage.csv**, but you can use any name that you want.

Importing Usage Data

Here are the first few lines of my **ec2_usage.csv** file:

```
Service, Operation, UsageType, StartTime, EndTime, UsageValue
AmazonEC2,PublicIP-In,DataTransfer-Regional-Bytes,01/01/09 00:00:00,
➥01/02/09 00:00:00,97625
AmazonEC2,RunInstances,BoxUsage,01/01/09 00:00:00,01/02/09 00:00:00,
➥24
AmazonEC2,ElasticIP-Out,DataTransfer-Regional-Bytes,01/01/09 00:00:0
➥0,01/02/09 00:00:00,558960
AmazonEC2,ElasticIP-In,DataTransfer-Regional-Bytes,01/01/09 00:00:00
➥,01/02/09 00:00:00,24449
⋮
```

The first line of the file provides the field names, while the other lines contain data: one record per line, with values separated by commas. PHP's `fgetcsv` function makes it easy to deal with CSV files. The function reads a line from a file, separates the fields at comma boundaries (respecting quoted strings), and returns an array of values. Here's what it returns for the first line of my file:

```
Array
(
  [0] => Service
  [1] => Operation
  [2] => UsageType
  [3] => StartTime
  [4] => EndTime
  [5] => UsageValue
)
```

The usage data files for each AWS service contain some common fields and some that are specific to a particular service. For example, the usage data files for S3 also contain a `Resource` field. This field associates the usage data with an S3 bucket.

Similarly, the usage data files for Amazon CloudFront use the `Resource` field to identify the account data associated with a particular CloudFront distribution.

Because the data format contains common elements and some service-specific variants, Amazon SimpleDB makes an ideal storage system for it. We will need a domain:

chapter_10/include/book.inc.php (excerpt)

```php
define('BOOK_AWS_USAGE_DOMAIN', 'aws_usage');
```

We can use a modified version of the domain creation program from Chapter 8 to create this domain:

chapter_10/create_domain.php (excerpt)

```php
$res = $sdb->create_domain(BOOK_AWS_USAGE_DOMAIN);
```

Let's put together a program to import data from one or more CSV files specified on the command line. Here's what we need to start off:

chapter_10/import_usage.php (excerpt)

```php
#!/usr/bin/php
<?php

error_reporting(E_ALL);

require_once('cloudfusion.class.php');
require_once('include/book.inc.php');

if ($argc == 1)
{
  exit("Usage: " . $argv[0] . " CSV_FILE ...\n");
}
```

The script expects to find one or more CSV files on the command line and the code above performs this check. It then outputs a helpful message if there are too few command line arguments.

We'll be storing data in SimpleDB, so we'll need an access object:

chapter_10/import_usage.php *(excerpt)*

```
$sdb = new AmazonSDB();
```

Then we can process each file using the custom `ImportCSV` function we'll be writing soon:

chapter_10/import_usage.php *(excerpt)*

```
for ($i = 1; $i < $argc; $i++)
{
  $file = $argv[$i];

  if (($ret = ImportCSV($sdb, $file)) !== false)
  {
    print("Imported ${file}: ${ret} records\n");
  }
  else
  {
    print("Did not import ${file}\n");
  }
}
```

Let's take a look at the `ImportCSV` function. The first step is to try to open the file; this will return `false` if it's unable to be opened:

chapter_10/import_usage.php *(excerpt)*

```
function ImportCSV($sdb, $file)
{
  $fp = fopen($file, 'r');
  if ($fp === false)
  {
    return false;
  }
```

Since the first line of a CSV file contains the field names, we read it into the `$fields` array. We'll need these names as we process and store each line of data. We'll also track the number of lines of data that have been read and processed:

chapter_10/import_usage.php *(excerpt)*

```php
$fields = fgetcsv($fp);
$recordCount = 0;
```

Now we can process each of the data lines:

chapter_10/import_usage.php *(excerpt)*

```php
while (($data = fgetcsv($fp)) !== false)
{
    $recordCount++;
```

As I discussed in Chapter 8, there's an art to the choice of SimpleDB keys. When I built this tool I wanted to be able to import the same data file, or multiple data files with overlapping dates, while retaining the integrity of the data. After some experimentation, I composed a key by concatenating the name of the service and the MD5 hash of the non-data fields (everything except the UsageValue). My algorithm produced keys like this:

```
AmazonS3_c8e3df29d22bca8b7e73fd3b35152133
AmazonS3_2efdc1f3ab71d5b11cb3aa5cb738909d
AmazonEC2_2a88d9d6945f7d081714f31abe610400
AmazonEC2_11ebe64d3b6b0cab959a6d91edaad8cb
```

Let's proceed. We start out with Key and KeyData variables:

chapter_10/import_usage.php *(excerpt)*

```php
$key     = '';
$keyData = '';
```

Then each field of each line is processed. Recall that the $fields variable contains the field names for the file. I also altered the format of the date fields (StartTime and EndTime) to allow for better range-based queries later. Here's the field processing code:

```
                                          chapter_10/import_usage.php (excerpt)
$attrs = array();
for ($i = 0; $i < count($fields); $i++)
{
  if (($fields[$i] == 'StartTime') ||
      ($fields[$i] == 'EndTime'))
  {
    $data[$i] = date_create($data[$i])->format('c');
  }

  $attrs[$fields[$i]] = $data[$i];

  if ($fields[$i] == 'Service')
  {
    $key = $data[$i];
  }

  if ($fields[$i] != 'UsageValue')
  {
    $keyData .= $data[$i];
  }
}
```

At the conclusion of this loop, the $attrs array contains the data to be written to SimpleDB, $key contains the prefix for the key, and $keyData contains the data to be hashed to form the remainder of the key. Here's a dump of the $attrs array for my data:

```
Array
(
  [Service] => AmazonEC2
  [Operation] => ElasticIP-Out
  [UsageType] => DataTransfer-Regional-Bytes
  [StartTime] => 2009-08-01T00:00:00-04:00
  [EndTime] => 2009-08-02T00:00:00-04:00
  [UsageValue] => 4982241
)
```

I should probably pad the `UsageValue` field to a fixed length. I had no plans to do any queries against this field, hence why I left off doing so.[1] Note how the field names from the input file directly control the way data is stored in SimpleDB.

Putting everything together, here's how to form the SimpleDB key:

chapter_10/import_usage.php (excerpt)

```php
$key = $key . '_' . md5($keyData);
```

Finally, we store the data in SimpleDB, taking care to specify that any existing attributes with the same name should be replaced:

chapter_10/import_usage.php (excerpt)

```php
$res = $sdb->put_attributes(BOOK_AWS_USAGE_DOMAIN,
    $key, $attrs, true);
```

A quick error check, and we're almost there:

chapter_10/import_usage.php (excerpt)

```php
if (!$res->isOK())
{
  $error = $res->body->Errors->Error->Message;
  print("Could not insert ${key}: ${error}\n");
}
}
```

The final step, after all the lines have been processed, is to close the file and return the record count:

chapter_10/import_usage.php (excerpt)

```php
  fclose($fp);
  return $recordCount;
}
?>
```

---

[1] This is probably short-sighted on my part, but I do need to leave some coding as an exercise for you to do yourself!

After you've downloaded all usage files to your EC2 instance, run the import program like this:

```
<dev>: php import_usage.php *.csv
```

It will process each file in turn, reporting on the record count for each one:

```
Imported cf_usage_year.csv: 242 records
Imported ec2_usage.csv: 138 records
```

Importing large files may take some time. You can run several instances of this program in parallel, one per data file, if you like.

Querying Account Data

With the data stored, the next step is to look at interesting ways of querying the account data. I took the simple query command (**query_usage_cmd.php**) from Chapter 8 and enhanced it so that it could retrieve all the results, rather than stopping after the first batch. I did this by tracking and using the `NextToken` value returned from each `select` call. Here's the main loop structure:

chapter_10/query_usage_cmd.php (excerpt)

```
⋮
$next = null;
do
{
  $attrs = ($next == null) ? null : array('NextToken' => $next);
  $res   = $sdb->select($query, $attrs);
  $next  = (string) $res->body->SelectResult->NextToken;

  if (!$res->isOK())
  {
    exit("Select operation failed\n");
  }

  foreach ($res->body->SelectResult->Item as $item)
  {
    $recordCount++;
    foreach ($item->Attribute as $attribute)
    {
      print($attribute->Name . ": " . $attribute->Value . ", ");
```

```
      if ($attribute->Name == 'UsageValue')
      {
        $totalUsage += (int) $attribute->Value;
      }
    }
    print("\n");
  }
}
while ($next != null);
```

Here's the command in action.[2] The first command simply retrieves all the usage data:

```
<dev>: php query_usage_cmd.php
Final query: select * from aws_usage
EndTime: 2009-08-02T00:00:00-04:00, UsageType: DataTransfer-Regional
➥-Bytes, UsageValue: 4982241, Operation: ElasticIP-Out, StartTime:
➥ 2009-08-01T00:00:00-04:00, Service: AmazonEC2,
EndTime: 2009-08-02T00:00:00-04:00, UsageType: BoxMonitoringUsage,
➥ UsageValue: 24, Operation: RunInstances, StartTime: 2009-08-01T00
➥:00:00-04:00, Service: AmazonEC2,
EndTime: 2009-08-02T00:00:00-04:00, UsageType: DataTransfer-Regional
➥-Bytes, UsageValue: 308692, Operation: ElasticIP-In, StartTime:
➥ 2009-08-01T00:00:00-04:00, Service: AmazonEC2,
```

Additional command arguments are added to the query, with a single where prefix. Here's how to retrieve usage data for a single service (note that the command line contains both double and single quotes):

```
<dev>: php query_usage_cmd.php "Service='AmazonS3'"
Final query: select * from aws_usage where  Service='AmazonS3'
EndTime: 2009-06-05T00:00:00-04:00, UsageType: StorageObjectCount,
➥ UsageValue: 2, Operation: StandardStorage, StartTime:
➥ 2009-06-04T00:00:00-04:00, Service: AmazonS3, Resource:
➥ aws-dev-relations,
⋮
```

Retrieving usage data for a single day for a single service:

---

[2] This looks a lot better on a wide-screen monitor, with no line wrapping.

```
<dev>: php query_usage_cmd.php "Service='AmazonS3' and
➥ StartTime like '2009-08-01%'"
Final query: select * from aws_usage where  Service='AmazonS3'
➥ and StartTime like '2009-08-01%'
EndTime: 2009-08-02T00:00:00-04:00, UsageType: Requests-Tier1,
➥ UsageValue: 291, Operation: PutObject, StartTime: 2009-08-01T00:
➥00:00-04:00, Service: AmazonS3, Resource: wsdot-bridges,
⋮
```

And finally, a month's worth of data for a single operation on a single service:[3]

```
<dev>: php query_usage_cmd.php "Service='AmazonS3' and
➥ StartTime like '2009-08%' and UsageType='DataTransfer-Out-Bytes'
➥ order by StartTime
Final query: select * from aws_usage where  Service='AmazonS3'
➥ and StartTime like '2009-08%'
➥and UsageType='DataTransfer-Out-Bytes' order by StartTime
EndTime: 2009-08-02T00:00:00-04:00, UsageType:
➥ DataTransfer-Out-Bytes, UsageValue: 57360567, Operation:
➥ GetObject, StartTime: 2009-08-01T00:00:00-04:00, Service:
➥ AmazonS3, Resource: jeffbarr-public,
⋮
```

So now we can slice and dice our usage data any way that we'd like. Although this section is focused on processing the usage data, it's worth mentioning how easy it was to import and query the data using SimpleDB. As new services (and associated usage reports) become available, no code changes will be needed to accommodate them.

Retrieving and Displaying Usage Data

Okay, the final step of our exercise is to display the data. Let's put together a little program to pull it out of SimpleDB and render it as an HTML table. Here's how it starts—the first step is to specify the usage value to be retrieved and displayed:

chapter_10/bucket_usage_page.php (excerpt)

```php
<?php

error_reporting(E_ALL);
```

---

[3] This little utility also turns out to be the ideal vehicle for experimenting with SimpleDB's SQL.

```
require_once('cloudfusion.class.php');
require_once('include/book.inc.php');

$usage = "DataTransfer-Out-Bytes";
```

I'll display outbound data transferred. This represents the number of bytes of S3 object data transferred from S3 to the outside world. Of course, feel free to replace the value in quotes with another type of usage such as `DataTransfer-In-Bytes` (the number of bytes of data transferred from the outside world to S3) or `StorageObjectCount` (the number of objects stored in the bucket), or even `TimedStorage-ByteHrs` (the number of byte-hours consumed by the data stored in the bucket).

By the way, a byte-hour is totally unrelated to the amount of time you spend in a dentist's chair. It represents the sum of the number of bytes stored multiplied by the number of hours they were stored. One of my buckets has a bytes-hour usage value of 14,597,270,160. This means that the bucket held about 608 megabytes for the 24-hour period starting August 18th, 2009.

The script will report on the usage for each S3 bucket, so we create the usual access objects and fetch the list of buckets:

chapter_10/bucket_usage_page.php (excerpt)

```
$s3  = new AmazonS3();
$sdb = new AmazonSDB();

$buckets = $s3->get_bucket_list();
```

Now we need to do some date arithmetic. We'll report on the range of dates starting from the previous day and going back six days before that, or a full week's worth of data. The following code sets up `$firstDay` and `$lastDay` for a date range query, and also creates the `$days` array, with a *year-month-day* representation of each date in the range. Here we go:

```
chapter_10/bucket_usage_page.php (excerpt)
```

```php
$today   = date_create("now");
$lastDay = $today->format("Y-m-d");

$days = array();
for ($i = 0; $i < 7; $i++)
{
  date_modify($today, "-1 day");
  $days[] = $today->format("Y-m-d");
}

$firstDay = $days[6];
```

We'll be using the $days array to generate the HTML table column headers.

Okay, now we reach the good part—fetching the usage data for each bucket and storing it in the $rows array for eventual generation of the table rows. The loop simply iterates over each bucket and calls a custom GetUsage function to retrieve the S3 usage data from SimpleDB. It looks like this:

```
chapter_10/bucket_usage_page.php (excerpt)
```

```php
$rows = array();

foreach ($buckets as $bucket)
{
  $dailyUsage = GetUsage($sdb,$usage,$bucket,$firstDay,$lastDay);
```

GetUsage will return an empty array if there's no usage data for the bucket within the given date interval. To keep the output compact, the code below simply skips such buckets. The usage data array is stored in the $rows array with the bucket name as the key. If there's no data for a given day an empty string is stored in the array. Finally, the daily total is also stored as the last array element for the bucket data array:

```
chapter_10/bucket_usage_page.php (excerpt)
```

```php
  if (count($dailyUsage) > 0)
  {
    $rows[$bucket] = array();
```

```
    foreach ($days as $day)
    {
      if (IsSet($dailyUsage[$day]))
      {
        $rows[$bucket][] = $dailyUsage[$day];
      }
      else
      {
        $rows[$bucket][] = '';
      }
    }
    $rows[$bucket][] = array_sum($dailyUsage);
  }
}
```

The remaining complexity resides within the GetUsage function. Here's what it looks like:

chapter_10/bucket_usage_page.php *(excerpt)*

```
function GetUsage($sdb, $usage, $bucket, $firstDay, $lastDay)
{
  $query =
    "select StartTime, UsageValue "   .
    " from " . BOOK_AWS_USAGE_DOMAIN  .
    " where"                          .
    " Service='AmazonS3' and "        .
    " StartTime >= '${firstDay}' and " .
    " StartTime <= '${lastDay}' and " .
    " Resource='${bucket}' and "      .
    " UsageType='${usage}'";

  $res = $sdb->select($query);
  if (!$res->isOK())
  {
    return null;
  }

  $dailyUsage = array();
  foreach ($res->body->SelectResult->Item as $item)
  {
    $attrs = getItemAttributes($item);
    $startTime = substr($attrs['StartTime'], 0, 10);
    $usage     = $attrs['UsageValue'];
```

```
    $dailyUsage[$startTime] = $usage;
  }

  return $dailyUsage;
}
```

This looks long but it's really simple. It builds the query, runs it, checks the result, and builds an array of the usage indexed by day. The array's returned as the value of the function.

The HTML template is the final component of our report page. It begins in the usual way:

chapter_10/bucket_usage_page.php (excerpt)

```
<!DOCTYPE html PUBLIC "-//W3C//DTD XHTML 1.0 Strict//EN"
  "http://www.w3.org/TR/xhtml1/DTD/xhtml1-strict.dtd">
<html xmlns="http://www.w3.org/1999/xhtml" xml:lang="en" lang="en">
  <head>
    <title><?php echo $output_title ?></title>
  </head>
  <body>
    <h1><?php echo $output_title ?></h1>
    <p><?php echo $output_message ?></p>
```

There are two parts to this template so let's look at them separately. First, we need to generate the table header row by iterating over the $days array:

chapter_10/bucket_usage_page.php (excerpt)

```
    <table>
      <thead>
        <tr>
          <th>Bucket</th>
          <?php foreach($days as $day): ?>
          <th><?php echo $day ?></th>
          <?php endforeach ?>
          <th>Total For Bucket</th>
        </tr>
      </thead>
```

Next, we generate the table body and finish the page:

```
                                   chapter_10/bucket_usage_page.php (excerpt)
        <tbody>
          <?php foreach($rows as $bucket => $cells): ?>
          <tr>
            <td><?php echo $bucket ?></td>
            <?php foreach($cells as $cell): ?>
            <td>
            <?php echo ($cell == '') ? ' '
                  : number_format($cell); ?>
            </td>
            <?php endforeach ?>
          </tr>
          <?php endforeach ?>
        </tbody>
      </table>
    </body>
</html>
```

With nested `foreach` loops, we iterate over the array of buckets and the array of cell data for each bucket. The `number_format` function adds commas to make the numbers look presentable. Empty table cells are filled with a single non-breaking space (` `). Figure 10.3 displays an example of the resulting table.

Bucket	2009-08-19	2009-08-18	2009-08-17	2009-08-16	2009-08-15	2009-08-14	2009-08-13	Total For Bucket
andybarr	1,645,631	165,231		6,670,625	7,293,265	8,004,750	7,252,952	31,032,454
carmenbarr				5,634				5,634
jharr-work			108	108	324	108	108	756
joffbarr	9,389,443	930,943	6,623,644	1,155	231	231	231	16,945,878
jeffbarr-public	178,547	17,547,404	37,132,329	34,348,975	54,950,788	94,055,525	202,764,048	440,977,616
jeffbarr_public		11,527		24,809	11,527	49,618	11,527	109,008
sitepoint-aws-cloud-book				17,629			231	17,860
wsdot-bridges	2,930,508	2,093,450	10,508,520	591	591	591	591	15,534,842

Figure 10.3. Outbound data transfer of each bucket per day

You should be able to modify this program to display other types of S3 usage with just a minute or two's worth of work. You could chart the data or flag outliers. With a little more work you could report on EC2, SimpleDB, CloudFront, or SQS usage as well.

Elastic Block Storage

We covered the basics of Amazon EC2's Elastic Block Storage feature in Chapter 5, where we learned how to create, attach, format, and mount EBS volumes on an EC2 instance. In this section you'll learn more about EBS. We'll cover command line usage, see how to do backups, learn about public data sets, and see how to increase performance or capacity by creating a RAID device on top of multiple EBS volumes.

EBS from the Command Line

You can perform all the EBS functions from the command line. You can create, attach, snapshot (back up), detach, and delete EBS volumes.

An EBS volume can be attached to any EC2 instance in the same Availability Zone. If you have a running instance, you can determine its Availability Zone from the AWS Management Console or from the command line. You can also retrieve this information (and a lot more) from the EC2 instance metadata, which we'll talk about later in this chapter.

With the Availability Zone in hand, here's how you create a new EBS volume from the command line:

```
$ ec2-create-volume -z us-east-1b -s 50
VOLUME   vol-73d4211a      50                  us-east-1b        creating
➥    2009-08-20T19:12:09+0000
```

The volume status is reported as "`creating`" immediately after execution of this command. The command also displays the volume ID (`vol-73d4211a` in my case). You'll need this ID later.

You need to wait (ordinarily just a matter of seconds) until the volume becomes available before proceeding. Here's how to check it:

```
$ ec2-describe-volumes vol-73d4211a
VOLUME   vol-73d4211a      50                  us-east-1b        available
➥    2009-08-20T19:12:09+0000
```

Now you need to attach the volume to your instance. You'll need the instance's ID, the volume ID, and a device name. Although Linux disk device names are essentially arbitrary, by convention they reside in the **/dev** directory and have names that start with **sd**, followed by another letter. The EC2 system disk is **/dev/sda** and the other local disks (on the larger-sized instances) are **sdb**, **sdc**, and so forth. **/dev/sdf** is a good device name for the first EBS volume attached to the instance (as "f" is far enough down the alphabet to avoid colliding with another device). Here's how to attach it:

```
$ ec2-attach-volume vol-73d4211a  -i i-da8f6db2 -d /dev/sdf
ATTACHMENT        vol-73d4211a      i-da8f6db2        /dev/sdf
➥attaching        2009-08-20T19:26:08+0000
```

The command accepts the volume ID, followed by -i and the instance ID, and -d and the device name. The volume status changes to "attaching." It will stay in this state for a few seconds before transitioning to "attached":

```
$ ec2-describe-volumes vol-73d4211a
ATTACHMENT        vol-73d4211a      i-da8f6db2        /dev/sdf
➥attached        2009-08-20T19:26:08+0000
```

At this point, we have done the cloud computing equivalent of procuring a disk drive, plugging it into a server, and attaching the data cable. The disk is physically connected and running; the operating system is aware of it, but the disk is raw (unformatted) and yet to be part of the file system.

The next step is to create a file system on the new volume and an attachment (mount point), and we can logically mount the volume on the instance's root file system. We'll follow the same procedure from the section called "Creating an EBS Volume" in Chapter 5 (you'll need to log in to your EC2 instance to run these commands):

```
<dev>: mkfs -F /dev/sdf
<dev>: mkdir /data
<dev>: mount /dev/sdf /data
```

You can mount an EBS volume on any location in your instance's file system. If you're planning to create and use a large number of volumes, you should take the time to plan out a logical name structure beforehand.

The volume is now ready for use. You can create directories, store files, and do whatever you need to inside of the **/data** directory hierarchy. I'm going to need some data in my **/data** directory for the examples in the next section, so I'm going to copy the contents of **/usr/lib** (about 250MB) over:

```
<dev>: cp -r /usr/lib /data
```

EBS Snapshots

Let's say that I want to create a backup of my EBS volume as it exists at this point. The first step is to make sure that any in-memory data has been written to disk:

```
<dev>: sync
```

If you're using the EBS volume to store database files, you should probably shut the database server down before you create the backup. This will ensure that the backup is complete and logically consistent.

Creating the backup—a snapshot in EBS terms—is very easy:

```
$ ec2-create-snapshot vol-73d4211a
SNAPSHOT            snap-c7e849ae    vol-73d4211a    pending
➡ 2009-08-20T19:52:35+0000
```

Once the snapshot has been initiated, it's safe to resume writing data to the volume. The snapshot may take some time to complete, but it will always represent the state of the volume at the time the snapshot was initiated.

You can check on the status of your snapshot like this:

```
$ ec2-describe-snapshots
SNAPSHOT            snap-c7e849ae    vol-73d4211a    pending
➡ 2009-08-20T19:52:35+0000
```

The first snapshot for an EBS volume is similar to a traditional, full backup. It contains all the information written to the volume. Second and subsequent snapshots are similar to traditional incremental backups. They contain only the information that's been changed since the previous backup. EBS takes care of all the details of this behind the scenes. Even if you delete the first snapshot, sufficient data will be retained to allow you to create new volumes from any of the other snapshots.

Snapshots are stored in Amazon S3 and take on all the desirable attributes that you'd expect. In particular, they're stored at low cost with high reliability.

The snapshot's state will eventually transition to "completed." The volume has been backed up:

```
$ ec2-describe-snapshots
SNAPSHOT        snap-c7e849ae    vol-73d4211a     completed
➡        2009-08-20T19:52:35+0000          100%
```

EBS snapshots can be used to create new volumes in the same or different availability zone. This is achieved by including the snapshot ID (snap-c7e849ae in my example) when the volume is created. I can create a new volume, with contents identical to the original at the time that I created the snapshot, as follows:

```
$ ec2-create-volume -z us-east-1b -s 50 --snapshot
➡ snap-c7e849ae
VOLUME  vol-00d72269    50          snap-c7e849ae   us-east-1b
➡        creating          2009-08-20T20:17:35+0000
```

Once the new volume's state turns to available, I need to attach it to an instance (in this case I'll use the same one that I started with, but they can be attached to any EC2 instance in the same Availability Zone), create a mount point, and then mount it, all in one fell swoop this time:

```
$ ec2-attach-volume vol-00d72269 -i i-da8f6db2 -d /dev/sdg
ATTACHMENT          vol-00d72269    i-da8f6db2       /dev/sdg
➡        attaching       2009-08-20T20:21:18+0000
```

Next, create a mount point:

```
<dev>: mkdir /data2
<dev>: mount /dev/sdf /data2
```

At this point /data and /data2 are exact duplicates of each other.

I can add more data to /data and then create another snapshot:

```
<dev>: cp -r /usr/java /data
```

```
$ ec2-create-snapshot vol-73d4211a
SNAPSHOT            snap-b1ed4cd8    vol-73d4211a    pending
➥ 2009-08-20T20:27:04+0000
```

I now have two snapshots (with different contents) of the same volume. I can create new volumes from either one:

```
$ ec2-describe-snapshots
SNAPSHOT            snap-c7e849ae    vol-73d4211a    completed
➥          2009-08-20T19:52:35+0000          100%
SNAPSHOT            snap-b1ed4cd8    vol-73d4211a    completed
➥          2009-08-20T20:27:04+0000          100%
```

On a production system you'll probably have lots and lots of snapshots. Take care to track the reason for each snapshot (for example, "Snapshot of development volume on Mack's instance before beta release 1.5"). You could write this on a sticky note and keep it under your keyboard, or you could write a little AWS program to capture the data in SimpleDB.

In fact, we can combine the snapshot and the logging. We will need a SimpleDB domain:

chapter_10/include/book.inc.php *(excerpt)*

```php
define('BOOK_SNAP_LOG_DOMAIN', 'snapshot_log');
```

Make sure you create this SimpleDB domain before you run the next script. You can use the **create_domain.php** script again. Here's all it takes:

chapter_10/snap_and_log.php *(excerpt)*

```php
#!/usr/bin/php
<?php

error_reporting(E_ALL);

require_once('cloudfusion.class.php');
require_once('include/book.inc.php');

if ($argc < 3)
{
```

```php
    exit("Usage: " . $argv[0] . " \"message\" VOLUMEID...\n");
}

$message = $argv[1];

$sdb = new AmazonSDB();
$ec2 = new AmazonEC2();

for ($i = 2; $i < $argc; $i++)
{
  $volId = $argv[$i];

  // Create snapshot
  $res1 = $ec2->create_snapshot($volId);

  if ($res1->isOK())
  {
    $snapId    = $res1->body->snapshotId;
    $startTime = $res1->body->startTime;

    $key = $volId . '_' . $startTime;

    $attrs = array('VolId' => $volId,
      'Message' => $message,
      'StartTime' => $startTime);

    $res2 = $sdb->put_attributes(BOOK_SNAP_LOG_DOMAIN, $key,
      $attrs, true);
  }
}
exit(0);
?>
```

The create_snapshot method initiates the snapshotting activity on the specified volume. The snapshot ID and the start time are extracted from the data that it returns, and the information is stored in SimpleDB.

Running the script is easy:

```
$ php snap_and_log.php "Important Backup"  vol-73d4211a
```

Just to be clear, this tiny program creates a near-instantaneous backup of a volume that can be up to one terabyte in size, stores the backup in Amazon S3 for safekeeping, and logs the salient information to SimpleDB. That's cloud computing (and the power of complete programmability) in action!

The EBS snapshots are stored in S3, but it's impossible to reach them using the S3 APIs. You can access them through the `ec2-describe-snapshots` command or you can write a program to call CloudFusion's `describe_volumes` method.

EBS Public Data Sets

You can also create EBS volumes from the EBS Public Data Sets. The data sets (listed at http://aws.amazon.com/publicdatasets/) contain public information for use with AWS. There's census data, genome data, economic data, and much more. Each data set is provided in the form of an EBS snapshot. Instead of spending hours or even days downloading and unpacking this data (some of the data sets contain hundreds of gigabytes of information), you can simply create a volume and start processing the data right away.

For example, the Wikipedia Page Traffic Statistics data set contains 320 gigabytes of hourly page statistics for the popular Wikipedia site.[4] Here's how to use it:

```
$ ec2-create-volume -z us-east-1b --snapshot snap-753dfc1c
VOLUME   vol-42d1242b     320      snap-753dfc1c    us-east-1b
➥        creating         2009-08-20T21:19:26+0000
$ ec2-attach-volume vol-42d1242b -i i-da8f6db2 -d /dev/sdh
ATTACHMENT          vol-42d1242b    i-da8f6db2        /dev/sdh
➥        attaching        2009-08-20T21:20:08+0000
```

```
<dev>: mkdir /wikipedia
<dev>: mount /dev/sdh /wikipedia
```

The data was available to me—in directory **/wikipedia**—in 20 seconds (quite literally, as fast as I could type).

A volume of this size will cost about $30 per month, so be sure to `umount`, detach, and destroy it when you no longer need it. Here's all it takes:

```
<dev>: umount /dev/sdh
<dev>: mount /dev/sdh /wikipedia
```

---

[4] http://www.wikipedia.org

```
$ ec2-detach-volume   vol-42d1242b
$ ec2-delete-volume   vol-42d1242b
```

I don't know about you, but the ability to materialize hundreds of gigabytes[5] of disk space on demand, seemingly out of thin air, is what I find really awe-inspiring and more than a little bit cool. Sure, at some point it's "just a bunch of hardware," and "just a few lines of code," but when you put it all together just right you can make some fairly cool stuff!

EBS RAID

In this section, you will learn how to assemble a set of EBS volumes into a single virtual volume known as a **RAID** array.[6] By doing so, you can create a virtual volume with some or all of the following attributes:

Increased Storage Capacity

A single EBS volume can be no larger than one terabyte. You can create a RAID array which spans any number of EBS volumes.[7]

Increased I/O Capacity

A RAID array can increase the overall **I/O** (input/output) throughput beyond what's possible with a single EBS volume by distributing accesses across multiple volumes.

Increased Redundancy

A RAID array can store multiple copies of the same data to ensure that a copy is still available if a hardware device fails. This RAID feature is inapplicable to EBS because EBS stores data redundantly "under the covers."

RAID arrays can be created in a number of different configurations, also known as levels. Here are some of the simpler and more popular configurations:

---

[5] Or even terabytes, since each EC2 account can create up to 20 times one-terabyte volumes by default.

[6] The example used draws information from Eric Hammond's post at http://alestic.com/2009/06/ec2-ebs-raid.

[7] A modern file system on a 64-bit system can theoretically handle a RAID array of any conceivable size. Practical considerations (such as the time to perform a disk repair using the `fsck` command) will come into play long before reaching any intrinsic limits of the file system.

■ RAID level 0 supports increased I/O capacity and increased storage capacity by *striping* data across multiple volumes. There is no additional redundancy.

■ RAID level 1 supports increased storage capacity and also increases redundancy by *mirroring* data across multiple volumes.

■ RAID levels 2 through 6 support increased storage and I/O capacity and also provide increased redundancy. The higher levels can even tolerate failure of multiple volumes or physical devices, generally at the cost of increased storage and retrieval time.

In this section we'll set up a RAID 0 volume. This is one of the simplest RAID levels, but the basic steps are the same regardless of the level. Here's what we need to do:

1. create the necessary EBS volumes
2. attach the EBS volumes to the EC2 instance
3. create the RAID volume on top of the EBS volumes
4. create a file system on top of the RAID volume

The first step is to create the volumes. As we've already seen, this is really easy once we know the desired Availability Zone and volume size. This example will use tiny (ten gigabyte) volumes, but you can use any size you would like up to the EBS limit of one terabyte. Let's create four lots of ten gigabyte EBS volumes in Availability Zone us-east-1b:

```
$ ec2-create-volume -z us-east-1b -s 10
VOLUME  vol-891de8e0    10                  us-east-1b      creating
➥          2009-08-23T17:19:39+0000
$ ec2-create-volume -z us-east-1b -s 10
VOLUME  vol-8b1de8e2    10                  us-east-1b      creating
➥          2009-08-23T17:19:57+0000
$ ec2-create-volume -z us-east-1b -s 10
VOLUME  vol-8a1de8e3    10                  us-east-1b      creating
➥          2009-08-23T17:20:07+0000
$ ec2-create-volume -z us-east-1b -s 10
VOLUME  vol-811de8e8    10                  us-east-1b      creating
➥          2009-08-23T17:20:18+0000
```

Now attach the EBS volumes to the instance:

```
$ ec2-attach-volume vol-891de8e0 -i i-d830dfb0 -d /dev/sdh1
ATTACHMENT        vol-891de8e0    i-d830dfb0       /dev/sdh1
➥        attaching        2009-08-23T17:22:54+0000
$ ec2-attach-volume vol-8b1de8e2 -i i-d830dfb0 -d /dev/sdh2
ATTACHMENT        vol-8b1de8e2    i-d830dfb0       /dev/sdh2
➥        attaching        2009-08-23T17:23:15+0000
$ ec2-attach-volume vol-8a1de8e3 -i i-d830dfb0 -d /dev/sdh3
ATTACHMENT        vol-8a1de8e3    i-d830dfb0       /dev/sdh3
➥        attaching        2009-08-23T17:23:35+0000
$ ec2-attach-volume vol-811de8e8 -i i-d830dfb0 -d /dev/sdh4
ATTACHMENT        vol-811de8e8    i-d830dfb0       /dev/sdh4
➥        attaching        2009-08-23T17:23:58+0000
```

Now we can glue the EBS volumes together into a RAID. We can make a bigger (in this case 40GB) volume using RAID 0:

```
<dev>: mdadm --create /dev/md0 --level 0 --metadata=1.1
➥ --raid-devices 4 /dev/sdh1 /dev/sdh2 /dev/sdh3 /dev/sdh4
mdadm: array /dev/md0 started.
```

We also need to add the following line to the **/etc/mdadm.cont** file (creating it if necessary):

```
DEVICES /dev/sdh1 /dev/sdh2 /dev/sdh3 /dev/sdh4
```

Then run the following command to add additional configuration information to the file:

```
<dev>: mdadm --detail --scan >> /etc/mdadm.conf
```

At this point the RAID volume (**/dev/md0**) has been created. It encapsulates the four EBS volumes (**/dev/sdh1**, **/dev/sdh2**, **/dev/sdh3**, and **/dev/sdh4**).

The next step is to create a file system on the RAID volume:

```
<dev>: mkfs /dev/md0
```

The mkfs command will produce a lot of output. Here's the most interesting part for our present endeavor:

```
Block size=4096 (log=2)
:
5242880 inodes, 10485696 blocks
```

Multiplying the block size (4096) by the block count (10,485,696) results in the value 42,949,410,816. We've created a 40 gigabyte RAID volume. As is the case with any file system, we wrap up by creating a mount point and mounting the volume on it:

```
<dev>: mkdir /data
<dev>: mount /dev/md0 /data
```

When using RAID volumes in production-level systems, you should keep a few things in mind:

1. An ext3 file system on a 32-bit Linux system is limited to a maximum size of eight terabytes (if the default 4K block size is used). You can use the xfs file system if you need to create larger file systems.

2. The larger the file system, the more time the `fsck` command will need to check and repair the disk after a crash or an unclean reboot.

3. Take extreme care when creating snapshots of the volumes used to create a RAID array. Be sure to defer all write activity, run the `sync` command, and initiate all the snapshots in succession. Track the snapshot IDs with care in case you need to put the volume back together later. If you do find that you have to put the volume back together, be sure that the ordering of the volumes within the RAID is preserved across the entire operation.

4. The `mdadm` command has many options. Spend some time studying it to learn even more about what you can do with RAID volumes. For example, you can add additional devices to a RAID 0 volume in order to increase its capacity. If you do this, you also need to do a logical resize on the file system.

EC2 Instance Metadata

Each EC2 instance can access run-time data about itself by making HTTP requests to the special address 169.254.169.254. The set of available metadata items has increased with each release of EC2. A GET request to the special address will return a list of versions and the special version latest.

The wget command can be used to make HTTP requests from the command line. Here's how to retrieve the list of available metadata versions:

```
<dev>: wget -r -q http://169.254.169.254
<dev>: cat 169.254.169.254/index.html
1.0
2007-01-19
2007-03-01
⋮
2009-04-04
latest
```

Retrieving one of these items returns a list of the available metadata:

```
<dev>: wget -q http://169.254.169.254/latest/meta-data
<dev>: cat index.html
ami-id
ami-launch-index
ami-manifest-path
⋮
security-groups
```

Table 10.1 shows what you can access.

Table 10.1. Available Metadata

Metadata Item	Description
ami-id	the ID of the AMI used to launch the instance
ami-launch-index	the numerical index of the instance within its reservation (the group of instances launched with a single request)
ami-manifest-path	the S3 path to the AMI used to launch the instance
ancestor-ami-ids	the ID of the AMIs used to bundle this instance's AMI
block-device-mapping	mapping of logical device names to actual device names
hostname	the instance's assigned host name
instance-id	the instance's ID
instance-type	the instance's type (m1.small, and so on)
kernel-id	the ID of the kernel used to launch the instance
local-hostname	the host name of the instance on the EC2 internal network (EC2 instances can use this host name to refer to other instances)
local-ipv4	the instance's local IP address on the EC2 internal network (EC2 instances can use this address to communicate with other instances)
placement/availabilityzone	the Availability Zone where the instance resides
public-hostname	the instance's publicly visible host name
public-ipv4	the instance's public IP address
public-keys	the public keys used to start the instance
ramdisk-id	the RAM disk (if any) used to start the instance
reservation-id	the ID of the reservation which contains this instance—a reservation collects all the EC2 instances launched with a single request
security-groups	the security groups attached to the instance

Here's how to retrieve some of the more useful values—the instance ID, its public IP address, and its Availability Zone:

```
<dev>: wget -q http://169.254.169.254/latest/meta-data/instance-id
<dev>: wget -q http://169.254.169.254/latest/meta-data/public-ipv4
<dev>: wget -q http://169.254.169.254/latest/meta-data/placement/
↪availability-zone
```

Note that these requests (and all other requests for instance metadata) must be made from within the instance itself. Here is the resulting metadata:

```
<dev>: cat public-ipv4
174.129.84.219
<dev>: cat instance-id
i-d830dfb0
<dev>: cat availability-zone
us-east-1b
```

You can also supply your own metadata when you launch an EC2 instance. This data is called user data. The AWS Management Console, the ElasticFox tool, and the ec2-run-instances command line tool each provide a way to specify this data. The AWS Management Console supports this function as an advanced option, as shown in Figure 10.4.

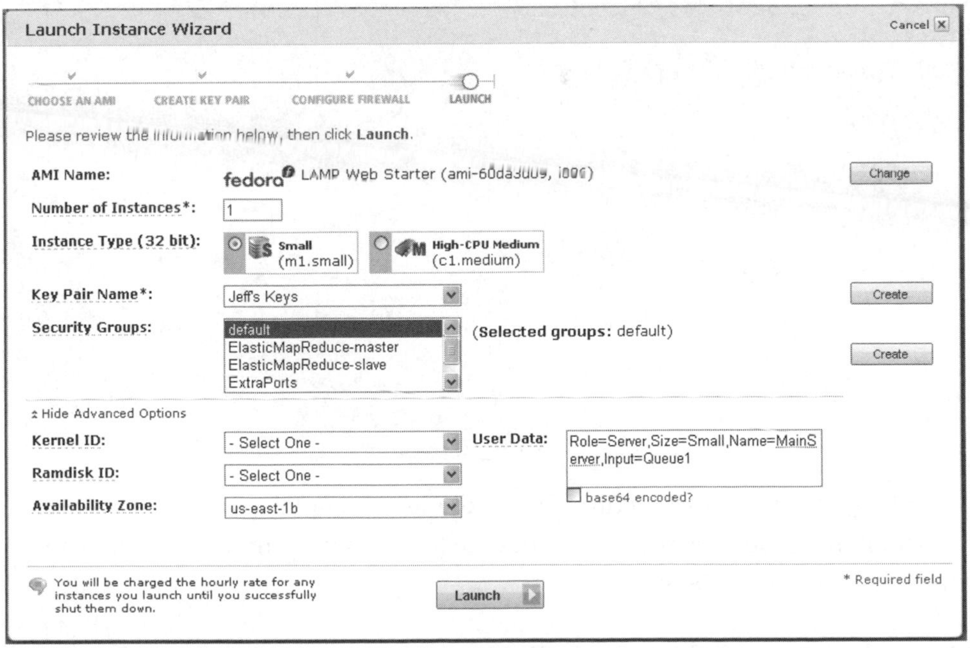

Figure 10.4. Launch an EC2 instance with user data

In this example, "Role=Server,Size=Small,Name=MainServer,Input=Queue1" is the string contained in my user data. I can retrieve this information immediately after my instance has launched, and use it to control the behavior of my instance.

Once launched, the user data can be retrieved like this:

```
<dev>: wget -q http://169.254.169.254/latest/user-data
<dev>: cat user-data
Role=Server,Size=Small,Name=MainServer,Input=Queue1
```

Of course, we can also retrieve and process the user metadata using a simple PHP program:

chapter_10/ec2_user_data.php *(excerpt)*

```php
#!/usr/bin/php
<?php

$userData = file_get_contents(
    'http://169.254.169.254/latest/user-data');
$options  = array();

foreach (explode(",", $userData) as $userDataItem)
{
  if (preg_match("!^([a-zA-Z]{1,})=([a-zA-Z0-9]{1,})$!",
                 $userDataItem, $parts))
  {
    $name  = $parts[1];
    $value = $parts[2];

    $options[$name] = $value;
  }
}

print_r($options);
?>
```

The file_get_contents function fetches the user metadata. The string is broken up at comma boundaries using PHP's explode function, producing name-value pairs in the form Role=Server.

You can use the user metadata facility any way you'd like. You can pass server names, server roles, SQS queue names, sizes, limits, and so forth. You'll need to create your own AMI. To go even further, you could have your custom AMI treat the user metadata as the URL of a script to be run when the instance starts.

Dynamic Diagramming

In this section we'll use the EC2 APIs to retrieve the list of running instances, the EBS volumes attached to each of the instances, and the snapshots of those instances, and draw a simple system diagram. You should be able to take this program and extend it in many different ways without too much trouble.

Let's make a start. The application is going to do a lot of drawing. I sketched out my layout on a piece of graph paper and then encoded the critical sizes as PHP constants:

chapter_10/ec2_diagram.php *(excerpt)*

```php
#!/usr/bin/php
<?php

error_reporting(E_ALL);
require_once('cloudfusion.class.php');
require_once('include/book.inc.php');

// Define shape geometry
define('LEFT_MARGIN', 16);
define('RIGHT_MARGIN', 16);
define('TOP_MARGIN', 16);
define('BOTTOM_MARGIN', 16);
define('TEXT_MARGIN', 4);
define('TEXT_LINE_HEIGHT', 14);
define('INSTANCE_WIDTH', 128);
define('INSTANCE_HEIGHT', 64);
define('VOLUME_WIDTH', 96);
define('VOLUME_HEIGHT', 64);
define('SNAP_WIDTH', 96);
define('SNAP_HEIGHT', 64);
define('VOLUME_GAP', 16);
define('SNAP_GAP', 16);
```

I decided to represent each running instance of EC2, the EBS volumes attached to the instance, and the snapshots for each volume as a series of connected rectangles.

I stacked the instances vertically, the volumes in a horizontal row, and the snapshots in a vertical column. Figure 10.5 shows a cleaned-up version of my sketch.

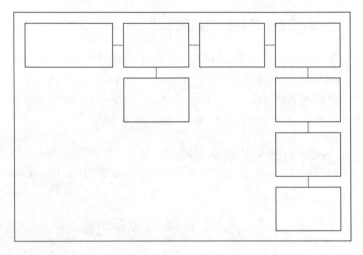

Figure 10.5. Design sketch for layout purposes

Each instance and its attached parts occupies a rectangular space on the final image, with a surrounding margin represented by `LEFT_MARGIN`, `RIGHT_MARGIN`, `TOP_MARGIN`, and `BOTTOM_MARGIN`. The instances, volumes, and snapshots are drawn as rectangles of size `INSTANCE_WIDTH` by `INSTANCE_HEIGHT`, `VOLUME_WIDTH` by `VOLUME_HEIGHT`, and `SNAP_WIDTH` by `SNAP_HEIGHT`, respectively. `TEXT_MARGIN` allows for some space between the edge of each rectangle and the text inside, and `TEXT_LINE_HEIGHT` is the space between lines of text. `VOLUME_GAP` is the horizontal space between volume rectangles and `SNAP_GAP` is the vertical space between snapshot rectangles.

As always, we need to create the objects that let us access EC2 and S3:

chapter_10/ec2_diagram.php *(excerpt)*

```
$ec2 = new AmazonEC2();
$s3  = new AmazonS3();
```

Next we fetch the list of EC2 instances, EBS volumes, and EBS volume snapshots like this:

```
                                        chapter_10/ec2_diagram.php (excerpt)

$resInstances = $ec2->describe_instances();
$resVolumes   = $ec2->describe_volumes();
$resSnapshots = $ec2->describe_snapshots();
```

This tiny code fragment retrieves all the important information about our system configuration. It never hurts to check for errors before proceeding, so let's do that now:

```
                                        chapter_10/ec2_diagram.php (excerpt)

if (!$resInstances->isOK() ||
    !$resVolumes->isOK()   ||
    !$resSnapshots->isOK())
{
  exit("Error retrieving system information.");
}
```

Unlike most of the other (and much simpler) programs in this book, I'm taking an object oriented approach here. I created classes to represent EC2 Regions, instances, volumes, and snapshots. Each class contains references to the objects that it logically owns or contains:

1. Regions contain instances
2. instances contain volumes
3. volumes contain snapshots

I chose to omit storing information about volumes that are unattached to instances or snapshots for non-existent volumes (which are perfectly legitimate situations).

The Region is the top-level object, so it's created first:

```
                                        chapter_10/ec2_diagram.php (excerpt)

$Region = new Region('us-east-1');
```

Next we can iterate through the list of instances, gathering the interesting attributes for each instance, using them to create an `Instance` object, and then adding the new object to the Region. Here's how to do that:

```
                                        chapter_10/ec2_diagram.php (excerpt)

foreach ($resInstances->body->reservationSet->item as $itemSet)
{
  foreach ($itemSet->instancesSet->item as $item)
  {
    $instanceId       = (string) $item->instanceId;
    $state            = (string) $item->instanceState->name;
    $instanceType     = (string) $item->instanceType;
    $availabilityZone = (string) $item->placement->availabilityZone;

    if ($state != 'terminated')
    {
      $Region->AddInstance(new Instance($availabilityZone,
          $instanceId,
          $state,
          $instanceType));
    }
  }
}
```

The code skips instances in the `terminated` state since they've been shut down.

Next, we can do the same sort of processing for each EBS volume:

```
                                        chapter_10/ec2_diagram.php (excerpt)

foreach ($resVolumes->body->volumeSet->item as $item)
{
  $volumeId         = (string) $item->volumeId;
  $size             = (string) $item->size;
  $availabilityZone = (string) $item->availabilityZone;

  if ($item->attachmentSet->item)
  {
    $instanceId = (string) $item->attachmentSet->item->instanceId;
    $device     = (string) $item->attachmentSet->item->device;

    $Region->AddVolume(new Volume($availabilityZone,
        $volumeId,
```

```
            $instanceId,
            $size,
            $device)));
    }
}
```

And the same for each snapshot:

```
                                    chapter_10/ec2_diagram.php (excerpt)

foreach ($resSnapshots->body->snapshotSet->item as $item)
{
    $snapshotId = (string) $item->snapshotId;
    $volumeId   = (string) $item->volumeId;
    $startTime  = (string) $item->startTime;

    $Region->AddSnapshot(new Snapshot($snapshotId,
            $volumeId,
            $startTime));
}
```

At this point the data structure is built. If you want to see what it looks like for yourself, dump it out like this:

```
print_r($Region);
```

My Region class has a Draw method. This method uses the GD library to render the instances, volumes, and snapshots to an in-memory image and then returns it:

```
                                    chapter_10/ec2_diagram.php (excerpt)

$image = $Region->Draw();
```

The final step is to write the in-memory image to the file system in GIF format, read the GIF into memory, and then store it in Amazon S3:

```
                                    chapter_10/ec2_diagram.php (excerpt)

$imageOut = tempnam("/tmp", "aws") . ".gif";
ImageGIF($image, $imageOut);

$imageOutBits = file_get_contents($imageOut);
```

```
$imageKey      = 'ec2_diagram_' . date('Y_m_d_H_i_s') . '.gif';
if (uploadObject($s3, BOOK_BUCKET, $imageKey, $imageOutBits,
    S3_ACL_PUBLIC, "image/gif"))
{
  $imageURL = $s3->get_object_url(BOOK_BUCKET, $imageKey);

  print("EC2 diagram is at ${imageURL}\n");
}
```

The image must be written to the file system because there's no direct way to turn an in-memory GD image into an in-memory GIF image. The prefix **ec2_diagram_** is appended with the current date and time, and the **.gif** file extension.

When I ran this program I had three instances running. Three EBS volumes were attached to one of the instances and I had four EBS snapshots. Figure 10.6 shows the resulting image.

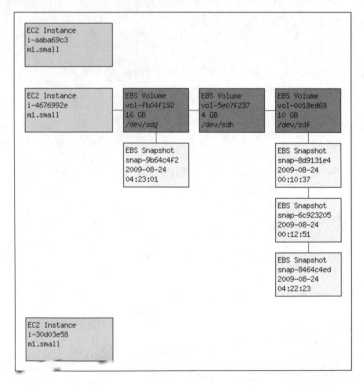

Figure 10.6. Diagram of actual instances, volumes, and snapshots

A 500-line PHP program can access your entire inventory of AWS assets, create relationships between the assets, and draw this nice picture. I think that's kind of
cool!

Now that we've taken a high-level look at this program, let's examine each classes.

Here's the basic structure of the `Region` class:

```
                                          chapter_10/ec2_diagram.php (excerpt)

class Region
{
  var $name;
  var $instances;

  public function __construct($name)
  {
    $this->Name      = $name;
    $this->Instances = array();
  }
```

The constructor simply stores the given Region name in a PHP instance variable
and creates an empty array to track the EC2 instances. The array will be indexed
by the ID of the instance.

Three simple methods are used to add `Instance`, `Volume`, and `Snapshot` objects to
the `Region` object. The `AddSnapshot` method searches through the instances until
it finds the one with the volume associated with the snapshot:

```
                                          chapter_10/ec2_diagram.php (excerpt)

  public function AddInstance($instance)
  {
    $this->Instances[$instance->InstanceId()] = $instance;
  }

  public function AddVolume($volume)
  {
    $this->Instances[$volume->InstanceId()]->AddVolume($volume);
  }

  public function AddSnapshot($snapshot)
  {
```

```
  foreach ($this->Instances as $instance)
  {
    if ($instance->HasVolume($snapshot->VolumeId))
    {
      $instance->AddSnapshot($snapshot);
    }
  }
}
```

The most interesting part of this class is found in the Draw method:

chapter_10/ec2_diagram.php *(excerpt)*

```
public function Draw()
{
  $totalW = 0;
  $totalH = 0;

  foreach ($this->Instances as $instance)
  {
    $thisW = $instance->GetDrawWidth();
    $thisH = $instance->GetDrawHeight();

    $totalW = max($totalW, $thisW);
    $totalH += $thisH;
  }

  $image = ImageCreate($totalW, $totalH);
  ImageFilledRectangle($image, 0, 0,
      $totalW - 1, $totalH - 1,
      ImageColorAllocate($image, 255, 255, 255));
  ImageRectangle($image, 0, 0,
      $totalW - 1, $totalH - 1,
      ImageColorAllocate($image, 0, 0, 0));

  $startY = 0;
  foreach ($this->Instances as $instance)
  {
    $instance->Draw($image, 0, $startY);
    $startY += $instance->GetDrawHeight();
  }

  return $image;
}
}
```

The code makes two passes through the `$instances` array. The first pass asks each instance for its width and height. This information is used to create a GD image of the appropriate size. The second pass asks each image to render itself to the appropriate location on the image.

Let's dive into the `Instance` class. Like the `Region` class, the instance variables and the constructor are very simple:

chapter_10/ec2_diagram.php *(excerpt)*

```php
class Instance
{
  var $availabilityZone;
  var $instanceId;
  var $state;
  var $instanceType;
  var $volumes;

  public function __construct($availabilityZone, $instanceId,
      $state, $instanceType)
  {
    $this->AvailabilityZone = $availabilityZone;
    $this->InstanceId       = $instanceId;
    $this->State            = $state;
    $this->InstanceType     = $instanceType;
    $this->Volumes          = array();
  }
```

As you can see, this code tracks a number of attributes for each EC2 instance. Each `Instance` object also tracks the attached EBS volumes, indexed by the volume's ID.

The outer levels of code need access to the ID of the EC2 instance, so we need an accessor method and access to the number of volumes attached to the instance:

chapter_10/ec2_diagram.php *(excerpt)*

```php
  public function InstanceId()
  {
    return $this->InstanceId;
  }

  public function VolumeCount()
```

```
{
  return count($this->Volumes);
}
```

The `AddVolume` method is used to add a new volume to the instance, while the `HasVolume` method is used to see if a particular volume is attached to the instance:

chapter_10/ec2_diagram.php (excerpt)

```
public function AddVolume($volume)
{
  $this->Volumes[$volume->VolumeId()] = $volume;
}

public function HasVolume($volumeId)
{
  return IsSet($this->Volumes[$volumeId]);
}
```

The code to draw an instance looks long but is quite simple. It outlines a rectangle representing the instance, fills it in, draws some text, and then asks each volume to draw itself:

chapter_10/ec2_diagram.php (excerpt)

```
public function Draw($image, $startX, $startY)
{
  ImageRectangle($image,
    $startX + LEFT_MARGIN,
    $startY + TOP_MARGIN,
    $startX + LEFT_MARGIN + INSTANCE_WIDTH,
    $startY + TOP_MARGIN + INSTANCE_HEIGHT,
    ImageColorAllocate($image, 0, 0, 0));

  ImageFill($image,
    $startX + LEFT_MARGIN + 1,
    $startY + TOP_MARGIN + 1,
    ImageColorAllocate($image, 0x60, 0xff, 0xcc));

  ImageString($image,
    2,
    $startX + LEFT_MARGIN + TEXT_MARGIN,
    $startY + TOP_MARGIN + TEXT_MARGIN,
```

```
        "EC2 Instance",
        ImageColorAllocate($image, 0, 0, 0));

    ImageString($image,
        2,
        LEFT_MARGIN + TEXT_MARGIN,
        $startY + TOP_MARGIN + TEXT_MARGIN + TEXT_LINE_HEIGHT,
        $this->InstanceId,
        ImageColorAllocate($image, 0, 0, 0));

    ImageString($image,
        2,
        $startX + LEFT_MARGIN + TEXT_MARGIN,
        $startY + TOP_MARGIN + TEXT_MARGIN + (2 * TEXT_LINE_HEIGHT),
        $this->InstanceType,
        ImageColorAllocate($image, 0, 0, 0));

    $startX += LEFT_MARGIN + INSTANCE_WIDTH;
    foreach ($this->Volumes as $volume)
    {
      $volume->Draw($image, $startX, $startY);
      $startX += VOLUME_GAP + VOLUME_WIDTH;
    }
  }
}
```

As you can see, some basic integer math is used to compute the proper position for each item.

The following pair of methods are central to the size computation process. They return the amount of space (width and height) needed to draw the instance, volumes, and snapshots. The width is dependent on the number of volumes and the height is dependent on the maximum number of snapshots found on any volume of the instance.

Here's the width calculation code:

chapter_10/ec2_diagram.php *(excerpt)*

```php
public function GetDrawWidth()
{
  $volumeCount  = $this->VolumeCount();

  return
    LEFT_MARGIN     +
    INSTANCE_WIDTH +
    ($volumeCount * (VOLUME_GAP + VOLUME_WIDTH)) +
    RIGHT_MARGIN;
}
```

And here's the height calculation code:

chapter_10/ec2_diagram.php *(excerpt)*

```php
public function GetDrawHeight()
{
  $maxSnapCount = $this->MaxSnapCount();

  return
    TOP_MARGIN      +
    INSTANCE_HEIGHT +
    ($maxSnapCount * (SNAP_GAP + SNAP_HEIGHT)) +
    BOTTOM_MARGIN;
}
```

Another simple method figures out the maximum number of snapshots found on any of the instance's volumes:

chapter_10/ec2_diagram.php *(excerpt)*

```php
public function MaxSnapCount()
{
  $maxSnapCount = 0;
  foreach ($this->Volumes as $volume)
  {
    $snapCount    = $volume->SnapCount();
    $maxSnapCount = max($maxSnapCount, $snapCount);
  }
```

```
    return $maxSnapCount;
  }
}
```

The Volume and Snapshot classes are quite similar to the Instance class so I'll avoid presenting them here. They are available in the code archive for this book on sitepoint.com.

The code, as presented here, draws a very simple diagram and there's plenty of room to extend it. Here are some ideas to start you off:

1. Draw additional attributes such as the Availability Zone of each instance (I left this out on purpose to give you a task).

2. Draw an appropriate icon with each item.

3. Retrieve and draw additional items, such as elastic IP addresses.

4. Partition the Region by Availability Zone and put each EC2 instance in the proper zone.

5. Capture the metadata at regular instances, store it in SimpleDB, and then use it to draw an animated version of the diagram (assuming that you're adding and removing instances, volumes, or snapshots over time).

6. Capture and graph CloudFront metrics for the instances as part of the diagram.

Conclusion

I hope that this chapter served as a good introduction to some of the more advanced aspects of AWS. We managed to use SimpleDB, EC2, S3, and the GD library in this chapter and we also learned an aspect or two about processing CSV files. I've always tried to find a way to learn new skills as part of every project. In this case I could have chosen to process the data in XML format, but thought that I'd give PHP's CSV handling function a try. Over the course of my career this willingness to explore new functions, libraries, systems, and languages has led me in some interesting and unexpected directions. I'd encourage you to do the same!

Putting It All Together: CloudList

In this chapter, we'll create a classified advertising application that I've named CloudList, using the Amazon EC2 infrastructure, S3, and SimpleDB. The sections of this chapter reflect my development efforts, so you should be able to see how I put the application together.

Designing the Application

Our project is to create a simple classified advertising application. The application will allow users in a number of cities to submit and view classified ads.

We need to track the following kinds of data:

- locations—a list of cities and states
- categories—a list of classified ad categories
- items—a list of classified ads

We'll store the following fields for each ad:

- City
- State
- Date
- Price
- Category
- Title
- Description
- Image (full-sized and thumbnail)

Since each SimpleDB attribute value is limited to 1,024 bytes, we will store the descriptions, images, and thumbnails in S3. In the pursuit of simplicity we'll avoid including any contact information (email address or phone number), but feel free to extend the application yourself.

Each type of data will need its own SimpleDB domain, so let's choose some good names:

cloudlist/include/cloudfunctions.inc.php *(excerpt)*

```php
define('CL_CITY_DOMAIN', 'cl_cities');
define('CL_CAT_DOMAIN', 'cl_categories');
define('CL_ITEM_DOMAIN', 'cl_items');
```

We'll put these constant definitions in the common file **cloudfunctions.inc.php**, to be included in all the CloudList application files. At this point we've yet to make any decisions about how the application will look or behave, but these considerations will have no effect on the data model.

Utility Functions and Programs

The next step is to create some command line utility programs to populate the SimpleDB domains with initial data.

To create the SimpleDB domains we will be using, we can simply modify the **create_domain.php** script from Chapter 8:

cloudlist/create_domain.php (excerpt)

```
$sdb = new AmazonSDB();

foreach (array(CL_CITY_DOMAIN,
         CL_CAT_DOMAIN,
         CL_ITEM_DOMAIN) as $domain)
{
  $res = $sdb->create_domain($domain);

  if (!$res->isOK())
  {
    exit("Create domain operation failed for domain ${domain}\n");
  }

  print("Domain ${domain} created.\n");
}
```

Now here's a script to add a new city—actually a city/state pair:

cloudlist/add_city.php (excerpt)

```
#!/usr/bin/php
<?php

error_reporting(E_ALL);

require_once('cloudfusion.class.php');
require_once('include/cloudfunctions.inc.php');

if ($argc < 3)
{
  exit("Usage: " . $argv[0] . " CITY STATE\n");
}

$city  = $argv[1];
$state = $argv[2];

$Key = $state . '_' . $city;
$attrs = array('City' => $city,
        'State' => $state);

$sdb = new AmazonSDB();
```

```php
$res = $sdb->put_attributes(CL_CITY_DOMAIN, $Key, $attrs, true);

if ($res->isOK())
{
  print("Added city ${city} in ${state}\n");
}
else
{
  $error = $res->body->Errors->Error->Message;
  print("Could not add city: ${error}\n");
}
?>
```

We'll also need a script to add a list of one or more categories:

cloudlist/add_category.php *(excerpt)*

```php
#!/usr/bin/php
<?php

error_reporting(E_ALL);

require_once('cloudfusion.class.php');
require_once('include/cloudfunctions.inc.php');

if ($argc < 2)
{
  exit("Usage: " . $argv[0] . " CATEGORY ...\n");
}

$sdb = new AmazonSDB();

for ($i = 1; $i < $argc; $i++)
{
  $category = $argv[$i];

  $Key = $category;
  $attrs = array('Category' => $category);

  $res = $sdb->put_attributes(CL_CAT_DOMAIN, $Key, $attrs, true);

  if ($res->isOK())
  {
    print("Added category ${category}\n");
  }
```

```
  else
  {
    $error = $res->body->Errors->Error->Message;
    print("Could not add category: ${error}\n");
  }
}
?>
```

Now we can use these command scripts to set up some sample data. First, we set up the domains:

```
$ create_domain.php
Domain cl_cities created.
Domain cl_categories created.
Domain cl_items created.
```

Then, we add some cities:

```
$ php add_city.php Bethesda MD
Added city Bethesda in MD
$ php add_city.php Redmond WA
Added city Redmond in WA
$ php add_city.php Boise ID
Added city Boise in ID
$ php add_city.php "San Francisco" CA
Added city San Francisco in CA
```

And then, we add the categories:

```
$ php add_category.php Cars Trucks Homes Furniture
Added category Cars
Added category Trucks
Added category Homes
Added category Furniture
```

If you remember from Chapter 8, each call to SimpleDB's select method can return up to 2,500 results, depending on the size and number of attributes returned. However, it is likely that we'll have to run SimpleDB queries that might produce long lists of results. So, let's create a function to make it easier to capture and process result sets of any size. Here's the code for the runQuery function:

cloudlist/include/cloudfunctions.inc.php *(excerpt)*

```php
function runQuery($sdb, $query)
{
  $next    = '';
  $results = array();

  do
  {
    $res = $sdb->select($query, array('NextToken' => $next));
    if (!$res->isOK())
    {
      return null;
    }

    $next = IsSet($res->body->SelectResult->NextToken) ?
      (string) $res->body->SelectResult->NextToken
      : '';

    foreach ($res->body->SelectResult->Item as $item)
    {
      $attributes = array();
      foreach ($item->Attribute as $attribute)
      {
        $attributes[(string) $attribute->Name] =
            (string) $attribute->Value;
      }

      $Key = (string) $item->Name;
      $results[$Key] = $attributes;
    }
  }
  while ($next != '');

  return $results;
}
```

This function accepts a SimpleDB query as a string, makes a series of calls to the select method to retrieve all the results, and then returns a PHP associative array that contains all the results. We can then write some very simple wrappers around this function to return arrays of all cities and categories:

```
                              cloudlist/include/cloudfunctions.inc.php (excerpt)
function getCities($sdb)
{
  $query = "select * from " . CL_CITY_DOMAIN;
  return runQuery($sdb, $query);
}

function getCategories($sdb)
{
  $query = "select * from " . CL_CAT_DOMAIN;
  return runQuery($sdb, $query);
}
```

The getCities function returns the city data like this:

```
Array
(
  [WA_Seattle] => Array
  (
    [State] => WA
    [City] => Seattle
  )
  [WA_Redmond] => Array
  (
    [State] => WA
    [City] => Redmond
  )
  ⋮
)
```

Of course, adding a new classified listing is a bit more complicated than cities and categories. It would be useful to be able to do this from the command line or from a web form. So, we will create a single (if a little complex) function named addCloudListItem to add a new item that can be called from the command line or a web page script.

In the addCloudListItem function, we'll make use of our thumbnailImage function from Chapter 4. Make sure you copy that function into the **cloudfunctions.inc.php** file. The thumbnailImage function also uses the value in the THUMB_NAIL constant to determine the thumbnail size, so we'll need to add that to our **cloudfunctions.inc.php** file as well:

```php
define('THUMB_SIZE', 200);
```

We'll also reuse our `uploadObject` function from Chapter 4 to upload the image files to our S3 bucket, so copy that function into the **cloudfunctions.inc.php** file too.

Let's take the `addCloudListItem` code apart and examine it step by step. Here's how it begins:

```php
function addCloudListItem($sdb, $s3, $city, $state, $date,
        $price, $category, $title, $description,
        $imagePath)
{
```

We need a unique key since the data is destined for SimpleDB. Let's take some of the fields, put them together into a string, and then compute the MD5 hash of the string, like this:

```php
$Key = md5($city . $state . $date . $price . $category . $title);
```

The next step (and it's a big one) is to process the image associated with the listing. The `$imagePath` argument to the function can be a URL to a remote image or a fully qualified path name to a local one. This is made possible by the PHP function `file_get_contents`. If there's no image associated with the listing, we'll pass `null` for the argument. Here's the code we need to download the image, create a thumbnail version, and store both images in S3:

```php
if ($imagePath !== null)
{
  $imageIn  = file_get_contents($imagePath);
  $imageMem = ImageCreateFromString($imageIn);

  $fileOut  = tempnam("/tmp", "aws") . ".aws";
  $ret      = ImageJPEG($imageMem, $fileOut, 100);
  $imageOut = file_get_contents($fileOut);
```

```
    $thumbOut = thumbnailImage($imageOut, "image/jpg");

    $imageKey = $Key . '.jpg';
    $thumbKey = $Key . '_thumb.jpg';

    if (!uploadObject($s3, CL_BUCKET,
          $imageKey, $imageOut,
          S3_ACL_PUBLIC, "image/jpeg") ||
  !uploadObject($s3, CL_BUCKET,
          $thumbKey, $thumbOut,
          S3_ACL_PUBLIC, "image/jpeg"))
  {
    return false;
  }

  $imageURL = $s3->get_object_url(CL_BUCKET, $imageKey);
  $thumbURL = $s3->get_object_url(CL_BUCKET, $thumbKey);
}
else
{
  $imageURL = null;
  $thumbURL = null;
}
```

We'll use the unique key we generated at the start of this function (in the variable $Key) for the SimpleDB item as the key for our images in S3 with a slight modification. We'll use $Key . '.jpg' for the full size image and $Key . '_thumb.jpg' for the thumbnail. This is convenient, but it means we're unable to handle more than one image per classified ad. That's fine for now; if we want to support more images per item in the future, it'll be easy to change.

The item description must also be stored in S3 (we'll use that $Key value again):

cloudlist/include/cloudfunctions.inc.php *(excerpt)*

```
if (uploadObject($s3,
      CL_BUCKET,
      $Key,
      $description,
      S3_ACL_PUBLIC))
{
  $descriptionURL =
```

```
      $s3->get_object_url(CL_BUCKET, $Key);
  }
  else
  {
    return false;
  }
```

Now that the two images and the description have been stored in S3, the next step is to store the classified ad itself in SimpleDB:

cloudlist/include/cloudfunctions.inc.php *(excerpt)*

```
$attrs = array(
    'City'        => $city,
    'State'       => $state,
    'Date'        => $date,
    'Price'       => $price,
    'Category'    => $category,
    'Title'       => $title,
    'Description' => $descriptionURL);

if ($imageURL !== null)
{
  $attrs['Image'] = $imageURL;
  $attrs['Thumb'] = $thumbURL;
}

$res = $sdb->put_attributes(CL_ITEM_DOMAIN, $Key, $attrs, true);
```

In the above code, we avoid creating `Image` or `Thumb` array items if the classified ad has no image, as there's no need.

The function should return `true` if all goes well or `false` if something goes wrong, so the final step is to check the status of the `put_attributes` call:

cloudlist/include/cloudfunctions.inc.php *(excerpt)*

```
  return $res->isOK();
}
```

Our `addCloudListItem` function is done.

Here's the command line wrapper around the function:

cloudlist/add_item.php *(excerpt)*

```php
#!/usr/bin/php
<?php

error_reporting(E_ALL);

require_once('cloudfusion.class.php');
require_once('include/cloudfunctions.inc.php');

if (($argc < 8) || ($argc > 9))
{
  exit("Usage: " . $argv[0] .
    " CITY STATE DATE PRICE CATEGORY \"TITLE\" \"DESCRIPTION\"
➡ [IMAGEURL]\n");
}

// Get item info
$city        = $argv[1];
$state       = $argv[2];
$date        = $argv[3];
$price       = $argv[4];
$category    = $argv[5];
$title       = $argv[6];
$description = $argv[7];
$imageURL    = null;

if ($argc > 8)
{
  $imageURL = $argv[8];
}

$s3  = new AmazonS3();
$sdb = new AmazonSDB();

if (addCloudListItem($sdb, $s3,
        $city, $state, $date, $price,
        $category, $title, $description,
        $imageURL))
{
  print("Added item ${title} in ${city}, ${state}\n");
}
else
{
```

```
    print("Could not add item!\n");
}
?>
```

The **add_item.php** script allows us to add an item like so:

```
$ php add_item.php city state date price category
➥ "Title" "Description" [image_url]
```

We need to create one more `Get` function; this one retrieves the entire list of classified ads for a given city and state:

cloudlist/include/cloudfunctions.inc.php *(excerpt)*

```
function getItems($sdb, $city, $state)
{
  $query =
    "select * from " . CL_ITEM_DOMAIN .
    " where City=\"${city}\" and State=\"${state}\"";

  return runQuery($sdb, $query);
}
```

In the interests of testing and monitoring, we'll write a utility script to call all three of our `Get` functions. This allows us to verify that the rest of our application is working as desired:

cloudlist/dump.php *(excerpt)*

```
#!/usr/bin/php
<?php

error_reporting(E_ALL);

require_once('cloudfusion.class.php');
require_once('include/cloudfunctions.inc.php');

$sdb = new AmazonSDB();

print("Cities\n");
print("======\n");
$cities = getCities($sdb);
print_r($cities);
```

```
print("Categories\n");
print("==========\n");
$categories = getCategories($sdb);
print_r($categories);

print("Items\n");
print("=====\n");
$items = getItems($sdb, "Redmond", "WA");
print_r($items);

?>
```

The **dump.php** script will print all the cities and categories, and all the items from a specific city.

With all this infrastructure in place, we can now insert an item using our command line utility:

```
$ php add_item.php Redmond WA 2008-08-29 11000.00 Cars "Scion XB"
➥ "Mint condition Toyota Scion XB, all accessories runs great,
➥ amazing car, hate to sell it." http://upload.wikimedia.org/wikipe
➥dia/commons/thumb/c/c1/2006_Scion_xB_.jpg/800px-2006_Scion_xB_.jpg
```

If we use our **dump.php** to output the data stored for this new item, here's what we see:

```
[8105daf1582a87084faf975d34e591e8] => Array
(
  [Title] => Scion XB
  [Price] => 11000.00
  [City] => Redmond
  [Description] => http://sitepoint-aws-cloud-book.s3.amazonaws.com
➥/8195daf1582a87084faf975d34e591e8
  [State] => WA
  [Date] => 2008-08-29
  [Category] => Cars
  [Thumb] => http://sitepoint-aws-cloud-book.s3.amazonaws.com
➥/8195daf1582a87084faf975d34e591e8_thumb.jpg
  [Image] => http://sitepoint-aws-cloud-book.s3.amazonaws.com
➥/8195daf1582a87084faf975d34e591e8.jpg
)
```

Because the Image, Thumb, and Description are all URLs that link to data stored in Amazon S3, we can paste each one into the address bar of our web browser to verify the content.

The Web Front End

Now that we've designed the data format and created some code to read and write items, it's quite easy to wrap it all up with a web front end. Our controller script is **cloudlist.php**. First, it'll assemble an array of all cities and states. Then, it will look for a city and state specified in the URL query string. If it finds one, it will assemble an array of all classified items for that location. Let's take it step by step:

```
cloudlist/cloudlist.php (excerpt)
<?php

error_reporting(E_ALL);

require_once('cloudfusion.class.php');
require_once('include/cloudfunctions.inc.php');

// Get city and state from request
if (IsSet($_GET['city'])  &&
    isSet($_GET['state']) &&
    preg_match("/^[A-Za-z\+ ]{1,}$/", $_GET['city']) &&
    preg_Match("/^[A-Z]{2}$/",        $_GET['state']))
{
  $currentCity  = urldecode($_GET['city']);
  $currentState = urldecode($_GET['state']);
}
else
{
  $currentCity  = null;
  $currentState = null;
}
```

This web page will accept city and state parameters in the URL query string, so the first task is to validate and capture them. The preg_match function is used to make sure that the city and state parameters only contain valid characters. This validation is a crucial step toward ensuring that the program avoids being compromised by bad input data.[1]

The code will access SimpleDB, so we need to create the access object:

cloudlist/cloudlist.php *(excerpt)*

```php
$sdb = new AmazonSDB();
```

Even though the images and descriptions are stored in S3, an S3 object is unnecessary. That's because we'll access them using GET requests to the appropriate URLs.

We'll also need a list of cities for the menu:

cloudlist/cloudlist.php *(excerpt)*

```php
$cities = getCities($sdb);
```

Next, we have to assemble an array of items ($itemCat) that match the city and state specified. If no city or state are specified, the array will be empty. We also reorganize the array so that the items are categorized by their category value:

cloudlist/cloudlist.php *(excerpt)*

```php
$itemCat = array();
if ($currentCity != '' && $currentState != '')
{
  $items = getItems($sdb, $city, $state);
  foreach ($items as $key => $attrs)
  {
    $category = $attrs['Category'];
    if (!IsSet($itemCat[$category]))
    {
      $itemCat[$category] = array();
    }
    $itemCat[$category][$key] = $attrs;
  }
}
```

The final job for our controller script is to include the HTML template:

---

[1] Because SimpleDB's select function only accepts a single statement, classic SQL injection attacks should be impossible. However, it's always best to verify critical input data.

```php
include 'cloudlist.html.php'
?>
```

Out template needs to generate three main items: a location menu, a link to add a new item, and a list of classified items by category. Firstly, let's look at the menu and new item link:

```php
<!DOCTYPE html PUBLIC "-//W3C//DTD XHTML 1.0 Strict//EN"
  "http://www.w3.org/TR/xhtml1/DTD/xhtml1-strict.dtd">
<html xmlns="http://www.w3.org/1999/xhtml" xml:lang="en" lang="en">
  <head>
    <title>CloudList Classified Ad System</title>
    <link rel="stylesheet" type="text/css" media="all"
        href="css/styles.css" />
  </head>
  <body>
    <h1>CloudList Classified Ad System</h1>
    <div id="menu">
      <ul>
        <?php foreach ($cities as $Key => $attrs):
          $menuCity  = $attrs['City'];
          $menuState = $attrs['State'];
          $link = "?city="  . urlencode($menuCity) . "&state=" .
            urlencode($menuState);
          $menuClass = (($currentCity == $menuCity) &&
            ($currentState == $menuState)) ? "activemenu" : "menu";
        ?>
        <li class="<?php echo $menuClass; ?>">
          <a href="<?php echo $link; ?>"><?php
              echo "${menuCity}, ${menuState}"; ?></a>
        </li>
        <? endforeach ?>
      </ul>
      <p id="newitemlink">
        <a href=\"add_form.php\">Add new item …</a>
      </p>
    </div>
```

The above code uses a `foreach` loop to output all the cities as an unordered list, with each item containing a link like so:

```
<a href="?city=Redmond&state=WA">Redmond, WA</a>
```

We also assign a special `activemenu` `class` value to the menu item if the current city matches; that way, we can add a visual style to indicate the currently viewed city in the menu.

The last element is a link to the form used to add a new classified listing. We will tackle that part of the application soon.

All that's left to do is output a list of items and format appropriately:

cloudlist/include/cloudlist.html.php (excerpt)

```php
<div id="items">
<?php foreach ($itemCat as $category => $items): ?>
  <div class="category">
    <h2><?php echo $category; ?></h2>
    <?php foreach ($items as $Key => $attrs): ?>
    <div class="item">
      <h3><?php echo $attrs['Title']; ?></h3>
      <?php if (IsSet($attrs['Thumb'])): ?>
      <a href="<?php echo $attrs['Image']; ?>" target=\"new\">
        <img src="<?php echo $attrs['Thumb']; ?>"/>
      </a>
      <?php endif ?>
      <p class="date">Listed <?php echo $attrs['Date']; ?></p>
      <p class="price">Priced at
          $<?php echo number_format($attrs['Price']); ?></p>
      <p class="desc">
        <?php echo file_get_contents($attrs['Description']); ?>
      </p>
    </div>
    <? endforeach ?>
    <div class="clear"></div>
  </div>
  <? endforeach ?>

</body>
</html>
```

The above code uses two nested `foreach` loops to list all the items, categorized by their categories. The array of items is dependent on the presence of the `city` and `state` arguments in the URL. Of course, if the arrays are empty we'll only see the city menu.[2]

I used `file_get_contents` to retrieve the description from S3. I could have used the S3 API, but there's really no reason to do so here.

That's our HTML sorted—feel free to add a few CSS styles. If you need a head start, you can find a CSS file (**cloudlist/css/styles.css**) in the code archive for this book that should have it looking good.[3]

Figure 11.1 shows what the finished page looks like.

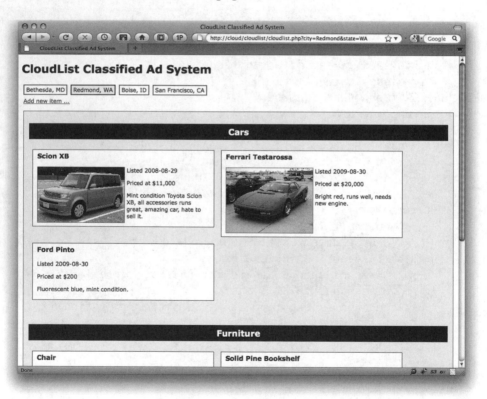

Figure 11.1. The CloudList page for Redmond, WA

---

[2] A relatively basic modification of the code presented in this chapter would allow for a two level presentation, viewing the classifieds either by state or by city within a state. I'll leave that change up to you!

[3] "Looking good" is a relative term here, since my sense of artistry is limited to selecting colors from a range of earth tones. I'm sure you can do better!

The New Item Submission Form

The **Add new item ...** link links to the **add_form.php** script. The script is invoked via HTTP GET or HTTP POST, and behaves differently for each method. When invoked via GET, it generates an empty form. When invoked via POST, it stores the new item form values in SimpleDB and S3.

Here's how it looks:

cloudlist/add_form.php *(excerpt)*

```php
<?php

error_reporting(E_ALL);

require_once('cloudfusion.class.php');
require_once('include/cloudfunctions.inc.php');

$s3  = new AmazonS3();
$sdb = new AmazonSDB();

if (isset($_POST['formsubmit']))
{
  : process POST data…
}
else
{
  $cities     = getCities($sdb);
  $categories = getCategories($sdb);
  include 'include/addform.html.php';
  exit(0);
}

?>
```

The script looks for a submitted value called formsubmit. If present, the form must have been submitted and we can proceed to process the form data; otherwise, we display the empty form. We'll examine the form processing code in a moment.

To respond to a GET request, the code above retrieves all the cities and categories from the database and then outputs the HTML template. Let's have a look at the template:

```
                              cloudlist/include/addform.html.php (excerpt)
<!DOCTYPE html PUBLIC "-//W3C//DTD XHTML 1.0 Strict//EN"
  "http://www.w3.org/TR/xhtml1/DTD/xhtml1-strict.dtd">
<html xmlns="http://www.w3.org/1999/xhtml" xml:lang="en" lang="en">
  <head>
    <title>CloudList Classified Ad System -- Add Item</title>
    <link rel="stylesheet" type="text/css" media="all"
        href="css/styles.css" />
  </head>
  <body>
    <h1>CloudList Classified Ad System -- Add Item</h1>
    <p>Please enter the new item information.</p>
    <form method="post" enctype="multipart/form-data" action="?">
      <input type="hidden" name="formsubmit" value="1"/>
      <input type="hidden" name="MAX_FILE_SIZE" value="2048000"/>
```

The form needs to have an `enctype` value of `multipart/form-data`, since it'll be
processing an uploaded file. We need to add the `formsubmit` hidden field because,
as we've mentioned, this acts as our trigger for form processing. We also include a
`MAX_FILE_SIZE` hidden field to ensure the maximum accepted file size is 2MB. Note
that there's a separate PHP limit—the variable `upload_max_filesize` in the **php.ini**
—that must be at least as large as the limit in this file in order for a maximally sized
upload to be accepted.

The remainder of the HTML displays all the form fields, including `<select>` menus
for the location and category fields:

```
                              cloudlist/include/addform.html.php (excerpt)
    <div>
      <label for="title">Title:</label>
      <input type="text" name="title" id="title" />
    </div>
    <div>
      <label for="price">Price:</label>
      <input type="text" name="price" id="price" />
    </div>
    <div>
      <label for="desc">Description:</label>
      <textarea rows="8" cols="40" name="description"
          name="desc"></textarea>
    </div>
```

```
  <div>
    <label for="category">Category:</label>
    <select name="category" id="category">
    <?php foreach ($categories as $Key => $attrs): ?>
      <option value="<?php echo $Key; ?>">
        <?php echo $Key; ?>
      </option>
    <?php endforeach ?>
    </select>
  </div>
  <div>
    <label for="statecity">Location:</label>
    <select name="statecity">
    <?php foreach ($cities as $Key => $attrs):
      $city  = $attrs['City'];
      $state = $attrs['State'];
    ?>
      <option value="<?php echo $Key; ?>">
        <?php echo "${city}, ${state}"; ?>
      </option>
    <?php endforeach ?>
    </select>
  </div>
  <div>
    <label for="statecity">Photo (optional):</label>
    <input type="file" name="image"/>
  </div>
  <div>
    <input type="submit" value="Add"/>
    <a href="cloudlist.php">Cancel &amp; return ...</a>
  </div>
  </form>
  </body>
</html>
```

Figure 11.2 shows the form: clean, no-nonsense, and ripe for some better styling.

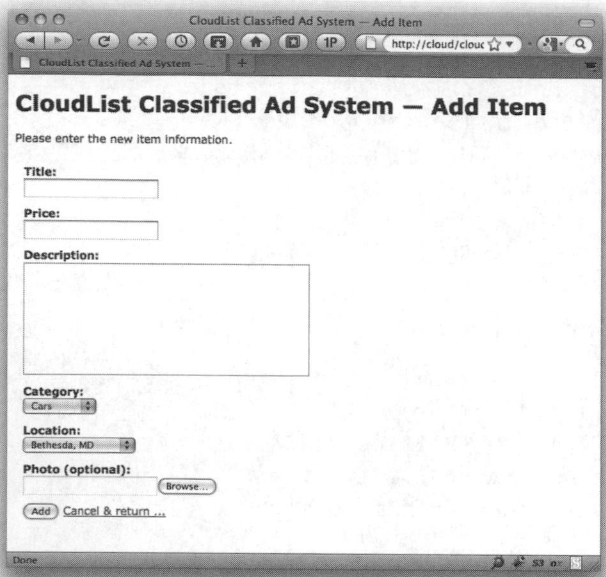

Figure 11.2. The Add Item form

The form processing code is simple to build, since we've already written our
`addCloudListItem` function to handle the heavy lifting. Here's the submission
handling code:

```
cloudlist/add_form.php (excerpt)

if (isset($_POST['formsubmit']))
{
  $stateCity   = $_POST['statecity'];
  $price       = $_POST['price'];
  $category    = $_POST['category'];
  $title       = $_POST['title'];
  $description = $_POST['description'];

  $date = date('Y-m-d');

  $state = substr($stateCity, 0, 2);
  $city  = substr($stateCity, 3);

  if (isset($_FILES['image']) &&
      is_uploaded_file($_FILES['image']['tmp_name']))
  {
```

```
      $imagePath = $_FILES['image']['tmp_name'];
    }
    else
    {
      $imagePath = null;
    }

    $success = addCloudListItem($sdb, $s3,
            $city, $state, $date, $price,
            $category, $title, $description,
            $imagePath);

    include 'include/addthanks.html.php';
    exit(0);
}
```

There's no magic here. The form sends the city and state as a single string, so we break it apart using the `substr` function. The form contains a file chooser for the optional photo. If a file was specified, it's available as a local file as named by `$_FILES['Image']['tmp_name']`. Recall that we built `addCloudListItems` to handle a URL or a local file? In this case a local file will be used.

Admittedly, the data validation and error reporting leaves a little bit to be desired here. A more sophisticated application would validate the form parameters and then regenerate the form (with appropriate error messages). I will leave that as an enhancement project for you.

Once the form submission has been processed, all that remains is to display a thank-you message if the submission was successful:

cloudlist/include/addthanks.html.php (excerpt)

```
<!DOCTYPE html PUBLIC "-//W3C//DTD XHTML 1.0 Strict//EN"
  "http://www.w3.org/TR/xhtml1/DTD/xhtml1-strict.dtd">
<html xmlns="http://www.w3.org/1999/xhtml" xml:lang="en" lang="en">
  <head>
    <title>CloudList Classified Ad System -- Add Item</title>
    <link rel="stylesheet" type="text/css" media="all"
        href="css/styles.css" />
  </head>
  <body>
```

```
    <h1>CloudList Classified Ad System -- Add Item</h1>
    <?php if ($success): ?>
    <p>New item accepted. Thanks!</p>
    <?php else: ?>
      <p>New item not accepted!</p>
    <?php endif ?>
    <p><a href="add_form.php">Add another...</a></p>
    <p><a href="cloudlist.php">Home</a></p>
  </body>
</html>
```

And That's It

I set out to create a simplified classified ad system, rather than a fully featured one, and I'm sure you'll agree that I did so! I believe that you can do a lot with approximately 500 lines of PHP, backed up by the power of AWS. Because the storage is handled by a combination of Amazon SimpleDB and S3, this application should be able to deal with hundreds of thousands of users and millions of items without too much effort. If the request rate were to grow too high for a single SimpleDB domain,[4] it would be very easy to spread the items across multiple domains, perhaps one per state or (when it's really busy) one per city. S3 has ample capacity and performance to serve up images directly, but I'd advise the use of CloudFront for production applications, since users will see the images more quickly.

The operational complexity of a large version of this application would be fairly minimal and you'd be able to spend your time adding features, doing marketing, or keeping the userbase happy. I think this is a wonderful example of cloud computing in action!

---

[4] A single SimpleDB domain can generally handle several thousand read or write requests per second. This is, of course, dependent on the complexity of the items.

Index